THE FOREIGN POLICY
RESEARCH INSTITUTE SERIES

The Foreign Policy Research Institute

University of Pennsylvania

NUMBER **3**

AMERICAN-ASIAN

FREDERICK A. PRAEGER

ENSIONS

edited by Robert Strausz-Hupé

Alvin J. Cottrell

James E. Dougherty

EW YORK

This volume is the third of a series of studies to be published by Frederick A. Praeger, Publishers, under the auspices of the Foreign Policy Research Institute at the University of Pennsylvania, established under a grant of the Richardson Foundation, Greensboro, North Carolina. This study was subjected to the extensive and critical discussion of the Associates of the Foreign Policy Research Institute. However, the views expressed in AMERICAN-ASIAN TENSIONS are those of the various authors.

Acknowledgments

This study was prepared under the auspices of the Foreign Policy Research Institute, University of Pennsylvania.
The editors and authors wish to acknowledge the research
contributions made by several graduate students who participated in the Seminars in International Relations offered
by the Department of Political Science. Olga Bendyna
prepared the original research for the chapter, "The United
States and Japan." Hedvah Shuchman and Frederick
W. Stutz collected research materials on the Middle
East countries. Indira Nalin read the final draft of the
chapter, "The United States and India," and offered valuable technical advice. Roger Smith read the chapter, "The
United States and the Philippines," and contributed helpful suggestions. Richard Kozicki supplied a valuable
critique of the chapter, "The United States and Indonesia." Thanks are owing to Dr. George Codding of the
Political Science Department of the University of Pennsylvania for the helpful suggestions which he made during
the early phases of the book's preparation. A special word
of gratitude is due Ward Morehouse, Executive Secretary
of the Conference on Asian Affairs, for his excellent de-
tailed critique of the second draft of the manuscript and
his invaluable editorial suggestions.

The Authors of the chapter, "The United States and
Japan," wish to thank Dr. Shen-yu-Dai, who contributed

a valuable paper on Asian attitudes towards American thermonuclear experiments in the Pacific, and Richard A. Steele for offering helpful insights into the politics of the Far East.

The authors are deeply indebted to Muhammad el Farra, Chief of the United Nations Section, Arab States' Delegation Office and Attaché, Syrian Delegation to the United Nations, who, while not endorsing all of the views expressed pertaining to the Middle East, contributed valuable source materials for the Arab countries, particularly on the Arab-Israeli conflict.

The authors recognize their deep indebtedness to the Associates of the Foreign Policy Research Institute who have furnished continuing intellectual stimulation, especially Dr. Hans Kohn, Dr. Paul Linebarger, Dr. Norman D. Palmer and Dr. Stefan Possony.

Finally, the authors and editors wish to express their deepest gratitude to Joy Mohrfeld for her excellent preparation of the many drafts of the manuscript which required consummate patience, skill and imagination.

Contents

PART II
The trials of cooperation

The United States and Japan
ALVIN J. COTTRELL, JAMES E. DOUGHERTY and ELLEN ERVIN

The United States and the Philippines
WALTER F. HAHN, JOSEPH A. PETERS and EDGAR ROSENTHAL

PART III
The neutralism of non-cooperation

The United States and Egypt
JAMES E. DOUGHERTY and ANWAR SYED

PART IV
General conclusions

Introduction

At this, the present stage of the Free World's struggle for peace and security, American foreign policy turns increasingly on the situation in Asia. In Western Europe, national economies have attained unprecedented high levels of productivity and individual standards of living, while the alliance that binds fifteen countries from the coasts of the North Atlantic to the shores of the Eastern Mediterranean marshals a powerful deterrent force against Soviet aggression. During the years of the patient European build-up after World War II, Asia was relegated to a secondary position. True, some economic aid had been granted to Asian countries, and in specific emergencies, such as the Korean War and Indo-Chinese crisis, the United States brought its military and diplomatic potential to bear in an effort to check communist aggression. Nevertheless, Europe never relinquished its place of primacy in our comprehensive foreign programs. This situation is now in the process of changing.

With the security of Western Europe much improved over what it was in 1948, the major American strategic effort is presently being directed to the vast area stretching from newly independent Libya to long independent Japan. The stakes are high: The tremendous human and natural resources of Asia must ultimately tip the scale one way or the other in the contest being waged for a new world order. The issue hangs in doubt, for communism, whose intellectual appeal has been exhausted and whose armed might has been checkmated in Europe, still poses either a military or a psycho-political threat to every Asian nation on the rim around the Sino-Soviet bloc. Since the death of Stalin, it has become obvious that Asia is to be the arena for the new phase of the "competitive co-existence" struggle.

Along with the shift of emphasis to Asia has come a realization how inadequate is the level of knowledge in the United States concerning the methods for winning the trust and friendship of the Asian peoples and for performing the military, economic and political tasks which must be performed in order to win their voluntary allegiance to the defense of the Free World. In view of the difficulties which the United States has encountered in dealing with other members of the Atlantic Community, it should come as no surprise that these tasks present a staggering challenge in regions of the world with which the United States maintained, up to the outbreak of the Second World War, some important commercial, but only tenuous cultural and political relations.

The purpose of this study is to help the student of Asian affairs to isolate the areas of tension in United States-Asian relations. For purposes of this work, *tension* was taken to mean a condition which reflects the pursuit of incompatible foreign policy objectives. Once this condition obtains, nations may be able to cooperate on specific *ad hoc* problems, but they cannot agree upon broad purposes such as mutual defense.

The five nations selected for presentation in this study are: India, Indonesia, Japan, the Philippines and Egypt. The choice of these five among the states of Free Asia appears warranted by the circumstance that each of the nations selected is representative of Asian responses to American Foreign Policy. The first section of this study entitled "The Temper of Neutralism," deals with India and Indonesia. These countries have played a significant role in the development of the so-called "neutralist" philosophy of international relations. The second section, "The Trials of Cooperation," examines the relations of the United States with two allies in the Pacific, Japan and the Philippines. Both of these nations, although sensitive to suggestions that Washington dominates their politics, have pledged them-selves to support American defense measures in the Far East. The last section treats of "The Tactics of Non-Co-operation" and focuses attention upon U.S.-Egyptian rela-tions during the Cold War. It will be noted that through-out the study considerable stress is placed upon official statements by the governmental leaders and editorial com-ments by the major newspapers of the countries in question. These expressions have been selected to indicate the tone of Asian-American tensions. They have not been accepted uncritically, but are carefully assessed against the back-ground of political, strategic, social and economic develop-ments. One caveat is in order: this study does not dwell on *all* the aspects of U.S.-Asian relations, and hence it should be remembered that the spotlight is turned on jarring tensions, not upon gratifying harmonies.

The authors have not taken refuge behind that non-committal "impartiality" which is so frequently equated with scholarly methods. Once conclusions were reached after careful research, there seemed to be little need to vitiate them by circumlocution.

PART I

The temper of neutralism

The United States and India

INTRODUCTION

In the Indian political world view, the contest for power between the United States and the communist bloc appears as the major source of the tensions which have arisen between India and the United States during recent years. Practically all of the points on which India and the United States take issue with one another, such as economic aid, color discrimination, the use of force in international relations, and the whole complex of questions usually called colonialism, take on their major meaning as far as the Indians are concerned within the context of the Cold War, in which every American action and decision is viewed merely as a move to gain an advantage over the communist bloc, regardless of the genuine interests of India and the Asian peoples. Indian leaders are convinced that to become embroiled in this bipolar struggle would be tantamount to losing everything that India has gained in her long struggle for national independence. India's determination to free herself from the coils of Big Power diplomacy began to manifest itself as soon as India achieved Dominion status in 1947, although its roots reach farther back into the history of the Congress Party.

Prime Minister Nehru summarized this aspect of his country's policy in a parliamentary address in 1952 when he said: "If there is a cold war today, certainly we are neutral. It does not matter who is right and who is wrong. We will not join in this exhibition of mutual abuse." [1] India's refusal to commit herself to either the communist or the Western side is founded not only upon moral conviction with which the policy is usually identified but also to a great extent upon the concrete facts of India's position in international society. Indian leaders are well aware of the military weakness of their country during the period of transition from a colonial to a national state. Although Indians are predisposed by virtue of the influence of ideas received from England and the other Western democracies, and by the immense prestige of the Gandhian doctrine of non-violent action towards methods of liberal persuasion rather than of coercion in politics, they cannot blink the strategic implications of geographical proximity to the two most powerful communist states in the world. They fear that partiality toward the West would lead to uncontrollable tensions on the Asian continent. Therefore, India has chosen to follow in the postwar decade what may aptly be called a policy of eclectic neutrality. (The Indians dislike the term "neutrality" because of its passive, negative connotations, and they insist that their position is really one of independent, constructive judgment relative to the merit of each issue.) This policy of neutrality seems all the more baffling to Americans because the slogans which the Indian leaders have stressed in their efforts to forge a unified national consciousness and to assume the leadership of the uncommitted nations of Asia, such as anti-colonialism, anti-racism, anti-militarism, etc., are pointed more against the West than against the communist bloc. Following a period of harmonious Indo-American relations just after the end of the war, the United States has found itself increasingly singled out as the *bête noire* of Indian public opinion—the foreign whipping boy on which nationalism exercises its muscles. Hard facts help to explain the phenomenon, without explaining it completely. Thus Western colonialism strikes the Indians as more offensive than the Soviet brand mainly because the former is the type which they have experienced firsthand in the past. Today, virtually any policy which is pursued by the United States, or by some of its NATO allies, or sometimes even by the United Nations, savors of historic colonial imperialism merely if it appears to the most sensitive Indian editor to involve a Western imposition upon any underdeveloped area which the Indians choose as a matter of course to regard as forming part of their community of interest. On the other hand, the Soviet Union's hold upon its eastern neighbors has caused relatively little stir, since the European satellites are geographically and culturally remote from the Indian sub-continent. Even the expansionist tendencies of Communist China have not alarmed Indians nearly as much as American policy. Indian spokesmen readily explain that the Chinese, far from being outsiders, share part of their Asian community of interest. Hence Chinese moves or threats to move in Asia since 1949 must be viewed as efforts either to consolidate the legitimate interests of China (Tibet and Formosa) or to support anti-Western movements toward forcible national unification (Korea and Indo-China). Thus one of the most serious causes of Indo-American tensions is, from the American viewpoint, the readiness of Indians, despite their avowed neutrality, to be more vocal in their criticisms of the West than of the communist bloc. The Indian might deem it to be the quintessence of neutrality to judge the United States by liberal Jeffersonian standards and to judge the Soviet Union by totalitarian standards. When the Indians do this, remarked Taya Zinkin, Bombay correspondent of the *Manchester Guardian,* "their reaction is always less favorable to the U. S. than to Russia, whose redemption they regard beyond hope." [2] Americans are likely to be at a loss to see how this particular display of neutral thinking is compatible with the strong moral tone in which India's foreign policy pronouncements are generally couched. There appears to underlie this misunderstanding a fundamental difference in the approach adopted by Indians and Americans in their analysis of the world's political problems at the mid-century point.

The nature of Indo-American tensions becomes apparent from a selection of statements on the following issues: The Korean War, Formosa, Indo-China, China, Kashmir, Pakistan Arms Aid, the New Course of American Foreign Policy, the United Nations, American Personalities, The South African Issue, Colonial Territories, Equality for Asia, and U. S. Economic Aid.

THE KOREAN WAR

Since the end of World War II Indians have looked upon Korea as an unfortunate victim of the Great Power Struggle. As early as 1945, *The Hindu,* an independent conservative newspaper, complained that "the interests and just rights of smaller peoples have to be subordinated to the prestige and power of the major nations," and cited Korea as an example of "how rivalry between the mighty postpones the dawn of independence to small peoples." The sufferings of the peninsular country were laid to the fact that "two major powers imagine that their strategic interests clash in her territory." [3] Throughout those critical years the tone of the Indian press remained constant. Meanwhile, India, although she supported the original police action against the aggressor in Korea, found it increasingly difficult to see eye to eye with the United States with respect to the measures subsequently taken to resist the aggression. Prime Minister Nehru on one occasion observed regretfully that "the world had gone to save Korea but, in the process, reduced Korea to mud and dust." He then went on to explain India's peacemaking effort as being "motivated by the misery and suffering of that country which had been reduced to shambles by countries which had ostensibly gone to help." Whenever there was any indication that the United States might attempt to extend the area of conflict, such as at the time the 38th Parallel was crossed and the Yalu power plants were bombed, it drew an agitated reaction from the Indians. Nehru once expressed the fear that Korea might be utterly devastated or "even blown off the map according to the whims of power-conscious politicians." [4]

Throughout the three years of hostilities the Indian Government, both in and out of the U. N., played an active part in trying to localize the conflict and bring about a peaceful solution. The actual silencing of the guns, however, did not result in the easing of Indo-American relations which many had expected. Two major factors which help to explain why the tensions continued were India's assigned role in handling the prisoner-of-war exchange and her prospective status in a Korean peace conference. Statements by leading U. S. Administration and Republican Party spokesmen raising doubts about the impartiality of the Neutral Nations' Repatriation Commission, of which India was the Chairman, deeply rankled the press of that country. The Indians had psychologically braced themselves to encounter Chinese intransigence and South Korean hysteria, but the American attitude came somewhat as a surprise which first perplexed and then angered them. Secretary of State Dulles' reference to the "so-called neutral" commission, as well as his remark that he was "not happy" about the work of the N.N.R.C., were taken in India as insults upon the nation's integrity or as insinuations that the South Koreans were quite justified in conducting their campaign of abuse. Calling Senator Knowland's assertion that India was "sabotaging the peace as she did the war" an extraordinary comment, *The Hindu* warned that "these leaders by their statements are encouraging the Rhee government in its policy of incitement." [5] Irate Indian editors began to sprinkle terms such as "sabotage" and "treachery" over their own editorial pages. If the United States stands for peace, asserted the *Free Press Journal*, "then it is high time that the antics of its spokesmen assumed a more reasonable, responsible and persuasive hue," or else drop all pretenses.[6] "The impression is strong," another editor noted,

> that the U. N. Command is very much influenced by, even if it does not share, the South Korean opposition to the armistice. . . . The U. N. Command, taking its cue from Washington, has not been as cooperative with the N.N.R.C. as it should be.[7]

Other newspapers were less restrained. "The question might as well be directed at this stage to the U. S.: Is it for peace or for war?"[8] The Prime Minister demanded that Washington denounce Rhee's irresponsible actions, and remained unsatisfied with the assurance that moderation and forbearance were being urged upon the South Korean government.[9] Indian public opinion remained perturbed for some time, but during the later stages of the prisoner-exchange program the impression grew that the United States was showing an increasingly sympathetic understanding of India's difficult role as the "honest broker" in Korea.

Indian public opinion was further chagrined at the insistent opposition of the United States to India's participation in a Korean peace conference on the grounds that she was not a belligerent. India preferred to look upon herself as something more than merely a non-belligerent nation. She pointed to her good offices as one of the prime factors which had smoothed the way toward an armistice. Nonetheless, a head-on collision over this issue was avoided almost at the last minute when India withdrew her candidacy for a seat at the peace conference table before the question came to a vote in the U. N. Assembly. Meanwhile, India stands committed to the creation of a unified, independent and democratic Korea with representative institutions. Nehru retains his confidence in the value of the open conference approach which was adopted at Geneva in the spring of 1954, when the Indo-Chinese settlement was negotiated, and when Korea was also on the agenda. As the day of settlement in Korea kept being postponed indefinitely, Indian misgivings about the situation continued to grow. As recently as January of 1955, the Congress Party called Korea "a source of grave danger which may lead to large-scale conflict," and in the same month V. K. Krishna Menon, leader of India's U. N. Delegation and Nehru's cabinet associate in foreign affairs, expressed a reminder that Korea was far from being settled:

> It is a mistake to think that we are free from trouble. South Korea has the largest and best equipped army in the whole of Asia, with the exception of China. It has an army of 21 divisions, or probably 27 divisions, a very considerable air force, and support of the Seventh Fleet. What is more, these men have been trained not only by very efficient instructors, but also they are seasoned in war. Our best efforts have failed up till now in taking any positive step. We have succeeded only in preventing its getting worse.[10]

One postscript to the whole Korean question perhaps merits being added here. Although the prompt U. N. condemnation of North Korea's aggression five years ago was the occasion of greatest Indo-American agreement over Korea during the last decade, there has recently appeared in India a tendency to seek justification for that aggression. Not long ago, elder statesman C. Rajagopalachari asked:

> Is it so completely clear that the partition of Korea into North and South was so good and permanent that we should consider any attempted unification to be an aggression? Of course, all violent efforts are to be condemned but can we maintain that the use of violence to unify

Korea should be deemed as a proof of unalterable communist aggressive spirit? [11]

FORMOSA

Indians regard this island as another pawn in the game of the Big Powers. The Indian press quite readily interprets American motives for retaining a hold over Formosa in terms of the power struggle. *The Hindu* has noted that "the strategically-located island can be used as part of a chain in a strategic line against Chinese and Russian mainland stretching from the Aleutians to Australia." [12] "The island's strategic importance is undoubted," said *The Statesman*, "and cannot be underrated so long as China is considered a hostile Power," but at the same time it characterized American involvement in that part of the Far East "one of the most regrettable aspects of the international scene." [13]

> America's commitment in Formosa is morally the weakest point in her foreign policy and the strongest in Peking's. The American presence in Formosa has been a godsend ever since the fighting in Korea, and thereafter Indo-China, died down. . . . Revolutions, once established, have been traditionally dependent on threats from outside to provide those cohesive and energizing forces so necessary for their survival.[14]

The feeling is widespread in India that the future of peace in the Far East hinges upon American intentions with respect to Formosa. The U. S. "keep-them-guessing" policy *vis-a-vis* the off-shore isles comes in for special criticism, and is considered highly dangerous, since "the result might be a major war which nobody wanted." [15] *The Times of India* remarked that "Washington would be capable of blundering into war [through some provocative move] without meaning to do so." [16]

The Government of India, of course, insists unequivocally that Formosa is part of China and must be restored to her in accordance with the Potsdam and Cairo agreements. Generally speaking, neither the Government nor the press has yet come fully to grips with the dichotomy which has developed between the legal and the strategic aspects of the situation since the time those agreements were made. Instead of suggesting alternative solutions that would commend themselves as realistic to the policymakers in the United States, India seems content to rely upon the thought that time and the biological facts of life are running against the United States and Chiang Kai-shek in Formosa. Public opinion is virtually unanimous in taking it for granted that the General must leave the island sooner or later, and the United States is roundly criticized for supporting him out of considerations of "loyal friendship." Any hope of reinstating this "unwanted" Chinese leader on the mainland is deemed ludicrous.

> The myth that China was lost to the Communists through Democratic bungling, that General Chiang Kai-shek has not been rejected by the Chinese people and that one day he will return in triumph to Peking is a self-deceiving invention. From it sprang the folly that he should be aided and abetted until his homecoming. . . . The number of American leaders who privately admit that Chiang has lost the "mandate of heaven" steadily grows.[17]

Indians can bring themselves to say only little, if anything, favorable about the Formosa regime. When Chester Bowles, former United States Ambassador to India and an American with whom Indians were often quick to agree, called the Nationalist Government's land reform program "a model for every free nation in Asia," and said that the Nationalists are determined to turn Formosa into a "model of economic development for Asia," [18] one Indian critic who reviewed his book could only conclude that Mr. Bowles "has had his joke at last." [19]

Indian opinion is not nearly so unanimous on the subject of Formosa's future. *The Statesman* has found it regrettable that "one of the tragedies is that those most entitled to a voice in the future of the island, the Formosans themselves, tend to be ignored by all except the recruiting sergeants of General Chiang's aging army." [20] The utmost that the moulders of public opinion might demand is a plebiscite, under the auspices of the U. N. or of neutral countries, to determine in an atmosphere free of Nationalist pressure the wishes of the inhabitants concerning their political future. Meanwhile, the Indian press hopes that Formosa can be isolated and that Chiang will call a halt to his "pointless" raids on the mainland until a settlement can be achieved. By the same token, of course, it looks to Peking to abandon its attacks upon Formosa. The feeling is rather strong that the initiative for a solution to the Formosan problem must now come from the United States, especially in view of Chou-en-lai's proposal for direct talks which he made at Bandung. According to *Amrita Bazar Patrika*, "it would be extremely regrettable if the opportunity provided by the Chinese Premier is missed or ignored by the U. S. Government." [21]

INDO-CHINA

India viewed the fighting in Indo-China primarily as an effort of a nationalist movement to throw off a foreign yoke. Doubtless the Chinese provided arms and encouragement in the "common desire to oust the Westerner," and in recognition of the "Communist viewpoint of the Viet-Minh leadership," [22] but in Indian eyes the American intervention was the more odious, for it involved giving material support to the continuation of the French colonial regime. Thus the military action in Indo-China took on essentially the appearance of a colonial war, rather than a communist aggression. In 1954, when the United States first flirted with the idea of full-scale intervention, grave apprehensions were voiced in India. American criticisms of Nehru for refusing to grant passage over Indian territory to the U. S. airlift of French troops considerably irritated the Indians, who recalled that one of Nehru's first acts as Foreign Minister back in 1947 had been to institute a policy of strict control over French planes flying over India, so that it could not appear that the Indians were acting against the people of Indo-China.[23]

Note has already been taken of that Indian view which favors the seizing of every opportunity to reduce international tensions through the conference device. The Geneva Conference on Indo-China generated a great deal of interest. Nehru's formula, which had the backing of the Prime Ministers who had attended the Colombo meeting, served as a basis for the eventual settlement reached at Geneva, where Krishna Menon played an active mediatory rôle. India welcomed the cease-fire and hailed the work of the conference as evidence that "international disputes could be solved by peaceful negotiation." [24] The newspapers, however, expressed some disappointment at the attitude of the United States, which seemed to act the part of a silent and disapproving spectator during the Geneva proceedings. *The Hindu* thought it was "premature to adopt the pessimistic American view that the settlement necessarily implied the communisation of the whole of Indochina." [25] Neither was it prepared to "assume in advance" that the communist promises would be broken. The distrust shown by the United States towards the Geneva agreement had many unfortunate repercussions, according to the Indians. They interpreted Mr. Dulles' organization of the South East Asia Treaty Organization as a hurried and an angry reaction to the peaceful settlement made at Geneva. India, of course, could not be expected to find a policy which distributes guns nearly as palatable as a policy which assumes that guns are unnecessary. SEATO, the Indians thought, contravened not only the spirit but also the letter of the Geneva agreement.

Later, the Indian Government expressed concern that the United States was putting pressure on South Viet Nam to evade the Geneva terms under which elections were scheduled to be held by mid-1956. It was reported that General J. Lawton Collins, President Eisenhower's Personal Representative in Indo-China, had advised Diem's Government that as a sovereign agent it was not bound by the decision to hold elections in conjunction with North Viet Nam.[26] *The Times of India* stated that the Americans were interested in South Viet Nam as a "permanent resistant to Communism," and seemed to be "building up the Diem regime to a point where it can function as a reliable 'bulwark' against Communism." The newspaper then went on to warn that "the objectives of the armistice cannot be achieved unless South Viet Nam orientates itself in a way that will facilitate cooperation with the Viet Minh."[27] To the Indians, American attitudes appeared to be more intransigent than those of many responsible people in France, who were willing to accept the reality of Viet-Minh and to develop cultural and commercial ties between North and South.[28] But not all of the press comments were carpingly anti-U.S. *The Statesman* attempted to appreciate Washington's point of view, noting that "the Americans must be the most pained and apprehensive observers of the present imbroglio and dissipation of South Viet-Nam's fighting strength," especially when analyzed in comparison with the situation in the North, where an increase of armed strength was taking place.[29] Current Indian thinking on the problem of the Indo-Chinese states was succinctly summarized in an editorial in *The Times of India* during Cambodia's change of government in March, 1955:

It is only because the tendency persists among the major powers to support certain factions within the Indochina states that crises of the kind that has occurred in Cambodia are of more than purely internal significance. Once again it needs to be reiterated that the principle of non-interference must be strictly applied if the armistice settlement is to enable the people of Indochina to evolve the shape and character of their own independence.[30]

The Indian press resents any insinuation that the International Supervisory Commissions, functioning in Indo-China under India's chairmanship, are not impartial, or that they are instruments through which India attempts to influence Indo-China's internal affairs. India is particularly sensitive to any allegations of what might be called cultural imperialism, even when such a policy is broached in words of encouragement rather than accusation. Recently, General Collins was reported to have argued that New Delhi should display a bit more concern over the independence and safety of South Viet-Nam and over the growth of communist influence in Southeast Asia. Apparently the General hinted broadly at India's historic cultural thrust into Thailand and Cambodia. *The Times of India* rejoined immediately by calling the General's remarks irrelevant and ludicrous:

> The American General inferred that increasing Communist influence should properly be a matter of serious concern for India. The point has still to be impressed on the Western democracies that New Delhi is completely uninterested in cultural or political spheres of interest and that its sole desire is that the States of Southeast Asia by becoming free and independent will automatically ensure the entire region peace and stability.[31]

CHINA

China looms large and important both in the Asian scene and in Indo-American relations. Shortly after the Chinese

communists came into power over the whole mainland,
Prime Minister Nehru told a group of reporters in New
York that "the happenings in China are such that they cannot be ignored." [32] Ever since that time, India has been
inclined to accord a certain amount of deference to the
Government of Red China, and she has been more than a
little puzzled by the U. S. policy of refusing to recognize
the Communist Government and refusing to seat that
regime in the United Nations. As far as New Delhi is concerned, it is mainly a question of Peking's being able to
maintain effective control over nearly six hundred million
Chinese and to rule the country with undisputed authority.

One of the major goals in India's foreign relations during
recent years has been not only to make the world more acceptable to China, but also to make China more acceptable
to the world.[33] Nehru and other spokesmen in ranking
positions have often reiterated their contention that there
can be no settlement of the problems of the Far East or of
Southeast Asia unless the central fact of the existence of
the People's Government of China is accepted and acted
upon by all the nations of the world which are concerned
with the stability of that sector of the globe.[34] On one
occasion Nehru went so far as to call the exclusion of Red
China from the United Nations "the root cause of all international troubles during the last four years." [35] *The Times
of India* spoke of the American policy of non-recognition
as "one of the most tragic and costly major mistakes made
by the democracies in recent years." [36] The *National Herald* characterized it as "a first-class blunder in history." A
number of newspapers have blamed the United States for
being so intransigent as to leave China no alternative but
to seek the close friendship of Moscow. The *Tribune,* in
the fall of 1951, lamented that so few Americans grasped
"the obvious fact" about Nehru's China policy, which was
"not designed to strengthen Communist imperialism but to
weaken it by demonstrating to the people of China that

their friends are to be found not among the Communist states alone but everywhere." [37] It should be recalled, however, that it was very difficult for the United States in the fall of 1951 to think of becoming any less intransigent toward a country with which it was engaged in mortal conflict. There is also the broader question, the answer to which can not now be more than conjecture, as to whether China was induced by the Soviet Union to enter the Korean War at least partially for the object of creating an unbridgeable gap between China and the United States, thereby postponing any such *detente* as India deemed desirable until Sino-Soviet ties were strengthened. Once the Korean War was over, the dominant tone of the Indian press was that there was no longer any excuse for delay in resolving the question of Peking's representation in the U. N. *The Hindu* commented:

> The future of Indochina and the stability of Southeast Asia depend on securing the goodwill of the Chinese. It is more than ever necessary that the international position of the Chinese Government should be recognized and that it should be associated with the efforts to bring about a lessening of world tension.[38]

A few voices dissenting from this majority position could be heard, nonetheless. *The Statesman* did not consider the reception of China into the circle of U. N. members so urgent as to justify overhasty action. Noting that Peking's "bellicose association has not subsided," the newspaper deemed it proper that "representation should wait upon China's disassociation from aggression against the Republic of South Korea and its sponsor and protector, the United Nations." [39] But by early 1955, even *The Statesman* had come to be critical of the continued exclusion of Red China from the world body.

The issue of the American airmen imprisoned in China furnished an occasion for the articulation of suspicions

that the United Nations was being too patently converted
into an instrument of U. S. policy. Most Indians believed
that the Chinese Government had a case which at least
merited a hearing in New York before the U. N. arrived at
a decision in the matter. *United Asia* concluded that it was
"abundantly clear . . . [that] the charges are on the
whole legitimate."

> Asian opinion has by and large accepted the Chinese
> version. The U. N. arbitration move indicated beyond
> question the growth of a dangerous bias in the U. N.
> organization, directed primarily against the Chinese Gov-
> ernment. For how can the U. N., by its own recent con-
> ventions, have any concern in so domestic a matter as the
> imprisonment of spies? And if it must, why was no move
> taken against the racial policies of South Africa, which by
> any standards are a greater sin against international eti-
> quette than the mere imprisonment of spies cloaked in
> uniform? [40]

From the American perspective, such an opinion does, of
course, presuppose acceptance of the Chinese version.
Furthermore, it contains certain equations and judgments
with which the American is hardly likely to concur. He
especially would take exception to the notion that the
"imprisonment of spies cloaked in uniform" in this concrete instance should be classified as the same sort of "domestic matter" as Stridjom's segregation policies. As for
the "sin against international etiquette," its meaning would
be lost upon the American, who prefers to distinguish both
sins and etiquette from law.

The Indian Government supported the visit of Secre-
tary-General Hammarskjold to China in the interests of
reaching an amicable settlement. Newspapers hoped that
even though no gains should be immediately apparent, at
least it might mark the beginning of a normalization of relations with China. Meanwhile, some editors wondered

about the motives of the Chinese in imprisoning the Americans. *The Hindu* thought that the incident might have been "a measure of retaliation to the recent pact between the U. S. and Marshal Chiang Kai-shek." [41] Later, the same journal declared that Peking's action was "obviously related to other Far Eastern problems such as the armistice in Korea, admission to the U. N., and the presence of the U. S. land and naval forces in the Pacific." [42]

J. K. Banerji, a columnist for the *Hindustan Standard,* wrote toward the end of 1950, just a few weeks after the Chinese entered the Korean War, that "the essence of the Far Eastern problem is the challenge of New China to the claim of the U. S. that the entire Pacific Ocean stretching right up to the shores of China is the security zone of the U. S." [43] This begins to touch the heart of the matter, as the Indians see it. Why should America be afraid of China, many of them ask. China, after all, has no fleet of long-range bombers or a navy which could pose any serious threat to the United States. On the other hand, India does not lack columnists who call attention to the other side of the coin:

> In the event of a war with the West, the Chinese will neither be easily destroyed nor forced into submission. This fact may carry no weight with those in the U. S. A. who believe not only in bargaining from strength but also in a show of strength, but people with reason throughout the world shudder at the thought of its possible consequences. [44]

The Indians do not dwell so exclusively upon America's emotional and adamant feelings about China that they are blind to the stubborn position adopted by China on a number of issues. But it is doubtless true to say that the Indians are predisposed to explain away the latter more than they are the former. The Indians themselves are emotional in their relations with China, but the emotions involved might best be described as familial. The two countries can be "touchy" at times, just as two brothers might be, but they can also be expected to close ranks when necessary to confront the outsider. To the Indians, the Chinese are fellow-Asians first, and communists second. This is only to say that at the present, the consciousness of being Asian, which really means to be in a similar plight, is stronger than the consciousness of being liberal-democratic, as distinct from communist. Some Indians, like Sardar K. M. Panikkar, former Indian Ambassador to Peking, and V. K. Krishna Menon, have even expressed doubts that the Chinese are properly to be classified as communists at all.[45]

Since the Bandung Conference in April 1955, Indians appear to have been under the impression that communist China was being "rapidly drawn into the orbit of Asian powers and to that extent identified less with a communist bloc dominated by the Soviet Union." This observation was made by *The Statesman*, which also took note of China's "pledge" to the ideals of the United Nations which was embodied by inference in the final communique issued from Bandung. That communique, said the newspaper, made Chou En-lai "a party to suggestions that the U. N.'s organization should be used in various beneficial ways and that the U. N. Charter should be upheld." [46] In Indian eyes, China has strengthened her claim to a seat in the international organization by identifying herself with these sentiments. It is reasonably safe to say, however, that Indian opinion would not regard the presence of "two Chinas" in the U. N. as a satisfactory solution of the problem. The Prime Minister, in a recent speech to the Parliament, said:

> It is patent that you cannot recognize two Chinas. You can only recognize one . . . obviously Formosa is not China. . . . It is a most extraordinary state of affairs that the U. N. calls the island of Formosa China. Geography seems to mean nothing to the U. N.[47]

This is not a new position for the Indians. It has been voiced frequently within the last two years. In November 1953, *The Hindu* commented that "Mr. Dulles' suggestion that Peking may represent China in the General Assembly, while Formosa (with the veto) will speak for the Chinese in the Security Council seems most improper and unhelpful." [48] The American evaluation of Formosa is understood in India to be crucial to the whole situation. It seems "pretty plain," said *The Statesman* recently, that "if a violent solution of the Formosan problem can be avoided, recognition of the Peking regime as China's true representative in the U. N. will not be very far off." [49]

KASHMIR

The Cold War, according to the Indians, has shaped the American position on Kashmir to the disadvantage of India. It must be remembered that the problem of Kashmir is a very intimate one for India, and therefore a high degree of sensitivity on this score is to be expected. A responsible and well-informed section of Indian public opinion is even ready to agree with the stand taken by Jacob Malik, the Soviet Delegate in the U. N. Security Council, on January 17, 1952, when he condemned "Anglo-American" interference in the internal affirs of Kashmir as a deliberate attempt to prevent a solution with the objective of turning Kashmir into "a trust territory . . . an imperialist war base." [50] An Anglo-American resolution in November 1952 which sought to reduce the number of Indian troops in Kashmir provoked considerable resentment in the Indian press, "already suspicious of Anglo-American moves and sensitive to their machinations." [51] An editorial in the *National Standard* a few weeks later criticized Britain and the United States for trying

> to draw the curtain across Pakistan's original act of aggression, and presented a way of escape for the Security

Council from the obligation of taking action against the aggressor. . . . The reason obviously was that the cold war strategists who dominate the U. N. today wanted to placate Pakistan, and enlist her aid in the campaign, even though they may have to condone instead of condemning aggression in the bargain.[52]

A report of Pakistan's alleged intention to join a Middle Eastern Defense Organization (MEDO) was taken as evidence that India's earlier suspicions were well founded. The MEDO project, however, was soon abandoned by a decision of Secretary Dulles. Indian resentment was next directed against the U. S. role in Kashmir's internal developments. The conduct of some American military observers was deemed "indiscreet, if not legally culpable." [53] There was popular suspicion that Americans, particularly Adlai Stevenson and Ambassador George Allen, played a sinister role in 1953 during Sheikh Abdullah's abortive attempt to take Kashmir out of the Indian Union and either form an independent state or join it to Pakistan. Denials followed, but the impression lingered that America was "mixed up in the grand conspiracy." [54]

As far as India is concerned, U. S. arms aid to Pakistan has given the Kashmir problem an entirely different meaning. Pakistani Premier Ali's reference to this aid as likely to make a settlement over Kashmir easier was "a plain enough hint," in the words of *The Statesman*.[55] It was feared that any military assistance to Pakistan was "bound to result in the exercise of undue pressure" on India.[56] Apprehensions mounted that it might strengthen Pakistan to the point where she would be emboldened to fight for Kashmir. The United States was accused of thwarting the peaceful settlement of the Kashmir problem by tilting the balance between the parties to the dispute.[57] Recalling President Eisenhower's assurance that he would undertake to forestall any misuse of the military aid for aggressive purposes, Nehru pointed out that the United States had condemned neither the aggressor nor the act of aggression in Kashmir when the trouble had started six years previously.[58] *The Hindu* was likewise unconvinced by the President's assurance:

> The U. S. has found it difficult enough to restrain even a puppet regime like Syngman Rhee's; it will be impossible for it to control a country like Pakistan, particularly on Kashmir.[59]

Nehru, while refusing in a speech before Parliament President Eisenhower's offer of arms aid to India, also called for the withdrawal of American military observers on either side of the cease fire line in Kashmir, saying that "they can no longer be treated as neutrals by us and hence their presence there appears improper." [60] Vedette, a columnist for *The Statesman*, thought that this was a moderately-worded statement, put forth "in the hope that the wise need no more than a hint." [61] Vedette went on to say that the "silence and mild comment" which greeted Nehru's speech in the United States meant either that the Americans appreciated the Indian case or "that opinion in that country has been shocked by a sense of guilt." [62] By way of contrast, the Indian newspapers were quick to respond to the Prime Minister's "hint". They urged the Indian Government to take vigorous measures if the parties concerned did not heed the admonition. As a matter of fact, the American military observers were subsequently withdrawn from the area by the U. N. Nonetheless, the stalemate continued and the Indian Government insisted that negotiations on Kashmir could not be conducted on an acceptable basis since Pakistan had received U. S. military aid.

U. S. ARMS AID TO PAKISTAN

Apart from its direct bearing on the Kashmir issue, the United States policy of arming Pakistan was opposed by

India on more fundamental grounds, for the Indians regard such arms aid as damaging to the best interests of the whole of Asia. This form of military help from one of the protagonists in the global struggle contradicts Nehru's idea of an uncommitted "peace area" outside the arena of the Cold War. He sees a policy of avoiding commitments to one side or the other as the key to India's security and hence Pakistan's alignment with the United States as setting up a focal point of tension right on India's borders. Such a development, it is feared, will have disastrous consequences for the security and the peace of Asia.[63] Nehru has frequently expressed misgivings about the unfortunate results which will inevitably flow from the American decision.[64] Here is a representative opinion on the subject from the pages of *The Hindustan Times:*

> To drag Pakistan into the Middle East Defense Organization will be to drag the whole of the Indian sub-continent into a war and no one can say that this is a matter which does not concern India. Any part of the territory of the Indo-Pakistan sub-continent cannot be dragged into military commitments elsewhere without India also being drawn into it.[65]

Beyond the fear that they might become involved in an unwanted war, the Indians objected strenuously to the U. S.-Pakistan alliance because it was equated in their minds with "resurgent colonialism." Bitter experiences of past arming and use of Asian nationals to fight imperialistic wars were recalled by the Indians, who felt that Pakistan, by accepting the help of a Western power, was deserting the anticolonial struggle of the Asian nations and thereby jeopardizing her own independence.

Newspaper opinion, although strongly critical of the proposed pact, reflected the "disappointment of a friend" rather than any overt hostility. The editors generally found it difficult to understand why the United States preferred the friendship of Pakistan to that of India. The tone of most comment was puzzled. *The Hindustan Times'* editorial was typical:

> We cannot believe that the object of Washington is to alienate India from the U. S. and weaken the forces of democracy in Asia. . . . We cannot conceive of a more unfriendly act toward India than the conclusion of the proposed agreement by the U. S.[66]

Even the most violent anti-communists in India found very little to say in favor of the American policy of arms to Pakistan. The pro-American periodical *Thought* called the U. S. decision foolish, and at the same time characterized the Indian Government's reaction as "pathologically narrow and inhibited," adding that "there is no doubt that this country's innate goodness and humanity will survive the present stupidity of the American Government and the hysteria of our politicians." [67] *The Statesman* acknowledged at least one merit of the proposed aid. "As a focus for the expression of the feeling of national unity it has served a useful purpose—the only one, as India sees it." [68]

Recently, the Indians have tended to think that the United States may be deliberately playing up Pakistan against India. Although the motives for such a U. S. policy are rarely made quite clear, all of the foregoing developments reinforce this conclusion in Indian circles. The exclusion of India in May 1954 from the clemency proceedings for the Japanese War Criminals was considered in New Delhi to be unjustified and bad enough, but the substitution of Pakistan for India in the same proceedings was tantamount to heaping insult upon injury. *The Hindu* commented that "perhaps Pakistan's voice is now preferred because her foreign policy follows that of the United States closely at the moment." [69]

THE NEW COURSE OF
AMERICAN FOREIGN POLICY

Relations between India and the United States took a turn
for the worse, at least temporarily, after the Republican
victory at the polls in November 1952. India saw in the
new Administration's foreign policy an increased emphasis on military factors. In retrospect, this attitude seems
paradoxical in the light of President Eisenhower's stress,
during his campaign and his early months in office, upon
ending the Korean War which had been the main source
of contention between the two countries. Prime Minister
Nehru appears to have taken it for granted that a military
leader would naturally resort to military means for the solution of major political problems. In an address before
the lower House of Parliament he made an obvious reference to the new President, regretting the "intrusion of
military mentality in the chancelleries of the world," and
called it a dangerous development that "statesmanship is
taking a second place and is governed more by military
factors than the normal factors which statesmen consider." [70] Nehru made these remarks just after the decision
to "deneutralize" Formosa and while the blockade of China
was being discussed. Nehru continued:

> Certain statements made in the U. S. by the highest
> authorities in regard to the Far East have caused grave
> concern not only to us here but in many countries all
> over the world. All this talk of the blockade of China or
> other such steps obviously is not talk that leads to peace
> or settlement, whatever else it might lead to.[71]

The Eastern Economist declared that the decision to
take the wraps off Formosa was "based only on domestic
public opinion," and that its lack of wisdom lay in "the acceptance of American opinion as being superior to [that of]
the rest of the world." [72] The *National Standard* doubted

that President Eisenhower cared very much about what America's allies thought of his policies, and then proceeded to score the Administration's "dictatorial attitude . . . [and] apparent unfamiliarity with accepted diplomatic traditions." [73]

The enunciation by Secretary Dulles of the doctrine of "massive and instant retaliation at times and places of our own choosing" evoked intensified criticism of the foreign policy of the United States in India. *The Hindu* in a leading editorial entitled "Time to Stop" deplored this sudden turn in U. S. policy, which made the threat of hurling atomic thunderbolts its cornerstone. [74] A columnist in *The Times of India* wrote that "the discriminating will not conclude that the U. S. is aggressively inclined or that the American people desire a thermonuclear war. But they do conclude that the U. S. relies on military power to the exclusion of everything else." He was of the opinion that the "belligerent sounding speeches of American leaders" were "a key factor in the deplorable misunderstanding that has developed between the U. S. and the independent democracies." [75] Meanwhile, the continuation of the American H-bomb tests in the Pacific area, Nehru's protests notwithstanding, did little to allay Indian apprehensions that the United States intended to place primary reliance on thermonuclear diplomacy.

India of late has shown herself to be perturbed by a spectre which at present appears to be more imaginary than real, namely, that the Western military alliance will extend its operations to her own borders. Generally speaking, India has refrained from excessive criticisms of NATO, but when she has objected to it she has done so in regard to the possible applicability of NATO's provisions to the defense of Goa, the Portuguese settlement on the West Coast of the sub-continent. Recent developments in French North Africa have led Mr. Nehru to believe that NATO is gradually being converted from an organization designed to defend Western Europe into "an organization to defend colonial territories." [76] He sees France's NATO allies giving their tacit approval to the employment of French NATO contingents to quell a colonial uprising. It is not hard to imagine how the Prime Minister would draw a lesson from the North African precedent which, in view of Portugal's membership in NATO, might at some future date be applied against India in the Goan crisis. Americans for their part might well wonder about the validity of Mr. Nehru's fears, since they understand the Indian philosophy to preclude the use of force in the settlement of disputes, and therefore they do not see how the NATO Treaty provisions could ever become operative in the Goan situation.

Whereas India does not object to the whole concept of NATO, but only one of its possible implications, the attitude which it adopts toward the Southeast Asia Treaty Organization is more vehement. V. K. Krishna Menon has branded SEATO as a violation of the meaning of the U. N. Charter, on the grounds that it is "not any regional organization, but an organization of some imperial powers and others to protect a region, a modern version of the protectorate." [77] *The Hindustan Times* elaborated the point in this way:

> The vast majority of the peoples inhabiting [this region] are not associated with it and it is signed mostly by nations farthest away from it. Consequently, it cannot claim to be a regional organization under the U. N. Charter. To thrust protection on those who do not want it is a direct repudiation of the principles of sovereignty of nations and self-determination to which the signatories pay lip homage.[78]

If SEATO was organized, said *The Hindu,* "not so much against open aggression, as against infiltration," it would give rise to many delicate political problems, since it "is

all too easy for reactionary regimes like those in South
Korea and Siam to call all their critics and opponents
Communists." [79] Hence the pervading Indian fear of Big
Power intrusion into the political affairs of the Asian states
manifests itself with respect to this particular U. S.-in-
spired alliance. The usual American rejoinder to this com-
plaint is that if India is unwilling or unable to exert her
influence to counter effectively the subversive movements
in the free countries of Southeast Asia, the United States
is left with no alternative but to take the initiative against
a China which is both able and willing to exert *her* influence in the area. It is true that since the end of the war in
Indo-China, Nehru's awareness of the problem of infiltration has been increased and he has personally negotiated
with Peking in an effort to define the status of the "overseas Chinese." He is inclined to think that the problem
will work itself out, for he is confident that communism
cannot bring about a successful revolution in that part of
the world except under the guise of a struggle to liberate
a nation from a colonial yoke, and the opportunities along
these lines are diminishing. Therefore, he is bound to look
upon SEATO as an unnecessary irritant in the Asian environment. Washington hopes that his analysis is correct,
but it has learned from unhappy experience that it cannot
base its policy in the Far East and in Southeast Asia on
hope alone, nor can it base it exclusively upon assessments
of public opinion reactions in India, even though it be the
most populous free country in the world.

The creation of SEATO has doubtless heightened Indo-
American tensions, so far as the Indians are concerned. In
a sense, SEATO represents what might be called a very
authentic tension, for it springs more from divergent analyses and less from mere misunderstandings than do
some of the other tensions dealt with in this study. But
beyond the cogency of the Indian position, which many
Americans are willing to concede to be one of the rational

alternatives, although not the one which they prefer, there lurks an emotionalism in the Indian reaction to SEATO which Americans tend to regard as a mark of immaturity. *The Hindustan Times,* for example, posed what appears to Americans as a false dilemma when it asserted that "what Southeast Asia needs today is peace and the economic betterment of her peoples, not arms and military guarantees." [80] The same newspaper described SEATO as a "guarantee of security to be imposed on other countries without their consent," and said that it was "offensive to national and democratic sentiment everywhere and, most of all, in Asia." [81] Americans, of course, cannot fully concur with the Indians when they affect to speak on behalf of all national and democratic sentiment throughout Asia, and this reflects an aspect of the tensions in the relations of the two countries which must be taken into account. The press of each country is bound to sound petulant at times when the other's policies are under review, but the United States, fortified with a long tradition of independence and free expression, can afford to show greater forbearance. There is no need for Americans to become greatly upset when *The Hindu* depicts SEATO as "a one-sided alliance against hypothetical aggression," [82] or when Nehru calls the allies of the United States in Asia little pigmy countries, mere camp followers of the huge giant. [83] Perhaps both sides could learn a lesson from a remark made in March 1955 by India's Elder Statesman, C. Rajagopalachari, to the effect that "the great difference between America and India is that the means America is adopting for establishing peace on earth do not appeal to India." [84]

THE UNITED NATIONS

The informed Indian has become disillusioned about the United Nations, thinking that it too is a victim of the Cold War. In his eyes, the world organization, American in its inspiration and in its location, has often been converted into an instrument of United States foreign policy. Prime Minister Nehru subscribes to the view that the U. N. "is influenced very much by certain powers, including America," but would not go so far as to say that it is "dancing to the tunes of the United States." At a press conference in March 1953, he said that the United Nations did not appear to be very successful in accomplishing things, but rather served merely to keep issues in abeyance. To illustrate this point, he cited the difficulties which Burma encountered in her effort to get the U. N. to bring about the evacuation of Chinese Nationalist troops from her territory, and added the comment that India's own experience with the U. N. had "not been very happy." [85]

This attitude stems from what India considers to be the failure of the United Nations to resolve satisfactorily such questions as Kashmir, representation of Communist China, South Africa's racial discrimination policy, and the Tunisia-Morocco issue. According to Nehru,

> It is becoming rather significant how discussions on particular vital matters affecting world peace are avoided in the United Nations General Assembly, and when something is discussed, previous decisions have been taken which almost appear to be imposed upon the United Nations General Assembly. That is not the way either to work the United Nations to fulfill the purposes of the Charter, or to remove the tensions of the world.[86]

In less diplomatic language, *The Hindu* asserted that "the present composition of the Assembly is such that no resolution unacceptable to the United States has much chance of success." [87] The U. N., in short, is looked upon for all practical purposes as a "pocket borough" of the United States. Americans must realize that much of this disaffection can be traced to the general Indian impression that on most of the issues previously mentioned the United States adopts a position opposed to that of India and most of the other Asian nations. Indians are irritated by the U. N.'s cautious approach to complicated colonial problems. V. K. Krishna Menon, India's U. N. delegate, uttered this warning in 1953:

> We should not, if I may put it bluntly, have the U. N. deteriorate into a holy alliance where the gospel is the monopoly of the three sovereigns. . . . It must not become a quadruple alliance where there is legitimism and the suppression of all colonial revolt under the name of communism.[88]

Indian displeasure at the U. S.-U. N. alliance doubtless reached its climax at the time the Kashmir dispute was before the Security Council. When India felt compelled to reject the Anglo-American proposal of November 1952, which sought to reduce the number of Indian troops in Kashmir, the *National Standard* ran an editorial deploring the Great Powers' manipulation of the U. N.:

> India feels sad at having to defy an international body, to the building and sustenance of which she has contributed her utmost. . . . If ever there was a decision by the Security Council which went against all canons of justice, fair play and international morality, it was this resolution, and India has rightly expressed her unwillingness to accept it as binding on her. . . . When, through the action of certain power-conscious groups, that international body is sought to be made an instrument of intrigue and foul play, she cannot countenance it.[89]

If India had held a permanent seat on the Security Council, the Anglo-American proposal, of course, would have been vetoed. This raises the interesting possibility, long viewed with favor in New Delhi, that India might be admitted to the Security Council as a permanent member able to represent the sentiments of Asia, which the Indians insist are not being satisfactorily represented by the Chinese Nationalists. Such a suggestion has been put forth by Chester Bowles, former U. S. Ambassador to India, in his book *Ambassador's Report*.[90] From time to time, it seems as if India's displeasure with the West springs from the rankling disappointment that too little importance is attached to her rôle as a world power within the United Nations. This sensitivity was reflected by *The Hindu* when it noted that Indians were underrepresented on the U. N. Secretariat while Pakistanis exceeded their quota. The newspaper deemed it "unfortunate if the U. N.'s Secretary General should create the impression that only those countries which side with the West in the Cold War would find favor in his eyes." [91]

AMERICAN PERSONALITIES

During the U. S. election campaign of 1952, it was evident that the liberal tone of Adlai Stevenson's addresses appealed to Indian intellectuals much more than did the military background of General Eisenhower. Following the Republican victory, there were strong misgivings in India over the fact that a soldier who had played a leading part in the forging of the Western alliance was now the head of the democratic world. A few weeks after his inauguration, the *National Standard* referred to President Eisenhower as being "unwise and inept." [92] *The Statesman*, in October 1953 at the height of the McCarthy controversy, portrayed President Eisenhower as "largely the prisoner of Rightist elements in the Republican Party." [93] The tone of the Indian press has gradually become more favorable to the President during the last year, in view of the end of the two wars in Asia, the new American emphasis on the peaceful development of atomic energy, and the good will and peaceful intentions manifested by the President in the period leading up to the "summit meeting" at Geneva.

The Indian attitude has not softened toward Secretary of State John Foster Dulles, who has been seldom credited with the same degree of understanding which the President has been said to display. This attitude probably had its origins in January 1947, when Mr. Dulles, then a U. S. Delegate in the U. N. General Assembly, stated that in India, "Soviet Communism exercises a strong influence through the Interim Hindu Government." [94] Nehru, then the head of the Interim Government, replied that Dulles' remarks indicated an ignorance of the facts. The Indians resented the term "Hindu" quite as much as the allegation of Russian influence, since the national government included five Moslem members and other minorities' representatives. Four years later, Mr. Dulles was guilty of another diplomatic *faux pas* as far as the Indians were concerned when he failed to consult Nehru while drafting the Japanese Peace Treaty. When Dulles was named Secretary of State, the *Indian Express* asked: "As Secretary of State what will he actually be—Dulles the moderate or Dulles the extremist." It depicted him as a man of "unpredictable potentialities" and "dual personality" who is quite capable of "trading on the proverbially short memory of the public." [95] *The Times of India*, picking up an American characterization of Mr. Dulles as a "God-fearing man," said that "the trouble with God-fearing men is that given power not a few of them tend to take unto themselves the lineaments of the Almighty." [96] But later the same newspaper said more temperately that it would not question "his sincere desire to serve the cause of peace," although it still felt constrained to describe him as "utterly incompetent to handle the affairs of nations with necessary tact and discretion." [97]

Generally speaking, the present Administration has not been as popular among the Indians as the Truman Administration was. The Eisenhower Administration got off to a bad start with New Delhi when it recalled Ambassador Bowles, who had won the affection and trust of the Indian

Government. India lamented the fact that in this case party politics were given preference over more cordial Indo-American relations. India perhaps overestimated the contribution which a single, affable personality could make to improve Indo-American relations, and this certainly exhibited a lack of realistic appreciation of the intimate connection which exists between American domestic politics and the appointment of persons to most high ambassadorial posts. It would seem that one of the best ways to effect an improvement in Indo-American relations is for both countries to develop a mature understanding of each other's total political situation.

THE COLONIAL TERRITORIES

Liquidation of Western colonialism in Africa, its last major stronghold, and the eradication of all its vestiges on the Asian continent are basic objectives of Indian foreign policy. It might even be more accurate to call them guiding principles, for India sees colonialism almost exclusively as an abstract moral issue rather than as a mosaic of concrete political problems. This distinction helps to explain why India, in her anticolonial policies, has come into serious conflict with the United States. India stands unalterably opposed to whatever savors of "white" colonialism, wherever it may be found, and she steadfastly refuses to conceive the problem in terms of what the West considers to be the realities of world politics. The Western nations, for their part, are unwilling to concede to India a monopoly of the moral approach in international affairs. The United States in particular will not accept the Indian belief in the good intentions of the Soviet Union and the People's Republic of China, nor does it wish to place its faith in the sufficiency of mere moral suasion where the rights of weaker peoples to chart their own future is at stake. Thus, since 1948, the United States has made NATO the cornerstone of international relations in the West. India, on the other hand, demands that the West accept the emancipation of colonial areas as the prime and absolute moral imperative confronting the world at this historical juncture, notwithstanding the expansionist threat of Soviet and Chinese Communism, and perhaps without fully realizing that acceptance of such a demand would involve the disintegration of the Western defense structure, both politically and morally. NATO would dissolve politically because it includes powers which have concrete colonial interests and these powers would surely be alienated if their chief ally were to adopt the Indian anticolonial philosophy. It would dissolve morally because a policy of unmitigated anticolonialism would only serve to turn loose countries that are totally unprepared to govern themselves under genuine democratic institutions. This would be tantamount to abandoning them either to native "strong-man" dictatorships or to penetration by an international force which the West cannot regard as moral in any guise.[98]

The connection that exists between colonial problems and the whole Western defense concept is an ever-recurring topic of official and journalistic pronouncements in India, although the American position on colonial questions prior to the Cold War, e.g., the Philippines and Indonesia, sometimes seems to be forgotten. Thus a columnist for *The Times of India* commented: "Wherever Washington is faced by the contending powers of communism and colonialism, it has invariably plumped for the 'lesser evil'—colonialism. . . . Unfortunately, no country has done more in the postwar world to identify itself with colonial regimes than the U. S., which itself cherishes no colonial ambitions." [99] Enlightened public opinion in India hardly believes that U. S. policy on Tunisia-Morocco and Indochina has been prompted by love for the French or by adherence to the principle of European domination over Asian peoples. Rather it holds that it is precisely the expe-

diencies of international politics that have shaped the
"equivocal" U. S. attitude toward colonialism. Said *The
Hindu:*

> Though many people still look up to the U. S. to help
> them in securing freedom from foreign domination, the
> U. S., unfortunately, seems often to be guided more by
> the requirements of global military strategy than by a
> strong attachment to the principle of helping countries
> toward their freedom.[100]

This statement goes to the heart of the matter, since the
United States is firmly convinced that the problem of the
political freedom of nations in the bipolar global struggle
of today cannot be settled except within the context of the
Cold War. Recently, an analyst for *The Times of India* presented the root difference between the two countries in
this way:

> Instinct in the American doctrine of the lesser evil is a
> willingness to compromise on essentials. Such compro-
> mises and contradictions make American policy difficult
> either to understand or accept. You cannot compromise
> with one kind of evil and be uncompromising before
> another kind.[101]

The other side of the coin would show an American analyst wondering whether the Indians have managed suc-
cessfully to be equally uncompromising in the face of both
kinds of evil.

The *Indian Express* contended that "the Asiatic nations,
like the African people, know to their cost that the Imperialist powers cannot hold on to their colonial possessions
without the material and military strength forthcoming
from the U.S.A." [102] The unmistakable inference is that the
main reason for the continued vigorous existence of the
colonial regimes is the fact that the United States is underwriting the interests of the colonial powers which would
be unable by their own efforts to withstand pressures to-

ward the abolition of the *status quo*. The Indians insist that the U. S. is thereby paying a heavy price by losing the respect of the colonial peoples and the support of the independent nations of Asia. Popular indignation reached a peak when the United States played a leading role in keeping the Tunisia-Morocco issue out of the Security Council's agenda. Instances like this inspired Nehru's conviction that a U. S.-dominated United Nations had "swerved from its original moorings and become gradually a protector of colonialism in an indirect manner." [103] Such instances also evoked editorial responses like these: "American policy seeks to prop up tottering colonial imperialism . . . in its hysterical drive against communism;" "So long as the campaign against Communism covers a multitude of sins, the mere promise of relief from the one without relief from the other holds no special attraction." [104]

There is some recognition in India of the fact that the United States, while publicly taking its stand at the side of the colonial powers, has been quietly exerting pressure on them to grant the right of self-determination and self-rule to the areas under their control. As a matter of fact, some of the key members of NATO believed that their chief ally had frequently gone too far, not only in exerting government-to-government pressure, but even in encouraging colonial nationalist leaders in their aspirations to independence. In 1951, Mr. Kenneth Younger, then British Delegate to the United Nations, had charged that the failure of the United States to support Britain more solidly in Iran had prompted the Persians to hold out against a settlement of their dispute with Britain. [105] The French have been no less vehement in their attitude toward certain American policies in the colonial territories. A *Le Monde* article in 1951 accused the United States of deliberately promoting Arab nationalism in North Africa and actually extending Voice of America facilities for local attacks upon the French administration there. [106] The Indian view, however, is that the United States has not done enough in this direction. Indians would like to receive active moral support from the United States on every colonial issue, and when this is not forthcoming, the Indians take American silence to be acquiescence in the perpetuation of colonialism. This interpretation recalls once again the Indian suspicion that "the long arm of NATO has even reached out to Goa, thereby committing the U. S. and the U. K. to the continuance of Portuguese rule on Indian soil." [107]

THE SOUTH AFRICAN ISSUE

Another basic moral tenet of India's foreign policy has been opposition to all forms of racialism. This anti-racialist attitude can best be shown by reviewing India's position on the *apartheid* in South Africa. India does not think that the United States has been outspoken enough with respect to the developments of the last decade in South Africa. "One of the reasons for India's misunderstandings with the USA," according to an article in *The Statesman*, "is America's silence over the issue of racialism, for it is wrong to suggest that another voice against South African policies would not make much difference." [108] India sees South Africa as the focal area of the racial problem, and the failure of the leading nation of the free, democratic world to condemn roundly the policies of Malan and Stridjom has given rise to strong criticism. *The Hindustan Times* recently aimed a subtle barb at the willingness of the Western nations in the U. N. to place their security interests above considerations of racial justice:

> It is unfortunate that many countries have been equivocal in their attitude in South Africa, as the proceedings in the U. N. General Assembly have come to underline. If that Western attitude based on political calculations of mutual interests has served to encourage the South African Government, it must nevertheless be recognized

by them that with all Africa and Asia bitterly resenting the policy of racial discrimination its repercussions are not to be discounted.[109]

The reference in that editorial to "mutual interests" doubtless grew out of the fact that the United States was at that time interested in extending its chain of strategic bases to the Union of South Africa.

Criticism of the U. S. stand on *apartheid* is by no means new. As early as August 1952, Raja Maharaj Singh, a former delegate at the United Nations, stated:

> The stand of the United States, in so many respects the foremost country in the world, has been weakened, as I have personally seen in the U. N. Assembly, vis-a-vis questions relating to human rights and colonial policies by the status of the Negro in the Southern States.[110]

Various other reasons have been offered to explain America's equivocation on the policy of the South African Government. An Indian fellow-traveler expressed the view that the U. S. motive was the availability of strategically important mineral resources, especially uranium, in that country.[111] *The Hindu* diagnosed the case by pointing out that South Africa has won the allegiance of the United States by sending a military force to fight in Korea.[112]

The Indians have not been oblivious of the fact that there has been a steady improvement in the legal position of the Negro in the United States during the postwar period, but they are nonetheless inclined to regard the American attitude on racial questions, especially in South Africa, as less forthright than that of the Soviet Union:

> The South African Government has also adopted the convenient practise of labelling all the patriots opposed to their tyranny as Communists, irrespective of whether they really are reds or not. U. S. support is available to all anti-Communists and it has not always condemned dictator-

ships of the right. Soviet Russia has steadily condemned
apartheid, in contrast to the U. S.[113]

In this statement, *The Hindu* exemplifies the Indian conviction that the United States has relegated the moral issue
of racial equality to a secondary position in the Cold War.
Americans might ask whether the Indians think that the
proper moral position adopted by the Soviet Union in this
case is entirely divorced from the realities of the Cold War.
If this is true, it indicates the existence of a serious divergence of views between India and the United States on the
fundamental facts of international relations at this point in
history.

EQUALITY FOR ASIA

Indians resent what they regard as the tone of superiority
assumed by the United States and the other Western countries in their dealings with the Asian nations. Nehru considers the emergence of the new Asia to be the major fact
of this age, and has frequently chastised the West for being reluctant to accept the great changes which have come
about and for continuing to treat Asia as though it were
the Asia of old.[114] The Prime Minister never tires of scor-
ing the Western tendency to ignore the wishes of the Asian
peoples. He is particularly sensitive to any suggestions of
continuing Western dominance in Asian affairs. This attitude was reflected in the spring of 1954 when Mr. Nehru
reacted to a statement by Walter Robertson, U. S. Assistant Secretary of State for Far Eastern Affairs, who was reported to have said that the United States must dominate
Asia for an indefinite period and maintain a military coun-
terpoise to China until the communist regime crumbles
from within. Nehru retorted in the House of the People:

> It is important that a responsible official of the United
> States should say it is their policy that the U. S. A. must

dominate Asia for an indefinite period. The countries of Asia and certainly India do not accept this policy and do not propose to be dominated by any country, for whatever purpose.[115]

The Times of India urged "a common line of action to resist such foreign intervention in the affairs of Asia as jeopardizes the peace and independence of the continent." It called upon the Colombo Prime Ministers to "explore the means to safeguard the area against military commitments which may involve it in a cold war or armed conflict between the big powers." [116] The *Hindustan Standard* appealed to the five Premiers to speak out against the "colossal blunder" committed by the United States in embarking upon this "new kind of colonialism." [117] *United Asia* noted the "Western attempts, overt as well as concealed, to prolong or renew the old type of colonialism . . . [and] to superimpose a new type on the flimsiest of pretexts." [118]

One of the most serious manifestations of India's belief that the West deems Asia inferior is the accusation leveled at Americans that they regard Asian lives as more expendable than those of white men. This feeling is based partially upon the fact that the United States dropped atomic bombs only on an Asian and not on a European country. Not a few Indians appear to suspect that the United States possessed atomic weapons in time to employ them against Germany, whereas actually the first successful test was made at Alamagordo during the Potsdam Conference, three months after the end of the war in Europe. Regardless of whether or not the United States had the bomb in time to use it against Germany, the impression prevails that the United States would not have used it against the Germans because of racial affinities. This impression was strengthened by post-war atomic and hydrogen bomb experiments, which were held exclusively in the Pacific. Asians concluded that no experiments were conducted in the Atlantic because it is a white man's ocean.[119] The Indian press devoted considerable attention to the contamination of wide areas of the ocean from the thermonuclear fall-out, and responded with emotion to the reports of the radiation illness of the Japanese fishermen, one of whom, it is alleged, became the world's first H-bomb casualty.

U. S. ECONOMIC AID

Indian reaction to U. S. economic aid has tended to take two main forms, which may not be entirely compatible with each other. On the one hand, Indians are apprehensive that American assistance is employed too often as a weapon of political warfare and therefore is made contingent upon the acceptance of "political strings." On the other hand, they are disappointed that the amount of aid extended has not been more substantial.

Indians have been concerned over the politico-military aspects of economic aid programs ever since the United States first made them an integral part of its postwar foreign policy. In 1947, they objected to the Truman Doctrine of assistance to Greece and Turkey, which was avowedly the initial step in the containment of Soviet communism, on the grounds that it set a "dangerous precedent" in bypassing the United Nations and carried with it the seeds of possible American "economic penetration" in the underdeveloped countries.[120]

India found the Marshall Plan for European recovery much less objectionable than the Truman Doctrine, since the former was put forward as a program which stressed the idea of mutual help and cooperative planning by the European nations. The Indians were able to agree more readily with a policy which was "not directed against any country or doctrine but against hunger, poverty, deprivation and chaos." [121] As the Indians saw it, ideological factors were minimized in this plan, in which even the Soviet Union was invited to participate. But since 1948, the Indians have watched with anxiety the gradual shift in the character of the U. S. aid program from economic to military. *The Hindu,* an influential moderate newspaper, stated:

> The truth is that the Eisenhower Administration, with its emphasis on the military aspect of the struggle for the containment of Communism, has not viewed economic development with the same urgency and vision with which General Marshall looked at the problem of rehabilitating Europe.[122]

Here once again is reflected the Indian preoccupation with the alleged emphasis upon things military in the Eisenhower Administration in Washington. The above statement by *The Hindu* will be viewed with amazement by thoughtful Americans because it would seem to disregard the fact that General of the Armies George C. Marshall's background was almost exclusively military (a pet peeve of the Indians against Eisenhower) and yet it did not prevent him from seeing the non-military aspects of world affairs, while the possibility that President Eisenhower might have such vision is being ruled out by his Indian critics on precisely identical grounds. As a matter of fact, the change in the aid program from an economic to a military emphasis occurred during the Truman Administration and was, in large measure, due to the outbreak of the war in Korea. The unfavorable comparison which the Indians draw between the Marshall Plan and the present aid policy highlights the basic point of departure for an analysis of Indo-American relations, i.e., the differing concepts as to what constitutes reality in present-day international politics. The Indians believe that aid programs should operate in a political vacuum, without any reference to the global struggle between the United States and the Soviet Union. The United States finds this assumption untenable.

The Indian press, while critical of the character of Amer-

ican aid and of its political implications, has generally
been more disturbed by the limited amount of economic
aid which has been made available to the underdeveloped areas. A New Delhi correspondent said that America's relatively meager assistance to certain Asian countries
"really embarrasses Indian friends of America." [123] India
resents what she considers U. S. tightfistedness as part of
the general pattern of U. S. neglect of Asia, whose interests are persistently subordinated to those of Europe. According to *Economic Weekly,*

> There was a possibility at one time that having put Europe
> on her feet with Marshall aid, America would direct her
> enormous resources to redressing the imbalance by de-
> veloping the other countries of the world. These possi-
> bilities have faded into the shadows of rearmament hang-
> ing over the Western world. It is difficult for India to fit
> into the new set-up as a neutral country.[124]

The *National Standard,* usually a strong critic of U. S. policy in Asia, implored the U. S. to aid India in order that the
Government might implement its first Five Year Plan, saying:

> India has shown her willingness to help herself. She is
> determined to fulfill the condition laid down for American
> aid. In return, the poor people of this country will ex-
> pect . . . [the] Republican Administration to help
> [them] to achieve democratic prosperity.[125]

The Hindu on several occasions during 1955 discussed the desirability of increased U. S. economic aid for
India. It blamed American niggardliness on the current
U. S. policy which "appears to contemplate the giving of
funds to countries who will hoist the anti-communist flag."
"India," it declared, "administratively and industrially the
most advanced [country in this region], has been able to
make the fullest use of foreign aid and would welcome
much more of it if offered without strings." [126] India has led

in suggesting that the Asian nations would greatly prefer to have all economic aid channeled through the U. N. in order to minimize the danger of economic imperialism.[127]

Finally, Indians detect a note of condescension in the attitude of Americans who promote, formulate and carry out U. S. aid programs. *Thought* complained editorially that there are "far too many Americans, like their counterparts in Europe, who seem to think of Asian countries as primitive lands peopled by half-civilized barbarians." [128] *United Asia* discerned shades of the British outlook at the height of empire:

> The Western approach to Asia has been rather like that of a newly rich person to his poor relations—domineering, patronizing and a shade too callous of the latter's feelings. . . . When the U. S. Congress votes an astronomical dollar appropriation for "aid to Asia," somehow the thing sounds very much like similar acts in the House of Commons in the palmy days of the British Empire.[129]

CONCLUSIONS

An objective analysis of Indo-American relations since the outbreak of the Korean War leads to the general conclusion that not only do tensions exist but they affect virtually every aspect of the relations between the two countries. If one central tension on which all others hinge is to be identified, it is that which arises from divergent analyses of the contemporary world political situation. Both countries are concerned with freedom. Both wish to see established a condition of order in which each people will be free to realize as fully as possible their own cherished values. But India and the United States part company when it comes to determining what constitutes the most formidable threat to this freedom at the present time. The United States and its allies are convinced that the prime threat is totalitarian communism, operating from a powerful Sino-

Soviet base. India disagrees, believing instead that the
vestiges of Western colonial imperialism in Asia, and the
resurgence of this imperialism in Africa, where European
communities appear to be developing new legal, social
and economic controls over the native populations, constitute the gravest obstacle to the achievement of political
freedom outside the communist orbit. Put first things first,
say the Indians, and make the free world really free. Nehru
put the problem this way:

> We talk about the crisis of our time and many people
> view it in different ways. Probably in the U. S. A., the
> crisis of the time is supposed to be Communism vs. anti-
> Communism. It may be so to some extent. But the crisis
> of the time in Asia is colonialism vs. anti-colonialism. Let
> us be quite clear about it.[130]

Americans are unwilling to concur in the characterization
of their policy as being merely anti-communist or pro-
colonialist. The United States, moreover, having made its
decision on the question of priority, refuses to jeopardize
the solidarity of the Western coalition by subscribing to
what it considers to be a doctrinaire and unrealistic position on the question of colonial territories. The United
States thinks that Indians place too much faith in the absolute purity of emergent nationalism; for the Indians are
confident that wherever colonial peoples can win their
national autonomy without having to engage in a physical
or even a psychological struggle against the Western Powers, communism cannot gain popular support. Americans
who have been following the performances of the Western European communist parties in their rôle as instruments of Soviet foreign policy during the last decade are
not as ready as the Indians to underestimate the resources
of communism in the less politically sophisticated areas of
Asia and Africa. The United States, therefore, cavils at
the assertion that colonial peoples everywhere are capable

of governing themselves without having attained the requisite economic and educational levels and of maintaining their freedom against the threats of native dictatorship or of infiltration or aggression. The United States deems its present policy more humane than a policy which would probably necessitate future military action to liberate these weaker areas from Chinese or Soviet rule, just as some of them had to be liberated from Japanese rule not more than a decade ago.

This Indo-American disagreement as to the priority of the struggle against communism over the struggle against "white" imperialism is a fundamental one, and it furnishes the framework within which other clashes of attitude take on meaning. It colors, for example, the frequently cited dichotomy between the moral mind of India, which disdains the use of force and the threat of force in international relations, and the technical mind of the United States, which relies heavily on military preparedness. India reacts with sharp criticism to what she regards as any evidence of sabre-rattling or the military mentality in American decisions, such as the conduct of H-bomb experiments, statements about massive and instant retaliation, the elevation of a general to the White House, and the extension of the network of alliances to her own neutral borders. In lieu of physical might, India would stress negotiation in conference as the most suitable means of solving international disputes.

The United States cannot minimize military preparations to the degree which the Indians seem to wish. There is a deep-rooted conviction in the American mind that successful negotiation requires effective bargaining power, and that any gratuitous retreat from a position of strength will create an impression of weakness and invite exploitation. Furthermore, Americans have inherited the traditional Western conviction that physical force is a legitimate instrument for the enforcement of right. Therefore, they will not accept pacifism as an operational concept in international relations. Actually, there is a piece of common ground on which the concepts of conciliation and preparedness overlap somewhat in the foreign policies of the two countries. The United States, for example, has exhibited a willingness to negotiate at Geneva, while India has recognized the need to maintain military fortifications along the Tibetan border and in the Kashmir sector.

At first glance, then, there would seem to be a bridge across the differences in approach, and if there is a bridge, it might be widened and strengthened. This development is not likely, however, for upon closer analysis it can be seen that the only cause for which the Indians appear ready to condone the use of force is not the cause of political freedom as the Western nations understand it, but rather the cause of emergent nationalism, i.e., the liberation of the colonial peoples and the unification or territorial consolidation of the new nations of the East. Thus India is ready, if necessary, to use force to defend the integrity of her own borders. The Indians did not protest the use of force when it was used to throw off the French yoke in Indo-China. They refused to brand the Chinese communists as aggressors in November 1950 for entering the Korean War to "protect their vital interests" against an attempt to unify North and South Korea under the auspices of the "Western-dominated" United Nations. Finally, many Americans think that, in urging the withdrawal of U. S. forces now protecting Formosa and in supporting the communist Government's claim to the island, the Indians have not voiced enough concern over the possible outcome, viz., a forcible effort by the communists to seize what they contend to be a part of their national territory. Such an effort would lead to a bloody struggle for the island and might touch off the very world conflagration which Indian foreign policy seeks to prevent.

The difference between the United States emphasis

upon the defense of the free world and the Indian emphasis on the liquidation of colonialism is so fundamental as to
indicate that in their foreign policies the two countries are
likely to be striving toward incompatible objectives for
years to come. The United States could accept the absolute principle of anticolonialism advanced by India only
by sacrificing the strategic value inherent in a position of
defense in depth, since the loss of Western bases in North
Africa and the Middle East might render the defense of
Western Europe, and ultimately the defense of the Atlantic Community, impossible. India, wishing to continue as
the spokesman of all underdeveloped countries, whether
colonial or newly independent, may find herself bound
more and more to press for the withdrawal of Western military power from this entire zone which the Indians take to
be their community of interest. The United States can
hardly expect to receive any meaningful support for its
global policy from New Delhi. But Americans must be
concerned if India fails to see in the Western defense system an instrument of peace and attempts to mobilize the
opinion of the Asian and African peoples against the United
States as the leader of the imperialist bloc. Indian diplomacy has sought, time and again, to thwart the efforts
of the United States to build a viable defense system in
Asia. If India were to hold to this course, then the United
States would be compelled to conclude that Indian foreign
policy coincides for all practical purposes with two major
Soviet objectives, viz., the psychological alienation of the
Asian and African peoples from the United States, and the
reduction of the U. S. strategic system. Furthermore, Indian foreign policy with regard to nuclear disarmament
seeks the same objective as Soviet foreign policy when it
calls for the immediate abolition of nuclear weapons
without apparently realizing that the U. S. could not ac-
cede to this policy except by removing the sole deterrent
to Soviet superiority in conventional armaments. The

Indian position was most recently stated by V. K. Krishna
Menon at the opening of the 10th General Assembly:

> Without meaning any offense, I would say, representing
> a country that is not an atomic power, that does not be-
> lieve in the balance-of-power doctrine, that does not
> believe that preparation for war creates peace or that war
> creates peace, that even if the Soviet Union and the
> United States were to agree that they should have atomic
> weapons, we would not think that that would be good
> enough for the world.
>
> We do not believe that there is more safety in two hydro-
> gen bombs than there is in one.
>
> Therefore, there is only one thing to do with the atomic
> weapon, and that is to throw it away.[131]

This peroration goes far to explain, albeit unwittingly,
why the United States resents the tone of moral superiority
which India assumes in her foreign policy pronouncements.
Americans will not concede to India a monopoly of morality
in world politics, for they insist that U. S. foreign policy
objectives have a genuine moral content, whether the Indians are able to recognize it or not. True, in recent years,
India, of all the countries in the world, has been the apple
of the American intellectual's eye. India, however, may find
herself increasingly alienating intelligent opinion in the
United States if she affects to speak with the voice of Asia,
carps about the contradictions of Western ideals and policies while rationalizing the power plays of China and the
Soviet Union, or erects anticolonialism into an absolute
symbol of hostility toward the West. The West has had its
fill of absolute symbols in this century and is trying to tran-
scend the narrow features of nationalism by laying the
foundations of a broader community based upon common
cultural values and mutual respect of differences. These
divergencies in Indo-American relations reflect deep-
rooted tensions, not merely superficial misunderstandings

which can be glossed over with routine appeals for the manifestation of a little good will by both sides. Both peoples, if they are not to compound the present and serious differences separating them, must face up to them honestly, in all their profound implications.

The United States and Indonesia

INTRODUCTION

The Indonesian Republic was established on August 17, 1945, shortly after the Japanese surrender. For the nationalist leaders who affixed their signature to the declaration of independence, the event was the culmination of nearly four decades of struggle against Dutch rule. The struggle, however, was not yet won. Only in December 1949, after an abortive military campaign against the Republic, did Holland recognize the United States of Indonesia as a sovereign partner in a Netherlands-Indonesian Union.

Throughout the first years of the Republic's precarious existence, the Indonesian leaders avowed abiding sympathies for the United States. In their discourses, they rarely failed to allude to the common heritage of the two countries in the struggle against tyranny and professed their gratitude for American efforts toward gaining for the new country quick and full acceptance in the family of nations.

These auspicious beginnings notwithstanding, Indonesian-American amity was shortlived. The deterioration of Indonesian-American relations has been attributed plausibly to the not uncommon resentment that a poor and insecure nation bears toward a powerful and rich one. To a greater measure, however, it was the repercussions of the world conflict which magnified what need not have been, under more benign circumstances, insurmountable barriers between a people emancipated from colonial rule and "anticolonialist" Americans. The Indonesian-American relationship thus conforms to the general pattern of divergent attitudes and objectives traced by the steadily worsening relations between the United States and the so-called "uncommitted" countries of Asia.

RESENTMENT OF AMERICAN INFLUENCE

Nationalism dominates Indonesian reactions to all political problems, and, as such, forms the root of Indonesian-American political and ideological differences. The one-word slogan *Merdeka* (freedom), omnipresent in Indonesian political literature, has connotations which make it a shorthand reference to independence, anticolonialism, neutralism in foreign policy, and nationalism. Intense national pride causes the Indonesians to react violently to any presumed threat to Indonesian independence or to the nation's complete freedom of action.

Thus Indonesians have indicated a strong sensitivity to any apparent attempt by the United States or any other powerful nation to influence Indonesian policy or to interfere in Indonesian affairs. In the case of the United States, moreover, this apprehension has been rationalized by an increasingly adverse view of America's role in the Indonesian struggle for independence. Walter H. Mallory summarized this turn-about, which contrasts sharply with the Indonesian leaders' avowed attitude on the morrow of independence, as follows:

> Virtually all Indonesians take it for granted that the United States never was their ally, but has actually sided with the Dutch. Thus they are convinced that it was not American sympathy, arms, and influence which assisted Indonesia in gaining freedom, but Russia's firm stand against Western imperialism.[1]

This version of the United States' true purpose gained currency in spite of expressions of American sympathy for the independence movement in and outside of the United Nations, near-unanimous public condemnation of the so-called "police actions" of the Dutch in late 1948 and 1949, United States pressure on the Dutch in connection with the Renville truce of January 1948 and the Round-Table Agreements in late 1949, United States recognition of the new government immediately on its establishment, and U. S. support of its admission to the United Nations in 1950.[2]

To the Indonesians fighting for independence, convinced of the total righteousness of their cause, however, American support appeared ambiguous, tempered as it was by the desire to reconcile the Dutch to the accomplished fact of Indonesia's independence and by United States support of the Netherlands as a member of the North Atlantic Treaty Organization. The Dutch troops fighting Indonesians had benefited from American training and carried arms of American origin. ". . . The United States . . . sought to harmonize the conflicting interests of Dutch and Indonesians and it alienated the sympathies of both." [3]

In 1952 a specific incident caused widespread criticism of the United States for exerting undue influence in Indonesian affairs.[4] Disclosure of secret negotiations between the American Ambassador and the Indonesian government on the grant of United States military aid produced a political crisis which toppled the Sukiman Cabinet. The Communist Party of Indonesia accused the Government of being completely subservient to the United States. Although the majority of Indonesians undoubtedly did not accept this view, the ill-advised project not only failed but also brought lasting discredit upon both its American and Indonesian sponsors. The Indonesians have not accepted military grants from the United States to this day. The political implications of American aid policies are less significant than economc ones, discussed at greater length below. Virulently anti-American elements ascribed the retention of Dutch military advisors in Indonesia to American connivance with alleged Dutch attempts to keep a strategic foothold in Indonesia.[5] Sutan Sjarir, leader of the small but influential anti-communist Socialist Party, expressed the fear that President Eisenhower is "looking at Asia from a military point of view." [6] The United States decision to permit greater freedom of action to Nationalist China in 1953, and President Eisenhower's speech expounding the "let Asians-fight-Asians" thesis were taken by some Indonesians as straws in the wind: The United States meant to keep the Asian pot boiling and to weaken Asia by internecine war.[7]

Mere rumor that Indonesian matters would be discussed at the Bermuda meeting of the heads of the American, British, and French governments in 1952 provoked Premier Ali Sastroamidjojo pointedly to remind the Western leaders that "Indonesia is an independent state and would view with concern any internal interference in its personal affairs." [8]

Thus far, accusations of United States interference in Indonesian *domestic* affairs have been confined to the economic area. Nevertheless, suspicions of American political chicanery persist. An ambiguous speech by President Sukarno in connection with a Cabinet crisis in late 1954 implicitly accused the United States of aiding and abetting Parliamentary opposition,[9] and a Government supporter accused the leading opposition party (the Masjumi) of being "influenced by McCarthyism." [10]

WESTERN COLONIALISM AND COMMUNIST IMPERIALISM

Virtually all Indonesians hold that the United States, together with the rest of the "Western bloc," is bent on perpetutating colonialism throughout the world. Because of

Indonesia's long experience with Western colonialism and her recent liberation from it, her identification with the Asian-African area and her sympathy for other Moslem countries, anticolonialism dominates Indonesia's foreign policy and, with it, her attitude toward the United States. It has been observed that "Indonesians do not think that the United States is anti-colonial at all, but the leading imperialist power." [11]

The assumption that the United States is a colonial power is expressed even by staunchly anti-communist Indonesians. *Duta Masjarakat*, an anti-communist journal which did not sympathize completely with the neutralist Ali Sastroamidjojo Government, neatly juxtaposed anti-communism and American "colonialism":

> In a society that is just and prosperous, Communism has no influence. We see the mistakes of the Western bloc in checking Communism. Instead of helping the countries in Asia to fight against poverty, the Western countries, including the U. S. A., depress the prices of the raw materials of the Asian countries and try to maintain colonialism there.[12]

The Asian-African conference held at Bandung, Indonesia, in the spring of 1955 provided the opportunity for criticism of the United States as a supporter of colonialism. The meeting, held without the "supervision of the U. S., Britain, France and the U. S. S. R." proved, according to *Indonesia Raya,* that the Western countries must "count their steps if they want to be respected by the countries of Asia and Africa." [13] *Berita Indonesia* charged that the Western countries were still attempting to cause discord among the countries of Asia.[14]

Although Indonesia remains greatly concerned with the condition of North Africans and other non-self-governing people, the most important colonial issue for anticolonial Indonesia is the dispute with the Dutch over Western New Guinea, or as the Indonesians call it, Irian. Until late 1954, the United States was only remotely involved in this dispute but it has been frequently suspected of supporting the Dutch claim to the disputed territory.

Irian, or Western New Guinea, is an inhospitable underdeveloped area of about 151,000 square miles. Its status was left in doubt by the 1949 Charter of the Transfer of Sovereignty between the Kingdom of the Netherlands and the Republic of the United States of Indonesia. By this agreement, the former granted the latter "unconditionally" the "complete sovereignty over Indonesia" but it was also stated that the *"status quo* of the residency" in Western New Guinea was to be maintained, subject to an explicit reservation. This reservation was that within a year from the date of the transfer of sovereignty, the two governments would determine, through negotiations, the future political status of the disputed territory. Conflicting Dutch and Indonesian interpretations of Article 2 have produced an impasse: the Dutch hold that the term *status quo* refers to the complete sovereignty over Western New Guinea which they wielded before the 1949 Charter of Transfer; the Indonesians contend that it refers only to temporary administrative control over an area subject to the terms of the Charter. The Indonesian Government finally made a formal request to the U.N. General Assembly in 1954 that it consider the matter.

The ensuing discussions in the First (Political) Committee of the General Assembly in late 1954 showed the disputants, the Netherlands and Indonesia, still at loggerheads but now enjoying the clear support of most of the colonial and anticolonial powers respectively. The United States, however, took no part in the debate in the First Committee and abstained on all votes concerning the Irian dispute in the First Committee and later in the General Assembly. Indonesia resented the position of abstention maintained by the United States and has heaped criticism upon it.

While it was Britain, France and Australia who sided actively against a resolution, one generally considered favorable to the Indonesian viewpoint was adopted by the First Committee on November 30.[15] Dr. Diapari, chairman of the Indonesian Government's Irian Bureau, accused the United States of "giving direct support to colonialism" by its abstention.[16] Foreign Minister Sunarjo criticized the abstaining countries for demonstrating that they were still in doubt on "this colonial question so vital to us." [17] When the resolution failed to get the necessary two-thirds majority in the General Assembly vote, Premier Sastroamidjojo stressed his disappointment at the stand of the United States, which had again abstained.[18]

On October 4, 1955, Indonesia won a long-sought victory on the Irian issue when by a 31 to 18 vote the General Assembly placed the question of Western New Guinea on its agenda. The United States was one of ten members which abstained in the voting.

Indonesia experienced the communist brand of imperialism in the fall of 1948. Armed units under the direction of the Indonesian Communist Party occupied the East Java town of Madiun, proclaimed the existence of a Soviet state, and attempted to take over the rest of Indonesia. The uprising came at a time when the forces of the Republic of Indonesia controlled only a small portion of the Island of Java, which was blockaded by the Dutch fleet and besieged by Dutch troops. The "stab in the back at Madiun," as Vice-President Hatta termed it, so discredited the Indonesian Communist Party that it remained long on the defensive, unable to remove the stigma of treason.

Nonetheless, the peace offensives of the Soviet Union and communist China have not been without effect. Russia is not held responsible for the actions of the Indonesian local Communist Party. Western references to Soviet and Chinese imperialism make little impression. For the Indonesians know Western colonialism from direct and vivid experience and regard Soviet Russia as the leading opponent of such colonialism. In short, the major Indonesian political parties generally regard communism as a domestic political problem, seldom as a local manifestation of an international conspiracy.

This does not mean that Indonesians look favorably on any prospect of Soviet influence on Indonesian affairs. Indonesian foreign policy strives for independence from the Soviet bloc as well as from Western influence. Thus the attempt to keep the "independent foreign policy" of Indonesia truly neutral does not lack sincerity.

NEUTRALISM AND RELATIONS
WITH THE U. S.

Indonesia's foreign relations are unqualifiedly based on the Indonesian version of neutralism: an "independent foreign policy." All major political groups—from the Moslem theocratic elements to the communists—endorse this general concept and profess to differ only as to its specific connotations.

The principle of non-identification with either the Soviet bloc or the West has guided Indonesia's foreign policy since the advent of complete independence in 1949. Even the government of Ali Sastroamidjojo (1953-1955), which was supported by the Parliamentary votes of the Communist Party, held to the principle of neutralism at least as strongly as had any previous Cabinet.[19]

The Indonesians invariably describe their policy as "independent," rather than "neutral." The term "neutralism" is seldom used and is deliberately avoided in contexts in which it might be confused with Indian neutralism or other versions of the concept. The policy goes further, Indonesians say, than the "negative" policy of "neutralism." Indonesia does not consider itself a member of any doctrinaire "third force" movement.[20] The Indonesian government, in an official statement from its Washington Embassy, stated its position as follows: "By carrying out an independent foreign policy, there will be more opportunity to provide mediation between the conflicting powers —of course, in cooperation with other countries which have the same outlook and ideas." But "the people do not believe in joining any 'third bloc' as a counter-poise to the Western and Russian blocs." [21]

The similarity between Indonesia's independent foreign policy and India's neutralism is apparent in the references to mediation, non-involvement, and the promotion of peace so consistently found in Indonesian statements on foreign affairs. But although Indonesia participates in the Colombo association and assumes a full share of responsibility for Asian and African movements such as the organization of the Bandung Conference, the "independent foreign policy" does not allow identification with India or with Indian-led groups of nations. "Indonesia's foreign policy is an expression of what is believed to be her national interest." [22]

Indonesia's associations with other nations have the avowed purpose of promoting world peace. Foreign Minister Subardjo stated that "We refuse to take sides with this or that nation or group of nations—except in the interest of international peace and understanding—and keep ourselves clear of all entangling alliances directed against third parties." [23]

The "independent foreign policy" has caused strained relations between the United States and Indonesia, and will undoubtedly continue to do so. Such a policy is a major factor in the economic tensions involving U. S. economic and military assistance (described below), since Indonesia's reluctance to receive American aid is motivated primarily by a fear of involvement with the "Western bloc." This attitude has prevented Indonesian participation in SEATO. "The only way to safeguard the existence of our nation [against] American political pressure on Asia," writes the journal of the influential Socialist Party (PSI), "is to stick to the course of our independent foreign policy." [24]

The tension caused by neutralism was recognized by the independent *Times of Indonesia,* a staunchly anti-communist paper. "Indonesia's future belongs primarily to Indonesia . . . Is this attitude necessarily a cause for indignation on the part of America? If there is a central, or majority, or 'average' viewpoint, it. . . . is that Indonesia must be no vassal or pawn in the titanic struggle all too roughly described as between East and West." [25]

The PNI (*Partai Nasionalis Indonesia*), which assumed control of the Government in July 1953, is, of all prominent parties, most insistent on Indonesian neutralism and also the one most friendly to China although the "independent foreign policy" was largely a Moslem Party and Socialist creation. *Merdeka,* a pro-PNI paper, has stated that the United States cannot "make us believe that the present struggle between East and West is a struggle between 'freedom' and 'slavery'." Indonesia is "not convinced that the methods and policies adopted by the Americans are the correct ones." [26]

On the other hand, former Premier Ali Sastroamidjojo, Ambassador to Washington before his appointment to the Premiership, and his PNI colleagues continued to express just as abiding a friendship for the United States as for Communist China. [27] The Burhanuddin Harahap Cabinet which replaced it in 1955 attempted to maintain the same spirit of cordiality.

CHINESE RELATIONS AND AMERICAN CHINA POLICY

The most critical tensions between Indonesia and the United States center on the question of China. Although only the Communist Party endorses the present regime in China categorically, all parties display a polite, if not a cordial attitude toward Peking.[28] Indonesia was among the first countries to recognize the Mao government. The Korean crisis and subsequent developments, however, have greatly complicated the issue. Indonesia abstained from voting in the United Nations on the resolution branding China as an aggressor in Korea, on the grounds that this resolution would not contribute to peace, and on the resolution imposing an embargo on the shipment of war material to Communist China. She has, however, abided by the latter since its adoption. Her U. N. activities during the crisis were largely confined to the use of U. N. machinery for establishing a cease fire. She opposed nine U. S. S. R. resolutions on the Korean issue, as well as the strongest Western-sponsored resolutions.[29]

Any American policy deemed likely to exacerbate Chinese-American relations is viewed with alarm. The *Times of Indonesia* feared the American-imposed blockade on China would lead to war.[30] At the height of the Quemoy-Matsu crisis early in 1955, the Indonesian government offered to act as mediator between the U. S. and Communist China.[31] *Suluh Indonesia* contended that these services had been specifically requested by Chou En-lai,[32] the Foreign Minister of Red China, and *Merdeka,* supporter of Sukarno's Nationalist Party, claimed Indonesia had prepared a peace plan for discussion provided the offer was accepted.[33] Significantly, *Abadi,* the Moslem Party organ, saw Chou En-lai and Dulles as equal partners in error and looked toward their respective enlightenment as the minimum result of Indonesian peace efforts.[34]

The Asian-African Conference at Bandung in early 1955, by bringing Chou En-lai to Indonesia at the outset of the large-scale global communist peace campaign, provided the stage for increasing Chinese-Indonesian exchanges. Chou was wined and dined at Jakarta for two days as the guest of the Indonesian government.[35] He signed a treaty on the long-standing problem of dual nationality of Indonesian residents of Chinese origin,[36] and issued a "joint declaration" with Premier Ali Sastroamidjojo, endorsing the "five principles of coexistence" on which he had obtained the agreement of Nehru of India and Premier U Nu of Burma.[37] Losing no opportunity to proclaim China's desire for "peace" and "coexistence" to Indonesian audiences, he formally invited Ali Sastroamidjojo to make a state visit to China in May, 1955. The Premier accepted and made a ceremonial visit to Peking later that month.[38]

Developments in 1955 prior to the fall of the Sastroamidjojo Cabinet seemed to indicate even more cordial relations between the Indonesian government—especially the PNI—and Communist China. It is possible to read into the Chou-Sastroamidjojo joint declaration a promise of Red Chinese support of the Irian claim in return for Indonesian support of the Chinese Communist claim to Formosa.[39] Although the contingency of such a policy of active cooperation with China passed temporarily with the fall of the Sastroamidjojo Cabinet, the long postponed first parliamentary elections produced a disturbing surprise. The elections resulted unexpectedly in a severe setback to the relatively pro-Western *Masjumi* (Moslem) Party. Contrary to expectations, the Nationalist Party (PNI) was a substantial victor. The PNI had dominated the coalition Sastroamidjojo Cabinet, and the policies of the Premier and the Cabinet were often assumed to reflect those of President Sukarno. Indeed, the voters' identification of the theoretically supra-party President with the PNI is probably the leading reason for the Nationalists' electoral success. The Communist Party did better than expected, while the capable and incorruptible anti-Communist Socialist Party of Sutan Sjarir received—as expected—little electoral support. Possibly the reverses of the moderate *Masjumi* are the reciprocal of the unpredicted success, especially in the most backward and rural areas, of the fanatical *Nahdatul Ulama* (Moslem Scholars League). The *Nahdatul Ulama* had participated in the Sastroamidjojo coalition while the Masjumi and Socialists had led the opposition. It had been expected that a *Masjumi* victory would lead to closer ties with the West and therefore to a cooler relationship with Communist China.[40] As the elections turned out, however, the increased power and undiminished prestige of Sukarno, the vindication of the PNI, whose left wing had been thrown out of office shortly before the election with the fall of the Sastroamidjojo Cabinet, and the gains in general of the more anti-Western parties at the expense of those relatively pro-Western, all presaged a domestic political situation likely to lead to increased American-Indonesian tension.

UNITED STATES FOREIGN ECONOMIC POLICIES

Indonesia's desire to remain "independent" in foreign policy and her extreme nationalism have contributed to differences with the United States on economic issues. Basically, however, the problem is one of two different economies and economic systems. The United States avows itself a capitalist country, while Indonesia considers her economy a socialist one. The United States is highly industrialized, has the world's highest per capita income, and is rich in capital resources, while Indonesia is a raw-materials-producing country with little industry, has an extremely low per capita income, and lacks capital.[41]

Tensions stemming from ideological divergence—a socialistically-oriented Indonesia contemplating a capitalistic United States—are difficult to assess; but their disruptive potential is, however, most real. This is all the more to be expected as the United States remains avowedly the champion of capitalism, a role which the articulate Indonesian, often as not an avowed Marxist, finds doubly suspect. Only recently the Secretary General of the Indonesian Ministry of Foreign Affairs pointedly wrote that "Colonialism is the offspring of capitalism. Therefore, for us, socialism is an essential ingredient of nationalism, since we believe that socialism offers our people the greatest escape from the poverties of our colonial heritage." [42] The social and economic philosophy that informed the founders of the Indonesian state, was expressed in the provisional organic law of Indonesia which provides that property is a "social function" (Article 26) and that not only shall the national economy be "organized on a cooperative basis" but that "branches of production of importance to the State and which vitally affect the life of the people, shall be controlled by the State" (Article 38).[43] It appears certain that when a new Indonesian constitution is drawn up and finally adopted these collectivist principles will be incorporated and probably expanded, underscoring some basic differences in attitudes between the United States and Indonesia and indirectly but profoundly affecting their political as well as economic relations. Differences in ideological outlook have tended to sharpen Indonesian distrust of United States foreign economic policies and of American trading practices. American economic and military aid programs have frequently been denounced in Indonesia as devices for increasing American influence or control over Indonesian affairs. President Sukarno expressed this attitude on May 19, 1955 in a speech delivered at a celebration of the 47th anniversary of the "Indonesian National Awakening":

> The United States wants to spend billions of dollars to aid in Asian-African development, but this effort will be useless as long as the United States does not understand the real desire of Asian-African nations. The Asian-

African nations are determined to eradicate all remnants of imperialism and colonialism. So long as the American nation does not realize that the Asian and African nations are living in an era of nationalism, an era of national sentiment, national ideas, an era of national aspirations, so long as the American nation does not realize this, then every dollar spent by America to help Asia and Africa, to bring freedom and justice to Asia and Africa, will be of no value.[44]

Because of the vague but strongly held notion that aid compromises the recipient's independence, Indonesia accepted little aid from the United States. For example, a loan of $100,000,000 from the Export-Import Bank in 1950 had still not been completely utilized by the beginning of 1954. Indonesia did agree, however, to accept several million dollars a year under the United States technical assistance program.

American aid was the issue of a 1952 Cabinet crisis in Indonesia. Under Section 511a of the Mutual Security Act of 1951, no country could receive American military aid on a grant basis unless it first signed an agreement, of a rather innocuous nature, forswearing aggressive designs. H. Merle Cochran, the American Ambassador to Indonesia, secretly negotiated such an agreement with the Indonesian foreign office. The subsequent public disclosure of the negotiations drew severe criticism of the Government from many Indonesian groups, especially the Masjumi (Moslem) Party. Although the Foreign Minister promptly resigned, the critics were not silenced, and the *Masjumi* forced the resignation of Premier Sukiman on February 23, 1952.[45]

The secret conduct of the negotiations was probably a larger factor in the political crisis than was the American requirement that such an agreement be made.[46] However, the fact remains that Indonesian nationalists regarded the refusal to accept this type of military aid as a victory for

Indonesia over "a form of American economic colonization which sabotaged the Republic's policy of active independence." [47]

The question of American aid has remained a prominent political issue. The Ministry of Information in the Ali Sastroamidjojo Cabinet consistently took pains to emphasize that only minimal American aid was received by his government. [48] Later, Dr. Harahap cheerfully admitted that he was more receptive to American aid than his predecessor Ali Sastroamidjojo. He told an American correspondent:

> I like the people of the United States. I am thankful for the help that they gave us toward winning our independence in the past. I will be thankful for any help they will be willing to give us in the future.[49]

American influence on the pricing of Indonesian export goods has been a more serious cause of tension, especially in the last few years, than the issue of American aid. The United States is now Indonesia's best customer, next to the Netherlands, receiving about 22% of Indonesia's exports and supplying 18% of her imports.

Rubber, once the source of much of the wealth of the Netherlands Indies, still represented 50% of Indonesia's exports during the Korean War, and rubber and petroleum together account for over 60% of exports from Indonesia today. Rubber has been consistently falling in price since the end of World War II. American stockpiling during the Korean crisis alleviated the situation somewhat, but since the cease-fire agreement the prices received for Indonesian rubber, which is not of the best quality, have fallen still further.[50] In 1953 Indonesian rubber was bringing only 24.2¢ per pound, in 1954, 22¢.

Since America purchases 40% of Indonesia's exported rubber,[51] the falling price of rubber has inspired considerable criticism of the United States. *Report on Indonesia,*

an Indonesian official publication printed in Washington
for American consumption, complained bitterly:

> Since other buyers were not in a position to counter the
> bargaining power of the United States, they were forced
> to withdraw from the world market. Now, as a single
> buyer, America can force producers to accept the lowest
> prices the U. S. is willing to pay.[52]

In the spring of 1953, at a meeting of the International
Rubber study group in Copenhagen, the producing and
consuming countries were unable to agree on measures to
improve the price situation. A leading Indonesian newspaper claimed the stabilization scheme was "rejected by
the Eisenhower Administration because it is composed of
big business representatives whose purpose it is to protect
the synthetic rubber industry." [53] *Abadi,* the *Masjumi* organ, warned: "Judging from the facts, the suspicion that
the United States wants Asian nations to remain always
in the same bad conditions so that they will always feel
the need of American aid and live on American charity is
well grounded." [54]

The influence of the American market on the prices of
raw materials other than rubber also creates an atmosphere of tension between Indonesia and America.[55] The
Masjumi organ *Abadi,* for example, complained editorially that "By cutting down the price of tin the United
States takes back with its right hand what it had given
away with the left—in the form of economic aid." [56] Tensions in this area can be expected as long as prices continue to fluctuate substantially in the prime market for
Indonesia's exports, i.e. the United States. Moreover,
there is little likelihood of an improvement since no radical change in the composition of Indonesia's foreign trade
is likely for some time. "Indonesia will continue her natural role as a supplier of raw materials and purchaser of
manufactured goods." [57]

The Communist Party, as can be expected, professes to see American aid and American "price fixing" as features of a plot to keep Indonesia in a state of "colonialism." Indonesia, along with other Asian and African countries, according to *Sin Po*, the Chinese-language communist journal, is subjected to Western control of its markets, and is compelled by the West to sell raw materials cheap but to pay high prices for imported industrial products.[58]

This attitude is not restricted to the communists. *Pedoman*, the socialist paper, declared that, "The Western Powers, along with the United States, are laying emphasis on the greatest possible production of raw materials in the countries of Asia, whereas Indonesia wants industries. Indonesia does not want to keep playing the old colonial role, supplying only the raw materials." [59]

DIFFERENCES IN CULTURAL PATTERNS

Great as are cultural differences between the United States and Indonesia, they are not in themselves significant enough to cause tensions.

Indonesia is a predominantly Moslem country—over 90% of its population is Moslem—but religious differences cause no particular animosity toward the United States.[60] Except for small bands of terrorists (the *Darul Islam*) conducting guerrilla warfare against the government, Indonesian Moslems are tolerant of other faiths in theory and in practice, and desire a state based on ethical-religious values but not governed by theocratic direction.[61] Thus the large Moslem Party (*Masjumi*) advocates "a state based on Moslem principles," but this does not mean advocacy of a theocratic state, and there is no religious-political issue dividing the *Masjumi* from other parties.[62] The 1955 electoral successes of the *Nahdatul Ulama* may presage the development of more theocratic attitudes, but this is not at present a significant tendency. The fifth point of the Pantasila, a body of five principles forming the theoretical background of Indonesian political conduct, is "belief in God," but this is an endorsement of religious values in general, not of Moslem doctrine.

Tensions stemming from religious differences are rendered politically harmless by a similarity of Indonesian and American attitudes on the place of religion in political and social life. However, Indonesia, as a Moslem country, has sympathies with other Islamic nations which affect her attitude toward the United States when its policy toward them is considered unfavorable, as, for example, in the Israeli-Arab or North African crises. "The United States . . . must expect to be regarded with less warmth [in Indonesia] than if she looked to Mecca, and with open hostility if she has any differences with any of the Islamic bloc." [63]

The North African independence movement aroused keen Indonesian interest. Indonesia has been active in the United Nations in supporting Arab-Asian efforts to have the question of Morocco and Tunis placed on the UN agenda. The abstentions on these issues of the United States have been strongly criticized, for Indonesians viewed the specific case of the Arabs in North Africa as part of the larger issue of Western colonialism in Asia and Africa. For example, according to the *Times of Indonesia*, the 1952 failure to put the Tunisian question on the UN agenda stemmed largely from the abstention of the United States. This leading Socialist journal expressed the hope that the United States "might now reconsider its stand" and accordingly "give its support" to renewed Arab-Asian efforts. "It is high time the West tries to be honest with itself—it cannot go on talking indefinitely about freedom and democracy, and not share them with others. The march towards freedom in Asia and Africa cannot be halted. . . ." [64]

There are several minor Christian political parties in Indonesia. The Catholic Party, the largest of these, has some influence in Parliament, because of the greater than aver-age prestige and economic status of most of its members.[65] It has associated itself with the Masjumi Party and with the Socialists, and joined these groups in opposition to the Ali Sastroamidjojo Cabinet.

Indonesians looked askance upon American support of the new state of Israel. Indonesia has not been willing to extend even *de facto* recognition to Israel and has invari-ably adopted a position akin to the Arab League states For example, a scheduled meeting of the Bureau of the Asian Socialist Conference, which was to have taken place at Bandung, Indonesia, in late April, 1954, had to be sud-denly postponed and shifted to Burma. The change was caused by the refusal of the Indonesian Government to issue visas to the delegates from Israel. Explaining the Government's action, the Foreign Minister informed the Indonesian Socialist Party that Indonesia has "not recog-nized the State of Israel and that the Government desires to avoid bad feelings in the Muslim world." [66]

As Indonesians are tolerant of different religious faiths, so they are tolerant of racial differences. There is little "anti-white" feeling,[67] and little evidence of discrimina-tion toward other races, despite some isolated anti-Chi-nese incidents, particularly in the early years of independ-ence.[68] Although the Indonesian Communists attempt to identify the United States with racial discrimination and to create "anti-white" sentiments,[69] there is no evidence of any appreciable amount of racial animosity toward America.

CONCLUSIONS

American-Indonesian relations are strained by basic and—at least for the foreseeable future—irreconcilable po-litical and ideological differences, not unlike those which the United States encounters in its relations with India.

Like India, Indonesia has won independence at the cost of a protracted and exhausting struggle. The legacy of this struggle is a well-nigh pathological sensitivity to any threat, whether real or presumed, to national sovereignty. Unlike India, however, whose efforts at self-assertion reveal a growing consciousness of power within the global struggle, the Indonesian outlook reflects awareness of weakness. The attitude toward the United States is, therefore, vaguely reminiscent of that of not a few among the Latin American nations, who view every movement by the "Colossus of the North" with a fear that borders on paranoia.

In the case of Indonesia, moreover, this fear finds a strong economic basis. It is the attitude of the poor toward the rich, of the raw-materials producer toward the industrialized giant. Finding herself completely at the mercy of world market prices, Indonesia tends to overestimate America's power in determining these prices. This has been a *primer movens* in the defensive attitude toward any manifestation of American economic influence, whether in the form of private investment or offers of government aid.

Like New Delhi, Jakarta finds a ready vocabulary for these attitudes. Protests against meddling on the part of non-Asian nations are grouped under the catch-all title of "anticolonialism." The response to the spectre of "colonialism" is a fever-pitched nationalism and, globally, a neutralism which goes under the somewhat euphemistic name of an "independent foreign policy."

To Indonesia's small ruling intelligentsia, survivors of the hard school of Dutch colonialism and products of the parlor-socialism of European universities, capitalism and colonialism have formed a single, inseparable identity. America is the most powerful capitalist nation in the world: by virtue of the Marxist law of over-production and under-consumption it must expand, whether this expansion takes the form of outright territorial colonization or a more surreptitious line of economic domination. By this crude equation the average Indonesian politician, administrator and journalist manage to identify the United States as the opponent of Asian freedom. This projection is strikingly illustrated by the facility with which Indonesian leaders peremptorily discount the historical facts of American support in the Indonesian struggle for independence, while stressing the continued tacit support by the United States of the colonial policies of its European allies.

The fundamental conflict between Indonesia and the United States, therefore, is one of differing short- and long-range objectives. Colonialism is the *bête noire* in the Indonesian's international field of vision. He cannot accept the American world view focussed on the cataclysmic confrontation of democracy and communism. The Western anathema of "Soviet imperialism" fails to stir his political imagination simply because he cannot associate "imperialism" with anything except the Marxist-Leninist texts. He does not feel threatened by the tentacles of the Cominform: he views the Indonesian Communist Party as perhaps an objectionable and sometimes dangerous faction in internal politics, but not as a local manifestation of an international conspiracy. Russia has earned, largely through the adeptness of the Soviet propaganda machine in Indonesia, the reputation of being the champion of the Asian and African peoples in their fight against classical colonialism. At the 1953 conference of the Economic Commission for Asia and the Far East held in Jakarta, for example, the Indonesian delegation did not once vote against the Soviet Union: when it could not vote *with* the Soviets, it abstained.

Thus, in the case of Indonesia, neutralism is the device adopted by a new and insecure country which strives simultaneously to protect and assert itself in a world of giant power blocs. It also expresses the ideological position of a ruling elite which prides itself on having chosen the "left-socialist" course and feels no compulsion to exercise an unequivocal option between two opposing economic systems. If anything, the system of the West, with its memories of oppression, seems the more repugnant of the two choices, if posed categorically.

In one important aspect, however, the Indonesian brand of neutrality differs from that of India. Indonesia's rulers, aware of their country's weakness, have viewed the power struggle within Asia with considerable trepidation. While siding consistently with the Asian-African bloc, for example, Indonesia has displayed a conspicuous reluctance to accept India as her spokesman, an attitude which undoubtedly contributed to Prime Minister Nehru's widely reported frowns during the Bandung Conference. While Indonesia was among the first countries to recognize Communist China as the legitimate claimant to the right of national self-determinations, the Indonesian delegates to the United Nations voiced their country's apprehensions of Chinese expansionism by voting with the West at the beginning of the Korean War. And at no time have the neutralist pronouncements emanating from Jakarta reverberated with that note of moral and cultural superiority which Indian spokesmen have been inclined to strike on not a few occasions. Indonesia's reticence in this respect cannot, however, alter the fact that the existing international framework allows for little compromise between the fundamental objectives of Indonesia and the United States. Indonesia may side—as it has in the past —with the West on specific issues; but, as long as the Cold War persists, Indonesia and the United States are not likely to find common ground.

PART II
The trials of cooperation

The United States and Japan

INTRODUCTION

Any study of Japanese-American tensions must at the outset take account of the fact that Japan, of all the countries
of Asia, has undergone a unique historical development.
All other Asian countries have emerged only recently
from colonial or semi-colonial status, and now find themselves at various stages of economic underdevelopment.
For the last fifty years, Japan has been a highly industrialized country and, up until defeat in 1945, Asia's leading
imperialist power. In its policies of quickly adopting new
scientific methods and productive techniques, raising the
material standard of living of its population, stressing the
importance of international trade, building a formidable
army and the third largest navy in the world after the
First World War, and launching upon the path of conquest and empire, Japan's conduct has not differed ma-
terially from that which the intellectuals in most Asian
countries are prone to associate with the European powers. If Japan has not incurred a censure as severe as the
West, it is doubtless because Japan has not achieved as
much economic and imperial success as the West, and
simply because Japan is an Asian nation. In the Asian historical perspective, Japan occupies a middle ground between the uncommitted nations of the East and the democratic nations of the West. This fact explains, at least
partially, why Japan is not psychologically prone to look

upon the questions of communism and anticolonialism within the same frame of reference as the one adopted by India and Indonesia. Furthermore, the Japanese are able to conceive the present international situation in strategic terms that are akin to those that are familiar to the West, for Japan has had to contend with Russian expansionist efforts for more than fifty years, and now, looking across the narrow seas, discerns a major threat to her independence in the shape of a newly unified China, ideologically and militarily allied with the historic foe.

Japanese-American tensions may be more easily grasped in their proper perspective if it is understood that Japan bears comparison not so much with any other Asian nation as with a European Power which has found itself in a remarkably similar position during the last decade, namely, Germany. Both countries embarked, after 1930, upon foreign policies to which no realistic limits were set. Both suffered heavily in a total war, waged for unlimited political objectives and ending finally in total defeat which left a regional power vacuum. Japan and West Germany, located strategically on the frontier of the Cold War, have gradually recovered their prewar vigor, thanks primarily to the moderate occupation policies, massive American economic assistance, and the generous peace terms of the Western allies. Neither of these vanquished Axis partners needs fear any longer a Carthaginian peace, because each has already received concessions from the West and because each has something which the U.S.S.R. deems worth bidding for. Both countries, as a result of their past performance, are still regarded with a certain amount of suspicion by their neighbors. Both countries have been centers of controversy between the advocates of rearmament and the advocates of neutralism. Their neutralism, however, can hardly be called ideological. It is not intimately related to their culture patterns. Rather, it has been largely a form of psychological reaction against the shocks of defeat and destruction, combined with a temporary sense of inadequacy in relation to the two superpowers. This neutralism is cut from a mould entirely different from that of the other uncommitted nations of Asia, which is linked to a deep-rooted disdain for the use of force and international power politics.

In view of the foregoing, it is to be expected that Japanese-American tensions will not turn on such issues as colonialism, or the nature of the communist threat, or equality for Asians, or pacifist neutralism or racism. It will be more profitable to look for the source of frictions and tensions in the complex of problems flowing from defeat, occupation, and Japan's efforts to recover her Great Power status.

THE QUEST FOR INDEPENDENCE FROM THE U. S.

A peculiar relationship has existed between Japan and the United States since September 2, 1945, the day of the surrender aboard the U. S. S. *Missouri*. Although all the victorious allies who had contributed forces toward the defeat of Japan participated formally in the occupation regime, the military government was for all practical purposes almost exclusively an American affair. The American policy was moderate. The Emperor was retained as the symbol of national unity, although the political theory of Japanese monarchy was revised radically.[1] The role of the American military authorities in the government of the country was gradually diminished, while considerable emphasis was placed upon the continued operation of existing institutions.[2] The Japanese people accommodated themselves with surprisingly good grace to a situation in which they were left free to carry out the directives which emanated from the Supreme Commander for the Allied Powers (SCAP). They were told to forswear militarism and to embrace the democratic spirit, and they attempted to comply with as much docility as any conquered people has ever displayed. On October 7, 1947, the lower house of the Diet accepted a completely American-inspired and a largely SCAP-drafted Constitution by an almost unanimous vote. The following May one of the most liberal organic laws of all time went into effect. The flag of the Rising Sun was again permitted to fly over the nation's public buildings. But despite the smooth relationships between the victor and the vanquished, the ubiquitous presence of the Americans sowed the seeds of national resentment. It is difficult for Americans, who have never known in their own lifetime or, for that matter, in their whole history an occupation by a culturally alien force, to conceive of what subtle and not-so-subtle frictions the very presence of the Western conqueror, no matter how enlightened and compassionate, must engender. A Swiss correspondent noted the average Japanese's response to what she deemed the average American's eccentricities:

> the Japanese consider our "natural" behavior barbaric and uncivilized . . . Even today, for instance, they feel embarrassed when foreigners kiss in public when saying good-bye, even in the case of mother and child or husband and wife. They find it disagreeable to be patted on the back or to see a man take a woman's arm with even the most polite intentions. All of this offends the Japanese sense of dignity and reserve.[3]

Despite the resentment which inevitably grows out of the intermingling of cultures, the leaders of all the major Japanese political parties have acknowledged the dependence of their country on the United States, especially for its economic well-being. This condition of dependence has been a natural consequence of Japan's loss of markets and raw material sources on the Asian mainland. To a lesser extent, the Japanese have looked to the United States for their own military security, although there have been some signs recently that they are ready to assume responsibility for their own defense. As long as the occupation lasted, the Japanese regarded their extraordinary dependence on American might as inevitable. To recognize the inevitable, however, does not necessarily render it more palatable to a people who were the first non-Westerners to be admitted to the international community of sovereign states. How Japan can restore her national independence and, at the same time, retain the benefits flowing from the conqueror's manifest concern with and stake in the welfare of the conquered, is, therefore, the crucial issue of Japanese politics. It may be expected that in a country where the parliamentary party system is relatively new, and where the large parties are not founded on serious ideological cleavages, this question of the degree of independence which the nation can wrest from the ex-occupying power is the most natural one to be exploited for partisan purposes.

Although the Japanese proved to be models of docility under the military government, their criticism of American policy has increased in severity in proportion to the degree of economic recovery and diplomatic maneuverability which they have achieved since the signing, in September, 1951, of the Peace Treaty of San Francisco, and the Security Pact and Administrative Agreement of February 1952, authorizing the establishment of American bases. Although it was now obvious to even the most dispassionate Japanese observers that the continued presence of the U. S. forces was a potential source of friction, the Yoshida Government justified its adherence to the agreement by pointing out that any alternative policy would create a "dangerous vacuum" in Japan and invite aggression from without and subversion from within.[4] Intellectuals, students, labor union leaders, and the socialists right and left were quick to criticize the Pact as an intolerable encroachment upon Japanese sovereignty. The *Nip-*

pon Times carried these quotes from the statements of people from all walks of life who were interviewed on the subject:

> Nothing can be said for a country which permits a foreign nation to station troops within its territory. Instead of having foreign troops here we should have our own defense forces at once.

> I am convinced that signing the pact when there is intensified rivalry between America and the Soviet Union will have the effect of giving impetus to the split of the world into opposing blocs.

> I am absolutely opposed to the security treaty. . . . It not only does not improve the position Japan held prior to its conclusion but rather it increases the pressure which is weighing heavily on our shoulders.[5]

Even conservative circles complained that, although substantial concessions were made to the United States, "no American commitment to defend Japan is incorporated in these conventions." [6] Not all comment, of course, was unfavorable. Some were inclined to look upon the security pact as a form of insurance against future hazards. According to an editorial in the *Mainichi*, Japan's second largest newspaper,

> Japan cannot remain in a state of military vacuum. In a peaceful world, no independent country welcomes garrisoning of foreign troops. But stationing of U. S. troops in Japan is necessary for the defense of Japan and of the whole free world.[7]

The general public exhibited neither strong hostility nor enthusiasm for the pact, although a concern over its long-range effects on the national economy was voiced in many quarters. Most of the press comment leaned to the unfavorable side. The Newspaper Association reported on March 6, 1952, that, out of a total of 64 editorials carried by member newspapers about the pact, only 7 approved it on the whole, while 15 treated it as "something to be tolerated under the present circumstances," and 42 expressed dissatisfaction.[8]

The critics became more vocal when the first steps were taken to implement the Security Pact and Administrative Agreement. The doubts most frequently voiced in Diet interpellations, newspaper editorials and public opinion polls revolved on these questions: (1) Would Japan be used as an atom-bomb base? (2) Would Japanese forces be despatched overseas to become involved in a "foreign war" in which Japan would have no strategic voice? (3) Under what specific circumstances would American forces be utilized for quelling "internal emergencies"? (4) Would U. S. military courts have exclusive jurisdiction over crimes committed by Americans on Japanese soil? [9]

Both the Japanese and the American Government felt compelled to allay these fears as quickly as possible. First, the United States gave prompt assurances that Japan was not destined to become an atomic base, while the Japanese Government denied that there was any intention to send the National Security Force either to Korea or to any other trouble spot on the Asian mainland.[10] The question of how to handle "internal emergencies" received the least attention, and it was doubtlessly thought the better part of wisdom to leave it unclarified until the clause should actually have to be invoked. The question of criminal jurisdiction proved to be the most immediately pressing one. The Administrative Agreement had provided that the "nationality principle" would be applied in determining jurisdiction over offenses involving American garrison forces. This provision implied that Japanese justice was inferior to American justice and was branded, therefore, by Japanese critics as an obnoxious instance of extraterritoriality.[11] A member of Tokyo University's law faculty declared

that the retention of jurisdiction by the United States over
any crimes committed by troops off duty or committed by
family relatives of troops was "unprecedented in the history of international law." [12] A stream of letters poured in
to newspaper editors condemning extraterritoriality as being just as unforgivable as colonialism and imperialism.
A group of 41 foreign missionaries and Japanese Chris-
tians addressed a telegram to Premier Yoshida protesting
against the criminal jurisdiction clause on religious
grounds.[13] Throughout 1952 popular opposition continued
to be expressed by most of the political parties, newspapers and nationalistic organizations in the country. It
was aimed directly at the United States. Since the Korean
War was being fought at the time, criticism was frequently broadened into an attack upon granting special
privileges to "U. N. Forces." The *Nippon Times* expressed
the prevailing mood as follows:

> The Japanese Government . . . is feeling tremendous
> domestic pressure which promises to give it a rough time
> in the Diet, if it gives the impression of being forced into
> ceding extraterritorial rights.
>
> The feeling among the Japanese people . . . has un-
> fortunately been closely bound with emotional factors.
> The rise of nationalistic sentiments coupled with the sense
> of inferiority brought on by war defeat have keyed the
> people up to a point where even a reasonable compromise
> may be looked upon as "capitulation." The people want
> to show that they are independent and are their own
> masters.[14]

Several quarters expressed the hope that some arrangements on criminal jurisdiction over military personnel similar to those incorporated in the NATO Pact be adopted in
the case of Japan. Under the NATO formula, if an act is a
crime only under the laws of the country in which the
military forces are stationed, the country's jurisdiction is
recognized. If the act is a crime only under the laws of the

nation stationing the forces, then the latter's jurisdiction prevails. If it is a crime under the laws of both nations, jursdiction is determined according to agreed stipulations.[15] In the fall of 1953, the Administrative Agreement underwent a revision which enabled the Japanese Government to exercise jurisdiction over all crimes committed by U. S. military personnel, except for the following classes of offenses: those committed while on duty, those committed on U. S. property; and those committed against other American troops.

Mainichi commented on the revision of the Agreement by warning that "after year-long wrangling" the friction arising from the presence of U. S. personnel in Japan had been reduced but slightly.[16] Apart from the understandable resentment against the maintenance of foreign forces in an overcrowded country, it has frequently been alleged within the last five years that the American troops have contributed to a marked decline in public morality, as reflected in the increased incidence of prostitution and drug addiction. Popular animosity in this regard reached its peak during 1952. The national chairman of the Japanese YWCA published an open letter to Mrs. Matthew Ridgway, wife of the then Supreme Commander of U. S. Forces in the Pacific, urging her to exert influence for higher moral conduct on the part of the occupation soldiers, who, she charged, "must bear the major responsibility for the growth of public prostitution after the war." [17] One village strongly protested the construction of army quarters nearby on the grounds that it "would immediately throw the life of this rural community into the whirl of depravity." [18] A committee of the Diet reported in November 1953 that more than half of the 3,000 prostitutes in the area of the Tachikawa Air Base were dope addicts and that they had contracted the habit from American GI's.[19] This situation confronted the U. S. authorities with a dilemma. If they declared the civilian areas off-limits, they would certainly have been accused of depriving the local communities of a large portion of their income, as Japanese journalists were quick to point out. The income derived by Japan from the American bases is by no means insignificant. While the public reacts unfavorably when the Government reveals that the total acreage pre-empted by the military runs to nearly 90,000 acres and involves an annual loss of 133,000 bushels of rice to the nation, it appears oblivious to the fact that the elimination or reduction in the size of American installations would also result in widespread economic dislocation in many parts of the country. The military authorities, in view of the necessities of the Korean campaign, were unable to give any serious consideration to the possibility of withdrawal or contraction at that time, either for moral or economic reasons. In fact, at the same time that the statistics cited above were published, it was announced that the Japanese Government had been requested to lease another 239,000 acres for the use of U. S. forces.[20] In the face of popular apprehensions over the morals of the children in the neighborhood of American bases, however, U. S. authorities co-sponsored the Association for Protecting Japan's Children, and sanctioned the establishment of local military-civilian councils to minimize the ill-feelings between bases and adjacent communities.[21]

Since the end of the war in Korea, and with the increased American insistence on Japan's assuming responsibility for a considerable share of her own defense, the prospects for the reduction of this particular source of friction have brightened. The concrete, visible signs of American presence and influence in Japan are gradually becoming less noticeable, although they cannot entirely disappear so long as the need for the maintenance of the twelve major air bases lasts. The complex of problems arising out of Japan's sense of dependence upon the United States continues to hang over the relations between the two countries. Two staff-writers for *Mainichi* recently summed up the prevalent mood in this way:

> As Japan enters into the fourth year of its "independence" it finds itself completely under the control of the American military police.

> Japan committed too much in signing the San Francisco Peace Treaty three years ago. For this incomplete independence, she has staked her freedom—the freedom of going her own way in this troubled world of today.[22]

U. S. NUCLEAR EXPERIMENTS

The American atomic and hydrogen experiments in the Pacific provoked the vehement protests of the neutral Asian nations. Official circles in Japan, the only nation ever to feel the blast of an A-bomb and the only one ever to suffer any casualties from the fall-out of an H-bomb, refrained from all but relatively minor criticisms. It is true that the Japanese people, and, to some extent, the press, prodded by leftists and opposition parties, have frequently voiced hostility to the testing of the weapons, to the whole American nuclear arms policy, and most of all to the possibility that Japan might be converted into an atomic base. Japanese governmental authorities, however, in all their official and diplomatic utterances, have carefully abstained from interfering with American decisions in this sphere.

Private sentiment in favor of banning all further atomic experiments was voiced in Japan as early as 1946, but there was very little open discussion about nuclear weapons in Japan during the occupation period. Pictures of Hiroshima and Nagasaki were published for the first time in the *Asahi Picture News* in August 1952, along with the following prefatory note:

One can hardly look at these terrible and dreadful pictures without covering one's eyes. The horribly great power of the atomic bomb, however, can never be diminished if we avert our eyes from these pictures. No! On the contrary, it is reported that the atomic bomb has been progressively improved until it now cannot be compared to the first bomb on which these pictures are based. Unfortunately, the Japanese were the first victims of the atomic bomb in the world. And yet how many of their own countrymen know the truth about the cruelty of the disaster? Possibly only a very few. Almost all of the rest know but a little about it through abstract writings and through some pictures of the great mushroom-shaped cloud. This has happened, however, because strict orders during the Occupation prohibited publication of the terrible facts. Here we publish . . . some selected pictures of the two cities, Nagasaki and Hiroshima, not because of mere inclination or curiosity, but because uncompromising reality far beyond an editor's private inclination demands it. If we can set aside awhile the pros and cons of rearmament, we want very emphatically to beg those who are not against rearmament to realize always that these same or much more cruel disasters will someday be our own.[23]

A few months later, the Japanese were overawed by the reports of the power of the H-bomb, and the popular reaction was one of horror. By early 1953, a ballet phantasy entitled "No More Hiroshimas" was playing in Tokyo, and listed high among the best-sellers was a book called *The Atom Bomb Children,* based on the impressions of children who had lived through the two blasts.[24] The high pitch of popular antagonism was reached in the spring of 1954, at the time of the Fukury-Maru H-bomb incident which resulted in radioactive injury to a number of Japanese fishermen, one of whom later died, and the contamination of their catch of tuna. Although Washington promptly proffered assistance to the stricken men, it did not come forth with an explicit apology and therefore left itself wide open to charges of "disregard of human feelings." [25] The U. S. Atomic Energy Commission aggravated the feelings of the Japanese by contradicting the report of the doctors who attributed the death to radioactive injuries, while one member of Congress suggested that the boat may have been in the area for purposes of spying.[26] The *Oriental Economist* was displeased at the alleged callousness of the American Government's attitude:

> It is reported that the United States is subjecting all tuna imported from Japan to rigorous tests against radioactivity, and certainly this is a justifiable step. However, competent U. S. authorities are entirely mistaken if they think that everything will be all right if only the imports into their own country are safe from danger. This is contemptibly shallow egotism.[27]

Notwithstanding widespread popular resentment, the Liberal Government of Premier Shigeru Yoshida issued a statement in support of American intentions to go ahead with further experiments when they were deemed necessary. The Japanese Cabinet not only rejected the proposal of the opposition parties for a full-scale investigation, but even urged the people to help protect the hydrogen secrets uncovered in the incident.[28] Tensions over this matter subsided somewhat for about a year, during which time no further tests were conducted in the Pacific, but the announcement, in July 1955, of the decision to transfer atomic-rocket equipped Air Force contingents to Japan aroused another popular uproar. A few weeks later, several internationalist groups, non-Communist as well as Communist, took part in an anti-atomic weapons conference in Hiroshima on the occasion of the tenth anniversary of the bombing of that city.[29]

The Japanese Government has not allowed itself to be swayed noticeably by the public outbursts and demonstrations which have been played up in the press. The most which the authorities have done is to ask the United States to modify its testing program by relocating the sites farther from Japan and by scheduling the tests during the intervals between fishing seasons. The Government does not express any opposition to the development of nuclear weapons on grounds of principle, as the Indians and Indonesians do, who regard the use of force in international relations as intrinsically immoral. When the Japanese Government protests against the experiments, it does so only insofar as they adversely affect the interests of Japanese citizens. Meanwhile, the Government takes the position that the problem of controlling these weapons is not so much one of marshalling public opinion against them as it is one of establishing a practicable system within the framework of the United Nations.

REARMAMENT AND DEFENSE STRATEGY

The problem of rearmament and defense did not emerge as a serious one for Japan until independence had been regained. Under the occupation, the policy of General MacArthur, of course, had been to disarm Japan, and to root out those conditions which would make it possible for Japan to menace the peace of the Far East again in the future. The new democratic Constitution was written in 1947, at a time when educators and statesmen were practically unanimous in agreeing that the inculcation of pacifist ideals was an indispensable feature of any demilitarization policy. The writers of the so-called MacArthur Constitution did their best to dramatize this departure from the aggressive tendencies which the nation had shown since 1931, and the provisions which they incorporated in the document provoked a great deal of comment at the time. Only a nation occupied by a foreign power which implicitly assumed the responsibility for its defense could ever ratify such clauses as these in its basic constitutional law:

> Aspiring sincerely to an international peace based on justice and order, the Japanese people forever renounce war as a sovereign right of the nation and the threat or use of force as means of settling international disputes.
>
> In order to accomplish the aim of the preceding paragraph, land, sea and air forces, as well as other war potential, will never be maintained. The right of the belligerency of the state will not be recognized.[30]

It was inevitable that such a constitutional provision, quite comprehensible during the period of military occupation, should give rise to considerable controversy when Japan again became a sovereign nation. It must be remembered that the Peace Treaty went into effect nearly two years after the military situation in the Far East had changed drastically as a result of the outbreak of the Korean War. The United States has been suspected in some quarters of pressuring the Japanese Government to amend Article 9 of the Constitution in order to legalize rearmament. Toshikazu Kase, a high Foreign Office official, summarized the Japanese attitude on this problem:

> As is well known, the present Japanese Constitution, prepared during the occupation, forbids our rearmament and this seems to give a legal sanction to the popular movement against rearmament. It is unfortunate that the inherent right of a sovereign nation to provide for her own national defense is disputed as a violation of the Constitution and that the issue of rearmament is replaced by and confused with that of upholding the basic law of the state. A vocal section of our public suspects that outside pressure is being brought to bear upon the government to revise the anti-rearmament clause of the Constitution. . . .[31]

The controversy dates back to the conclusion of the Security Treaty, which was signed along with the Peace

Treaty in September 1951. Under this pact, the United States declared that it was "willing to maintain certain of its armed forces in and around Japan, in the expectation, however, that Japan will itself increasingly assume responsibility for its own defense." [32] During the following months, while discussions were taking place over the Administrative Agreement which was to implement the pact, the Government found it difficult to arouse much enthusiasm for the new military link with the United States. Premier Shigeru Yoshida's Liberal Party was able to muster only a narrow majority in the Diet in favor of ratification.[33] Initially, the opposition to the security agreement sprang from the popular aversion to its overtones of extraterritoriality, the fear that American forces might intervene in the event of domestic disturbances, and related questions of sovereignty and independence which have already been treated in these pages. As time went on, however, and as it became more urgent for the Japanese Government to start fulfilling its obligations under the Treaty by laying plans for a national defense force, the basis of opposition to the program both from the other parties in the Diet and from the press shifted to constitutional and neutralistic arguments. Looking back now, it seems unfortunate that Article 9 of the Constitution had not been modified in some way prior to the ending of the occupation. The communists, the socialists, and all the other anti-rearmament forces were able to point to this article to justify their stand. They assumed the pose of staunch defenders of the American-inspired liberal Constitution, while the pro-American Liberal Party was driven into the awkward position of appearing to subvert it. At the height of the debate, Dr. Kotaro Tanaka, Chief Justice of the Supreme Court, declared:

> Japan has a right to self-defense against foreign attacks.
> Moreover, since she has allied herself with the free world,
> she is under obligation to defend the free world, of which

she is an integral part. If Japan is attacked by Red imperialism, therefore, it means an attack on the free world itself. . . . The San Francisco treaty imposed on Japan the obligation of defense. For Japan to remain in a military vacuum is to shirk her responsibility to the free world. Therefore, the best and most effective way for Japan to fill the vacuum was to sign the security treaty with the U. S.[34]

That statement contains a rather curious line of reasoning, which is indicative of the difficulty confronting the Japanese after six years of education under the occupation authorities who had instructed them to cultivate peace-loving, democratic and constitutional attitudes. They did not find it easy to reconcile their postwar indoctrination with the sudden need to defend themselves as American troops were being withdrawn to fight in Korea. The proximity of Soviet troops on South Sakhalin and the Kuriles made it imperative that some counterforce be maintained in Japan. This situation led to a request by SCAP for the creation of a National Safety Force. The initial step was to recruit 75,000 men for a two year period. The reaction of the public to rearmament was hard to gauge. Public opinion polls in the Spring of 1952 revealed that nearly fifty percent of the people thought that rearmament would entail a revision of the Constitution.[35] Since a considerable doubt prevailed as to the possible outcome of a popular referendum, which is required for a constitutional amendment, the Yoshida Government decided not to make the test if it could be avoided. Hence the program was presented as a "gradual" increase in defense potential, rather than as rearmament.

In September 1954, *Mainichi*, anticipating the forthcoming electoral contest, adopted a critical tone toward all of those in the Diet who attempted to justify the possession of a war potential for self-defense as being compatible with the Constitution, and accused them of "making arbitrary interpretations while planning to increase the defense power to a point where such amendment is necessary." [36] The parliamentary election of February 1955 yielded enough seats to the opponents of rearmament, especially the Left and Right Socialists, to persuade the government to drop the much-debated amendment. The only course of action which the Government could follow was to continue to by-pass the constitutional issue, and to take its stand on the common-sense grounds that the Constitution, although it prohibits arming for aggressive war, permits arming for defense, since the latter right inheres in sovereignty. To a certain extent, the problem has largely become an academic one. Japan has already placed in uniform 130,000 men, and has recently agreed to raise the number to 180,000 by 1960. Disagreement between the United States and Japan still exists: Washington would like to see a Japanese force of 350,000 by 1962, but the present Tokyo cabinet remains reluctant to consent to this request for a variety of political and economic reasons. (The economic considerations will be dealt with in a later section of this chapter.)

From outward appearances, the Japanese appear to have become reconciled to the need for a defense establishment. They continue, however, to express, from time to time, fears that the National Safety Force might someday have to be sent abroad to take part in a peripheral war after the pattern of Korea. While the Korean action was in progress, parliamentary leaders and newspaper editors left the United States in no doubt about the national mood. Ichiro Hatoyama, who later became Premier, declared in late 1952:

> I will fight Prime Minister Shigeru Yoshida when there is some specific issue worth fighting about, as, for example, if and when he should try to send the National Safety Force out to enter the war in Korea.[37]

This statement may have been designed for domestic partisan consumption, but its importance should not therefore be minimized. His position was reinforced by an editorial in *Mainichi* a few days after the election of President Eisenhower, referring to a notion expressed during the latter's campaign:

> The slogan that Asia should be defended by Asians is a beautiful slogan as a matter of principle. But the Korean War is not essentially an Asian war.
>
> We believe that increase of defense power in accordance with the national strength is necessary in view of the unpredictable international situation. The expansion, however, should be limited within the framework of self-defense.[38]

Shinichi Hasegawa, Associate Editor of the *Nippon Times,* expressed these misgivings about American intentions vis-à-vis Japan's role in the Pacific strategic system:

> Few Japanese expect Eisenhower to "end the Korean War honorably" through talks at Panmumjom. More Japanese anticipate the brilliant general would rather try to end it through force. Is Ike going to demand reinforcements from Formosa alone, or from Japan too? That's the question which makes many Japanese worried. . . .[39]

Quite naturally, these fears have subsided since the termination of the fighting in Korea and Indo-China. Nonetheless, it is to be expected that the Japanese will continue to look with suspicion upon any development which contains the slightest hint that the National Safety Force is to be used as a "cat's paw" by Washington. Japan wishes it to be clearly understood that it does not want to become entangled in any future military action on the Asian mainland under circumstances over which Japan has no control. Hence American plans to integrate Japan into the Asian defense structure have encountered considerable difficulties. Many Japanese were afraid during 1953 and

1954 that the NSF would be utilized in America's efforts to organize the defense of Asia if Mutual Security Aid were to be accepted. *Mainichi* took the Yoshida Government to task for permitting Secretary Dulles and other American leaders to influence its concept of the NSF:

> The basic objective of the Mutual Security Act is to defend American security as it is clearly stated in the law. If then the change in the NSF mission is related to the acceptance of MSA, the ultimate objective of the new mission becomes painfully obvious.[40]

There is little reason to doubt Japan's willingness to assume the responsibility for its own defense, but it appears definitely opposed to becoming involved piecemeal in any treaty organization similar to SEATO. Since the United States has never spelled out the reasons why it deems a more extensive NSF essential, the Japanese wonder whether the primary U. S. objective is merely to enhance the strategic value of its own forces in the Pacific area by releasing them from their defense obligations in Japan and thereby making them available for deployment elsewhere in Asia. There is much more involved here than a difference in the estimate of what the defense of Japan requires. What is really at stake is the prospect of Japan's regaining its Great Power status through successful negotiations with the Soviet Union and its Chinese communist ally, now that it is approaching the point of diminishing returns in its negotiations with the United States. The Japanese are not oblivious of their growing bargaining power in view of the new emphasis in Soviet policy upon the neutralism of the key nations of the free world upon which American strategy hinges. Kase has put the problem succinctly:

> For the paramount aim of the Communist effort is to detach Japan from the United States, then to neutralize her, and eventually to win her over to the Communist camp.

> Thus our situation is closely analogous to that of West
> Germany. The fate of Europe will be decided by the dis-
> position of the German question; the destiny of Asia will
> depend on the orientation of Japan.[41]

The Japanese recognize their strengthened negotiating
position, and doubtless realize that any major increase
in the size of the NSF would constitute a serious obstacle
in the path to the restoration of Japanese power, for it
would reduce the opportunity of gaining favorable peace
treaty terms from the U.S.S.R., and at the same time it
would make U. S. forces available for deployment elsewhere in Asia. This latter contingency might increase the
likelihood of "little wars" and compel the Japanese to commit themselves too soon, thereby closing the door on the
possibility of regaining Great Power status through diplomatic bargaining. Any military action in Asia, such as a
resumption of hostilities in and around Formosa, would
doubtless involve U. S. operations from Japanese soil. This
would put pressure on Japan to close ranks with the
United States. The use of Japanese bases by American
strategic air forces, now that Japan has achieved her national independence, would be fraught with vaster implications than it was at the time of the fighting in Korea. Like
England, Japan cannot absorb many nuclear strikes. Tokyo
must reckon with the fact that the Sino-Soviet Treaty of
Friendship, Alliance and Mutual Assistance of 1950 contains a clause directly aimed at Japan:

> In the event of one of the contracting parties being at-
> tacked by Japan or any state allied with it, and thus being
> involved in a state of war, the other contracting party
> shall immediately render military and other assistance by
> all means at its disposal.[42]

This could mean that even in a limited war which might
be precipitated in Asia, the Soviet Union, while not committing its own forces, might make nuclear weapons avail-

able to the Chinese. While all the implications of the Sino-Soviet treaty are not clear, it is certain that the U.S.S.R. could not continue to negotiate a peace settlement with a Japan which allowed U. S. forces to use its facilities against the Chinese mainland. Thus, Japan can be expected at this time to try to minimize the chances of another peripheral crisis like the one circumvented, in 1954-1955, in the Formosan Straits. Considerations such as these appear to have prompted Toshikazu Kase's pessimistic diagnosis:

> . . . A psychological gap seems about to develop between Japan and the United States. In the American view, the international situation is still grave, and especially in East Asia. Consequently, the United States urges Japan to fulfill her obligations . . . [but] our people incline to take a more hopeful view of the global situation. Not believing in the imminence of war, they do not feel the same urgency that the American military command does to increase Japanese defense efforts sharply.[43]

THE JAPANESE ECONOMY AND U. S. POLICY

One of the major differences between the foreign policy of Japan and that of the other Asian nations derives from the emphasis which the Japanese are compelled to place upon considerations of international trade. This manufacturing nation, whose population of eighty-eight millions is rising at the rate of 1.5 percent each year, and whose land area is equivalent only to the size of Wisconsin, depends nearly as much as Great Britain does upon the export of manufactures in order to keep needed food and raw materials flowing in. It is not surprising, therefore, that some of the frictions in Tokyo-Washington relations during recent years relate to the same matters which have frequently been subjects of disagreement between Washington and

London: American tariff policy and the dollar gap, the cost of defense establishments, and trade with the communist countries. For both of these island workshops, the American market represents the chief source of "hard currency." Yet both of them import from the United States considerably more than they are able to export to this country. The United States tariff excludes many Japanese and British products which would otherwise find their way here for sale. For political and strategic reasons, the United States frowns whenever its transoceanic partners manifest interest in doing business with the communist countries. Americans are quite happy to let the English and the Japanese carry on a thriving exchange with all nations of the world that lie between the protected American market and the state-controlled communist market. The chief obstacle to that fortuitous solution is the fact that such a large portion of the in-between area is underdeveloped and hence in a poor position to buy manufactured commodities. U. S. loans and military expenditures abroad helped to reduce the gap between exports and imports, but these devices have now passed the point of maximum effectiveness. Public opinion in the relatively self-sufficient United States, which does not depend heavily upon the export of finished goods to meet its requirements of foodstuffs and basic raw materials, does not readily appreciate the crucial importance of foreign trade to other countries. Less fortunate peoples find it difficult to agree with the conclusion of the Randall Commission on Foreign Economic Policy: "Taken by and large, our trade restrictions are certainly no more of a cause of payment imbalances than the rigidities maintained by other nations." [44] Whatever validity such a judgment might have, it furnished small comfort to America's allies, especially Japan, whose long-range trade problem was not referred to at all in the Randall Report.

Japan's plight is worse than Britain's. Britain is able to

rely more fully than the Japanese on income from shipping and insurance services, as well as from foreign investments, to take up the slack and bring her foreign trade into balance. Furthermore, Britain enjoys a pre-eminent position in the Commonwealth and reaps the benefits of a widespread trade preference system. Britain has not felt the loss of the China market as much as Japan has. Japan moreover has lost valuable sources of rice in Korea and Formosa, as well as fishing grounds around the Kuriles and elsewhere. On top of everything, the development of synthetic textiles like nylon, orlon and dacron have reduced Japanese silk exports from 550,000 bales in 1935 to 75,000 in 1954.[45] No matter which way the situation is analyzed, Japan emerges as the one processing nation in the free world whose long-range economic prospects appear rather bleak. In the Fall of 1954, economic experts in the State Department in Washington calculated that Japan could strike an export-import balance within five years at the level of $2.1 billion dollars, but only by restoring its merchant marine to full efficiency, increasing its annual sales to Asia, by nearly 50 percent, exporting an additional $100 million worth of goods to the United States (mostly textiles, metals, chemicals and machinery), and reducing its own imports by at least $300 million.[46] This amounts to advising the Japanese that they can accomplish the impossible merely by breaking it down into a number of nearly impossible components. After all the calculations have been made, the Japanese are still inclined to blame American tariff barriers for a $600 million trade deficit. Even the often-discussed Marshall Plan for Asia, much as the Japanese would like to see it materialize, would be "hardly more than a vinegar sold under a wine label" if the United States were to extend the aid without simultaneously lowering its tariffs. *Mainichi* warned: "You cannot blame the Japanese if they laugh at what they call American self-complacency." [47]

The Japanese, of course, take exception to the cheap labor argument which is frequently invoked by American textile companies, and when they ponder this long enough they begin to remember certain unfriendly aspects of immigration legislation. The editor of a New York textile trade paper, speaking to an audience in Yokahama, conveyed the unwelcome news that "our important textile executives are frantic in their fear of the unloading of Japanese textile exports on the United States." [48] He then proceeded to advise the Japanese to increase their sales in Asia and Africa as much as possible. But such blandishments are not received too well by the people who depend on the export of fabrics for their livelihood. They keep on asking such skeptical questions as these: 1) Are not Japanese exports only a negligible portion of America's domestic supply? 2) How can Japanese wages ever be raised if the nation must reduce her imports to achieve a balance of payments? 3) If Japanese exports are really a source of "frantic fear" because they pose such a disastrous threat, would the United States care to specify the amount which will endanger domestic industries? [49] Within the last three years, the textiles problem has come in for some heated discussions on both sides of the Pacific. Japanese newspapers prominently featured Senator J. Strom Thurmond's remark in 1953 to the effect that he was "vitally interested in protecting the employers and employees of South Carolina textile industries against low-grade and low-price imports from Japan." [50] Somewhat later, strong protests were raised against American efforts to limit the importation of Japanese silk scarves under the category of inflammable goods. The American protectionists scored a major victory when the George Amendment to the Administration's reciprocal trade program extension bill, by merely shifting the base date for purposes of statistical calculation, effectively deprived Japan of the benefits anticipated under the authorized 15% tariff reduction. [51] Certain unusual purchasing policies of American importers have given the U. S. textile industry a serious scare during 1955, and consequently the clamour for quotas has increased in intensity. During 1954, for example, the flow of Japanese cotton goods into the United States was maintained at a rather even average rate of 6 million yards per month, only about one-eighth of the amount of cotton goods which this country was exporting to Japan. But during the summer of 1955, American manufacturers, many of whom probably tried to turn out as many finished products as possible before the new federal minimum wage law would go into effect in March, 1956, placed orders for 85,000,000 yards of Japanese cotton within a two month period. The reaction of the American textile interests has been unfavorable, to say the least. The Trade Bureau in Tokyo, fearing the imposition of quotas, has suggested that Japan itself should restrict its exports to figures that are safely below the "recrimination level." [52]

Perhaps the most serious trade issue between Japan and the United States concerns the question of economic relations with the communist bloc, and especially mainland China. While the American market confronts Japan with protectionist policies as stringent as those before the war, the China market shrank in 1949 quite suddenly to the vanishing point, just as Japan's ability to support herself by exporting was being restored. Before China was conquered by the communists, its market absorbed 28% of all Japan's exports. In the first eight months of 1955, the figure was 2.9%, or 60 million dollars, and even that represented a sizeable increase over the total of 18 million dollars for all of 1954. [53]

The Japanese, however, do not regard the reopening of the trade with China as a panacea for their economic troubles, because they are aware that they could not exchange their surplus of manufactures for Chinese food and raw materials on a pure business basis, much less on the old basis of Japanese political dominance in the coastal areas. In 1951 the *Nippon Times* carried an editorial entitled "How Essential is Trade with Red China?":

> Efforts are being made to instill in the Japanese people the feeling that trade with Red China is absolutely essential to their national welfare. This is in itself the employment by the Reds of trade as a political weapon. As important as the Red China trade may be, it would be unfortunate if the Japanese people allow themselves, through an overestimation of its value, to be browbeaten into doing business with the Reds.[54]

There was a general realization that the communists would subordinate trade to political considerations, that particular difficulties were likely to arise from the fact that Japan did not maintain diplomatic or consular representatives in China, and that any trade would have to fit the pattern of requirements of the Chinese total planners.[55] The *Yomiuri Shimbun* warned businessmen not to be overoptimistic on the possibilities of trade with Red China. If such trade were to be revived, the newspaper declared, it would be a poor bargain if it led to the severance of friendly Japanese-American relations, "the lifeline of the country." [56]

Nonetheless, the Leftist Socialists have maintained a steady effort to keep the question of trade with China at the forefront of public attention. At the Asian Socialist Conference in January 1953, the Japanese delegation declared:

> We must change the present form of Japan's economy, which is dependent upon the American procurement program initiated during the Korean War. We must import raw materials from neighboring Asian nations. For this it is indispensable to have economic cooperation with Asian nations, including Communist China.[57]

An interesting insight into the Leftist Socialists' reasoned case against the restrictions of trade with China was contained in a letter to the *Mainichi* "Readers' Forum" in the spring of 1953:

> It is all right for Americans to use anti-socialist slogans. It is not befitting for us Japanese, living in present-day Japan, to use such double-edged words. We merely hurt ourselves or end by making ourselves ridiculous. Of course, the Americans want us to believe in the idea of a divided world because they do not want us to regain our former power through free trade with China and other Asiatic countries. But we don't have to be such dopes as to believe in silly slogans meant for gullible Americans and their European satellites. Americans can't teach us about things Chinese.[58]

The Japanese, even though they did not place great hopes in trade across the China Sea, contended for a long time that the restrictions upon their exports to the communist areas should be eased at least to the level permitted to the exporters of the West European nations. When trade control was handed over to the Japanese government shortly before the Peace Treaty went into effect, the transfer was made under the strict understanding that the same restrictions which had obtained during the Occupation period should be continued. The Export Control Guide, an embargo list furnished by the outgoing GHQ, was much stricter than the list applied to other nations, despite the fact that the loss of the China market had hit the Japanese more seriously than any Western countries. When Secretary Dulles in the fall of 1953 hinted that the list of prohibited items might be considerably liberalized, Japanese business circles tended to regard his speech as a purely political utterance, and complained that "the mitigation of drastic restrictions on trade with Red China will be in exchange for future reenforcement of the NSF." [59]

Early in 1954, the Japanese were placed on a footing of equality with the other nations engaged in trade with China, but the economic picture did not brighten much as a result. A staff writer for *Mainichi*, after lamenting the fact that it had taken so long to achieve equality of restrictions, analyzed his country's plight thus:

> As long as control over trade with Communist China and the Soviet bloc exists, Japan will have to seek other markets. Unless the United States, the Commonwealth nations and others are considerate and cooperative in affording Japan an opportunity to cultivate her markets, Japan's foreign trade will never recover from its present slump, and what is worse, clamors against Western policies will become more and more vociferous.[60]

As long as Japan suffers from economic troubles, businessmen will look wistfully, if not realistically, to the mainland for outlets. The Communists and the Leftist Socialists will continue to play up the prospect of improved economic relations with Peking for all that it is worth. That prospect becomes more alluring to Japan as American off-shore procurement orders dwindle. When the Korean War ended, it was hoped that the inevitable decline in U. S. military purchases might be compensated by increased South Korean purchases in Japan. But Rhee's Government made it clear as soon as the rehabilitation program was under way that, because of the dispute over fishing rights and other questions at issue between the two countries, it would not spend its dollars in Japan, as it was urged to do by Washington.[61] American spokesmen like Harold Stassen have repeatedly urged Japan to try to become self-sustaining by working out its problems with its non-Communist neighbors in South Asia and Southeast Asia in a way that would foster expanded commercial exchange with them and thereby reduce the importance of the China trade question.[62] This, of course, is easier to pro-

pose than to accomplish. Great Britain views with no little
concern the increase of Japanese competition in Asian
markets. It was the United Kingdom more than any other
member of the General Agreement on Tariffs and Trade
(GATT) which held up the entry of Japan into that international organization, while several other nations, including some members of the Commonwealth, were reluctant
to extend most-favored-nation treatment to Japan for fear
that it might adopt dumping policies.[63] Another bar to the
economic penetration of Southeast and South Asia by
Japan is the postwar residue of anti-Japanese sentiment,
particularly in Burma, Indonesia and the Philippines, which
have been engaged in prolonged wrangling with Tokyo
over reparations payments. The problem of Burmese
reparations has recently been settled with an arrangement
that suggests a sort of Japanese-sponsored Point Four program for the country formerly occupied by Nipponese
forces. Japan has agreed to send $2 billion worth of equip-
ment and technical aid to Burma over a ten-year period,
and it is expected that this will contribute greatly toward
the establishment of a sizeable market for Japanese manufactures.[64] Hence at the present time, Southeast Asia appears to hold the greatest promise for future Japanese trade,
although gains in this direction cannot be expected for
several years, since there are decided limitations to the rate
at which underdeveloped economies can grow.

Meanwhile, the Chinese question will continue to haunt
the national scene. The *Oriental Economist* warned in
September 1954 that, even though the commerce with the
Chinese mainland should remain relatively unimportant,
Communist propaganda would make it likely "that it will
assume a place in the Japanese mind quite out of proportion to its actual worth." [65] The Hatoyama Government,
having pledged itself to explore all legitimate avenues of
expanding the Chinese trade, has looked more favorably
upon the activities of the private trading groups which

were beginning to exchange unofficial delegations. Although Premier Hatoyama rejected Chou En-lai's suggestion of July 1955 that representatives be sent to Peking to discuss "normalising relations," the unofficial Japanese business delegations have reached the proportions of *de facto* governmental bodies. Unless the United States can make its economic policies toward the Communist bloc more palatable to the Japanese by providing them with realistic alternatives before it is too late, Japan may be alienated once again from the Western nations over the matter of exports and imports. It does not seem likely that Japan will turn economically toward Red China. It appears, however, highly likely that Japan will be induced both by considerations of almost desperate need and by American encouragement to forge substantial economic ties with the neutralist nations of South and Southeast Asia. If this happens, it will mean that Japan will begin to look upon countries like Burma and Indonesia as a vital segment of her community of interest. In order to maintain their economic goodwill and allay their political suspicions, Japan would undoubtedly feel constrained to assume increasingly, on the plane of international politics, the behavior pattern of an "uncommitted" nation.

Japan's economic situation is, of course, intimately related to her capacity and willingness to rearm. From the very beginning of the period of national independence, objections were raised not only on political but also on economic grounds against the establishment of a defense corps capable of replacing the U. S. security forces. Throughout the latter part of 1952, leading newspapers regularly carried editorials stressing the necessity of keeping the NSF within such limits as would not entail a heavy fiscal burden upon the people. The problem was one of balancing rifles with rice. Here are some representative opinions expressed at that time:

Naturally, Japan should rearm as a free nation. However, with her present economic strength, she cannot afford to maintain any sizeable defense forces. Reasonable aid must come from America.[66]

Rearmament cannot be considered a true rearmament when it is prepared out of proportion to the nation's economy. And, when the nation's livelihood is threatened under the heavy pressure of rearmaments, there will arise a danger of fatal collapse from within the nation. "Butter" for the people, therefore, is just as important a weapon as munitions.[67]

But for Japan, this problem is not a clear-cut case of attempting to stretch funds to cover both the needs of rearmament and of reconstruction and the people's livelihood. Japan must also take heed of the dent which the repayment of prewar debts and of reparations will make in the nation's pocketbook for several years to come. The three-way pull of the three R's—rearmament, reconstruction and reparations—upon the economy will not come easy.[68]

The Japanese press frequently gives the impression that the danger of Soviet aggression is not regarded too seriously, especially when the threat of inflation, which would result from the aggravation of Japan's unfavorable balance of payments, is given precedence over strategic considerations. *Mainichi,* for example, in the spring of 1954, noted that the "people are doubtful of both the propriety and advisability of holding such an expensive armed force, no matter how 'impending' the 'danger' is, under the current economic capacity of the nation." [69] American officials, however, do not appear to entertain much doubt that Japan does have the ability to rearm while at the same time maintaining a stable economic structure. Secretary Dulles voiced his disappointment over Japan's defense efforts, and hinted that the economic argument was merely being employed as a shield for lethargy or reluctance. The Japanese rejoinder to this was that America failed to recognize the enormous gap in living standards between the two nations, and that this difference made it impossible to evaluate Japanese internal revenue policies in terms of U. S. taxing rates.[70]

Meanwhile, the increased U. S. emphasis on the need for rearmament has been accompanied by a shifting emphasis in the nature of American aid programs, away from purely economic and toward more military aid. According to an analysis made by the *Asahi Evening News* early in 1955, the ratio of economic to military aid in Asia, which was as high as 10 to 1 in 1950, is now only 8 to 10. This, it was contended, more than offset the gain indicated by the threefold increase of Asia's share in the total of America's foreign assistance expenditures during that five year period.[71] The apparent decline of American interest in the Point Four Program reinforced the Japanese in their conviction that Asia was on its way to becoming a purely military object of U. S. foreign policy. *Mainichi* gloomily predicted that "if the existing situation is left as it is, there is danger that the standard of living of Asian peoples will fall, leading to social unrest and greater exposure to communism." [72]

The Japanese have frequently taken offense at some of the technical aspects of American defense aid. Whereas they had anticipated a "liberal" interpretation of MSA funds agreements, they were surprised and irritated by the strict attitude adopted by American officials, who authorized the disbursement of funds only to the arms industries and related basic industries, and who insisted that the loans, originally made in yen, were to be repaid with three percent interest on the basis of their dollar value at the time they were made.[73] The Japanese Government has been placed in an embarrassing position more than once by promises to the Diet of future economic concessions from Washington, only to find out, when the time came, that Washington was hard to impress with threats of growing economic unrest in Japan. The effort by the Government to pare down the national share of the costs of keeping U. S. troops in Japan furnishes an apt illustration. The Japanese share of these joint defense costs was originally allocated in the form of a fixed annual amount. This procedure was adopted at the request of the Japanese Government itself in order to avoid delay in budget computation. Apparently the Yoshida Cabinet had misled the Diet and the people into thinking that, later on, the downward revision of Japan's share would be quite easy to achieve. The businesslike tone assumed by American officials during the subsequent negotiations over this point was not exactly what the Japanese had been expecting. Beginning with the fiscal agreements for 1953-54, the Americans did bend a little, and acquiesced in a reduction of the Japanese share. The concession has been repeated for every fiscal year since then, and never for more than a year at a time. The preparation of the annual budget has to be deferred to the conclusion of the negotiations with Washington.[74] *Mainichi* saw fit in the spring of 1955 to complain that "the nation was given the impression that Japan, three years after it recovered independence, is still under American control in the disposition of such key matters as the national budget." [75]

THE ISLANDS ADJACENT TO JAPAN

When Japan was a Great Power, part of its might and its prestige lay in the possession of a number of smaller island territories which helped to guard the avenues of approach to the main island group. Defeated Japan was shorn of practically all of these outlying possessions: the Kurile Chain, the southern half of Sakhalin, the Habomai and Shikotan groups, the Bonins and the Ryukyus. Within

the last few years the question of these islands, to which
the Japanese have asserted either historic ownership
rights or rights of occupation short of ownership, has been
gradually emerging as what may be called the primary
source of likely Japanese-American tension. The United
States is not directly involved in all of the island problems.
It continues to occupy the Bonins, of course, and it has a
particularly vital interest in one of the Ryukyus, viz.,
Okinawa, which serves as the most important U. S. strategic air base in the Pacific area. But the United States,
in view of its special postwar connection with Japan, also
finds itself drawn into the disputes over other islands for
a variety of diplomatic and strategic reasons, many of
them having their origin in the Cold War.

Before taking up the more serious island questions, it
may be instructive to examine a relatively insignificant
dispute which casts some light on the potentially explosive character of the island problems. This dispute relates
to two barren chunks of rock in the Sea of Japan which
the Japanese call Take. For several centuries, fishermen
from both Japan and Korea have taken refuge on Take in
emergencies. There were never any serious difficulties
over Take until the postwar period. During the occupation, American authorities had drawn the so-called "Mac-
Arthur Line" in such a way as to include Take within the
area assigned to Japanese fishermen. Early in 1952, just as
the occupation was being terminated, President Syngman
Rhee drew his own boundary of Korea's territorial waters
50 to 60 miles offshore in order to prevent the intrusion of
Japanese fishing vessels into Korea's fishing grounds. Rhee
later dispatched military forces to occupy Take. The Japanese Government, the fishing industry and the press fulmi-
nated against this unilateral action which, they argued
vehemently, violated the three-mile rule set by international law.[76] When General Mark W. Clark's Headquarters established a Sea Defense Zone around South Korea

in September 1952, the Japanese accused it of underwriting the Rhee Line. Although General Clark announced that the purpose of the defense zone was to prevent attacks on the coast and the running of contraband, the order, since it operated against Japanese fishing vessels but not against Korean boats, was open to charges of discrimination. The dispute assumed major proportions when a Korean ship fired upon a Japanese fishing vessel which had entered the defense zone, arousing a wave of popular indignation throughout Japan.[77] Doubtless the question of accessibility to fishing grounds was the main issue at stake for Japan, which felt that its fishing rights had been seriously encroached upon by the Soviet Union, the United States, Canada, and most intolerable thought of all, Korea.[78] Both Korea and Japan have appealed for the mediation of the United States, which quite understandably prefers to remain neutral and inactive in the dispute. During Vice President Nixon's visit to Japan in November 1953, he was presented with a petition by representatives of the fishing industry, in which the view was urged upon the United States that it was the most logical country to act as mediator, and that should mediation fail, the United States should step forward and break the deadlock. The United States remained cool to the suggestion. The Take Island dispute, like the Japanese-Philippine reparations dispute, illustrates the dilemma with which the United States sometimes finds itself confronted in its relations with Asian nations who look to the United States for leadership but are locked in a conflict of interests among themselves.

The second island dispute relates to one of the key U. S. bases in the Far East, i.e., Okinawa. Although Okinawa's continued occupation by the Americans as a strategic trust territory was sanctioned by the San Francisco Peace Treaty, the Japanese have repeatedly urged its early return to their control. The United States actually did return some of the Ryukyu Islands, the Amami Oshima group, to Japan on Christmas Eve, 1953.[79] This action, however, has not satisfied the Japanese' desire to regain full possession of their former islands which are now held by the United States. As a leading American student of the Ryukyus has pointed out, the "rationale for the separation of the Ryukyu Islands from the rest of Japan is for the most part one of official silence and astute circumvention." [80] The warrant for this "official silence" can be construed from the circumstance that the Ryukyus were never mentioned either in the Cairo, Yalta or Potsdam agreements of the allied powers, or in the surrender terms accepted by Japan in 1945. The first time they came up for discussion was at the time of the Peace Treaty talks in San Francisco. The Treaty placed the Ryukyus under the immediate control of the United States, and suggested a trust status under the United Nations. The United States, however, probably to avoid subjecting its strategic interests in that sector to international scrutiny and also to hold out to Japan the prospect of eventually returning the islands, has not placed them under the Trusteeship Commission.

It would seem that the popular discontent has been gradually mounting, ever since the time in August 1951 when, a month before the treaty was signed, a delegation of Ryukyu Island officials asserted that a majority of the Ryukyu population desired to be reunited with Japan as early as possible.[81] Premier Yoshida, in the address which he delivered at the San Francisco Peace Conference, said that the disposition of the territories was a cause of "pain and anxiety," and expressed the hope "that the administration of these islands will be put back into Japanese hands in the not distant future with the re-establishment of world security, especially the security of Asia." [82] Apart from legal arguments as to ownership, the Japanese have alleged mistreatment by Americans of the native population of Okinawa in an effort to justify their demands for the return of the islands. The Civil Liberties Association of Japan, reporting on its investigation of administrative practices on the island, was especially critical of the land purchase system under which U. S. authorities, operating on a rather tight budget, appropriated, at low rentals, farm land from the natives for the construction of airfields. The only rejoinder which the Americans were able to make was to say that the Association had not even visited Okinawa during the course of its "exhaustive ten-month investigation." [83]

Just how intense the popular feeling is on this matter is hard to evaluate. Nor is it clear what the Japanese mean when they demand that Okinawa and the other Ryukyu Islands be returned to their own control, for it is difficult to reconcile the demand for a Japanese-Ryukyuan civilian administration of the islands with the exigencies of U. S. military planning, especially in the case of Okinawa, where air installations take up such a sizeable part of the land area. If the ultimate withdrawal of American bases is implicit in the demand for Okinawa's early return, then that demand would touch upon American strategy in the Pacific Area and might thus engender serious frictions between the two nations. At the present time, Okinawa is of central importance to the West's global defense structure. Ralph Braibanti has shown how complex is the problem of modifying Okinawa's political and legal status:

If the geography of Okinawa were like that of Japan proper, joint control of this important base might be feasible. In reality, however, the entire southern third of Okinawa is a vast network of American military installations intertwined with Okinawan economy and vitally affecting every aspect of Okinawa's life. To cut through this maze of relationships and isolate those elements which are essentially military and those which are civilian would be exceedingly difficult . . . [and] the difficulties of language, differing cultural values, and clashing political and economic objectives would tend to make for a disarticulation which might spell the end of orderly, responsible government.[84]

Quite obviously, so long as the strategic significance of the Ryukyus grows with each successive crisis in Asia, the United States will not acquiesce in any alteration of their status that would diminish their availability to the Far East Command in Tokyo. The feeling generated against American retention of the islands may, up until this time, deserve to be regarded as nothing more serious than a harmless by-product of the domestic political process of blowing off steam against an indulgent United States, without full awareness of the future implications of such tactics. In the past, the Government of Japan appeared to be resigned to its inability to change the situation drastically.[85] Within recent months, however, there had been some indication that the Japanese are beginning to discern at least a possibility of using shrewd diplomatic bargaining methods to regain some of their former island possessions from both the United States and the Soviet Union. This leads to a consideration of the third, and in many respects the most intriguing of island questions.

This third set of island questions in which the Japanese are vitally interested grew out of the Yalta Conference. At Yalta, the strategic Kurile Islands chain, the Southern half of Sakhalin Island, and the Habomai and Shikotan Islands (an extension of Hokkaido, northernmost of the four main components of the Japanese Archipelago) were given to the Soviet Union. While the Soviet claim to Southern Sakhalin was based on the fact that Japan had seized it from the Czars after their victory in 1905, the Japanese title to the Kuriles is incontestable. The Soviets had demanded this chain, which provides a screen for their maritime provinces, as their price for promising the United States to enter the war in the Pacific "two or three months" after the termination of European hostilities. Japan pressed for the return of these islands during the peace treaty negotiations which it carried on with the Soviet Union in London in June 1955.[86] But at that time, Japan, not wishing to be regarded as a puppet of the United States, was acting strictly on her own, and had to bank almost exclusively on the contingency that the Soviet Union would be willing to make concessions to her in order to restore diplomatic and commercial relations and, if possible, to neutralize Japan. During the negotiations, Tokyo gave assurances that if the Soviet Union were to return the islands, Japan would guarantee that no U. S. bases would be constructed on them.[87] Japan was able to give such an assurance because the defense of Hokkaido, the northernmost home island, had already been handed back to Japan by the United States Far East Command. While the Soviet Union was unwilling to evacuate the Kuriles and South Sakhalin, it apparently held out some hope for the eventual return of Habomai and Shikotan. It is becoming clear that Soviet policy is aimed at purchasing the neutrality of the Japanese by proffering a territorial token which has small strategic value from the Russian viewpoint, but to which the Japanese may attach considerable symbolic importance. During the Cold War, neither the Soviet Union nor the United States made any serious effort to raise the island question, because each must have realized that any accusations hurled at the other would surely boomerang, since both countries occupied some of Japan's former possessions. But the Soviet Union is cautiously starting to use the islands for bargaining purposes, showing its ability to capitalize now on the concessions which seemed so modest when the Allies made them at Yalta to draw the U.S.S.R. into the Pacific War. If this tactic should be developed, and Habomai and Shikotan are returned, the Japanese will be likely to exert strong pressure on the United States for the abandonment of islands which are of much greater strategic value, namely, Okinawa and Ogasa-wara. In brief, the Soviet Union appears to be in the process of contriving an issue which could within the next few years confront the United States with a dilemma. The United States may then have to choose between undesirable alternatives: either to continue to hold the islands at the risk of alienating Japanese opinion, or to be outmaneuvered in that area by Soviet policy which seeks gradually to roll back the forward line of U. S. strategic bases on which the Western policy of defense through air-nuclear deterrence rests. The question of the islands thus remains in abeyance, and, although it has not yet generated strong emotional responses by the Japanese government and people, it nevertheless is fraught with serious implications for the future of Japanese-American relations. It is almost inevitable that, as time goes on, Japanese politicians of all parties, in their search for meaningful and stirring issues, will fasten upon these unredeemed possessions of Japan. As a matter of fact, the Yalta Agreement has already been erected into a sort of domestic shibboleth by Foreign Minister Mamoru Shigemitsu, who assured the people that the Government would not consider itself bound by the Allies' pact of February 1945.[88]

In the Washington talks of September 1955, Foreign Minister Shigemitsu attempted to convince Mr. Dulles that, in view of the Japanese assurance that an army of 180,000 will soon be created, the United States could with safety withdraw from its Japanese bases. At present, the United States sees the need for a Japanese army at least twice that size. Even if such an army of some 350,000 ground troops were mobilized by 1962, the American strategists doubtless would question the Japanese assumption that ground forces could by themselves ever furnish an adequate substitute for the loss of any vital air bases. Within the next few years, therefore, this potential source of tension, if it should be maximized by the Kremlin, may give rise in the Far East to a situation strikingly analogous to that which now obtains in the case of West Germany, where the desire for the redemption of alienated national territory has become the most burning issue in the country's politics.

CONCLUSIONS

The difficulties which have arisen between Japan and the United States since the Peace Treaty went into effect hardly deserve at the present time to be called *tensions,* at least not within the meaning assigned to that term in this study, namely, *the pursuit by two nations of incompatible foreign policy objectives.* Whatever strain has appeared in Japanese-American relations during recent years can be traced largely to issues which the American people should not find very mystifying. These issues are the traditional economic and political ones, familiar to statesmen and diplomats, rather than the more elusive ideological conflicts which color U. S. relations with the newer nations of Asia. Up until now, differences of opinion between Tokyo and Washington have focused upon questions of sovereignty, territory, and trade rather than upon questions of neutralism in the Cold War, pacifism in the H-age, and anticolonialism.

Japan's main goal during the last four years, like Germany's, has been to regain her former economic, political and cultural pre-eminence in a large segment of the world. The United States has no reason as yet to regard the pursuit of this objective by Japan as incompatible with its own vital interests, but the United States must recognize that the Japanese, again like the Germans, can regain their former power positions only through negotiations with the communist bloc. It is this emerging fact which is fraught with the possibility of serious Japanese-American tensions during the years to come. Thanks to the generous occupation policy and peace treaty terms granted by the United States, as well as American economic and military aid, Japan has been strengthened up to the point where the Soviet Union now finds it important to start bargaining with Tokyo.

The purpose of Soviet diplomacy is to reverse the drift of Japan into a permanent commitment to the American security system in the Pacific. Because of the major part played by the United States in the winning of the war against Japan, and because of the deployment of American forces in the Japanese isles and in Korea, the Soviet Union would have been at a distinct disadvantage had it attempted to reach a final peace settlement with Japan at any time between 1945 and 1953. During those years, Japan benefited from the political and economic concessions made by the United States. But the negotiations with the United States have reached the point of relatively diminishing returns, for any significant new concessions by Washington, in the absence of a firm Japanese link-up with SEATO, would jeopardize America's strategic posture in this corner of the globe. From now on the major concessions that Japan will seek to wrest from the United States will probably be 1) the return of her pre-war island possessions on which U. S. air power is based; 2) a reduction in the cost of the national defense establishment as the crisis in Asia abates; and 3) approval of trade with Communist China. Japanese diplomats are likely to encounter stiffening resistance from Washington when they request modification of American policy along these lines.

The Soviet Union has not yielded Japan anything since 1945, and can be expected to hold out the prospect of some tempting rewards in its bid for the neutralization of its former enemy. The Soviet Union is still holding large numbers of Japanese war prisoners. It has a firm grip on some highly-prized island territories, especially the Kuriles and South Sakhalin. As time goes on, Moscow may come forth with some tempting suggestions for the alleviation of Japan's economic problems, especially its dearth of markets. But the U.S.S.R., not wishing to appear over-anxious, is moving with caution. It has been careful not to appear too eager for a settlement with Japan. Obviously, the Kremlin thinks that time is on its side, and that the longer it makes Japan wait, the higher the price it will be able to extract. Here again, the parallel with West Germany's situation is striking. Russia holds something that the other country cherishes more ardently with each passing year. In contrast to Soviet foreign policy tactics with respect to countries like France and Italy, where heavy reliance is placed upon the domestic political power of mass Communist parties, the Kremlin, in dealing with West Germany and Japan, stakes the success of its neutralizing policy upon such bargaining assets as prisoners, territory and trade.

The prospects of the Kremlin are bound to improve as the cultural frictions engendered by the occupation trigger and exacerbate the post-occupation resentment of continued dependence upon the United States. American trade discrimination, demands for increased Japanese arms and defense programs, requests for the confiscation of farmland for the construction of air bases, training practices such as the use of Mount Fuji as an artillery range, the implacement of "Honest John" atomic rockets on Japanese soil, constitute so many sources of irritation and antagonism.

There are several other issues that are likely to favor increasingly the U.S.S.R.'s design, namely the neutralization of Japan. If the United States should deem it necessary to conduct another series of thermonuclear tests in the Pacific, the Japanese press, the leftist political parties, and various pacifist and neutralist organizations can be counted upon to resuscitate the ghosts of Hiroshima and Nagasaki. The Government, which has been sympathetic to the American experiments in the past, will be under manifold pressures to take a firmer stand lest it run the risk of losing face. The Japanese Government may well find itself forced into apologizing for the military operations of the United States, especially if the era of the Soviet policy of smiles should be prolonged. If the Japanese Government, for reasons of domestic politics, deems it expedient to be critical of U. S. policy, it will probably attempt to confine its criticism to non-strategic areas. Instead of demanding the withdrawal of American air bases, for example, it will voice complaints against U. S. administration of the Ryukyus. Instead of protesting the continued presence of American troops in Japan, it will argue about Japan's share in the joint defense costs, and ignore studiously the insinuation of the opposition parties that the United States is interfering in domestic budget matters.

During the next few years, the United States can expect to hear more frequently the expression of Japanese misgivings over the Security pact, which was concluded when Japan was not on an equal footing with the United States. The United States will be confronted by a mounting sentiment in favor of the revision of the Constitution, to which the Government has referred recently as an "occupation-imposed" instrument. Perhaps the heaviest attacks will be launched on the international trade front for Japan seems inclined to believe that she is being deprived of the most promising markets and sources of raw materials. In this regard, the United States appears to be abetting unwittingly Soviet policies toward Japan. First, the United States is alienating many Japanese through the refusal to lower its tariff. Secondly, the United States embargo on trade with China increases Japanese resentment. Rightly or wrongly, the major part of the blame for the loss of the Chinese market is being assigned to the United States. The United States has urged Japan to look toward Southeast Asia for the development of markets and sources of raw materials. In a way, this represents the most natural solution to Japan's economic problems, for Japan would expand her influence in the same area which she had once carved out for herself as the "co-prosperity sphere." If Japan's trade with Southeast Asia were to increase, Japanese policy and the policies of the Southeast Asia nations, now largely neutralist, would gradually converge. Japanese policy may veer temporarily toward neutralism for the sake of cultivating good relations with Burma, Indonesia, and India. Then, as time goes on, these latter countries may gradually seek a rapprochement with a Greater Japan. Japan apparently perceives the opportunities which lie in that direction, and is seeking to exploit them with imagination and enterprise, as well as with capital resources which cannot be equalled by any other nation in Asia.

It goes without saying that the situation contains a number of elements that favor amicable and cooperative Japanese-American relations during the coming years. This study has not been directly concerned with the bonds of friendship woven between the two countries since 1945, nor with the grateful response of the Japanese to the many magnanimous aspects of the United States policy in the occupation and post-occupation period, nor with the Japanese continuing admiration for American techniques, enterprise, and liberality. No mention has been made of U. S. land reclamation programs in Japan, or of the extensive educational exchange program, or of the persistent support given by the United States to Japan's application for admission to membership in the United Nations. The United States has by no means exhausted its fund of good will which it created between 1945 and 1951. The Soviet Union has a long way to go before it can dissipate the historic antipathy which Japan has felt toward Russia for more than half a century. The Japanese, firmly committed to capitalist enterprise, are likely to maintain an attitude of intransigence toward domestic communism as an organized ideology for a long time to come. They will, however, watch internal developments in China with keen interest, and will prove more susceptible to ideological influence from Peking than from Moscow. But these are long-range speculations. In the short run, the maximum objective which the communist strategists dare to aspire to is the neutralization of Japan. As the tug-of-war continues in the Far East, an imposing number of factors—economic, military, diplomatic and political—will exert pressure upon Japan to move farther away from any sort of alliance with the United States and into a position of neutrality which cannot but weaken the position of the United States and its allies in the Pacific.

The United States and the Philippines

INTRODUCTION

How a Western-Asian colonial relationship can be liqui-
dated without leaving deep scars in the psyche of the former colony and without provoking the new nation to
espouse a foreign policy based on rejection of the former
governing country and all its works, this, perhaps, is the
moral contained in the story of post-war Philippine-American relations.

The Philippine colonial status had already been modified before World War II by the Philippine Independence (Tydings-McDuffie) Act of 1934. The Philippine
Commonwealth which it established fought against Japan
as a free nation and a full member of the great alliance.
After the war, Congress formalized the *de facto* independence. A joint resolution on June 29, 1944 pledged complete
independence and authorized the President to proclaim it
prior to July 4, 1946.

Only a short time elapsed between this date and the
beginning of the Cold War. In this struggle the Philippine
Republic participated as a wholehearted and fully committed member of the Free World. As one of the three
Asian members of the SEATO organization, the Philippines mounted one of the most important outposts of
Western strategy in the Far East.

One primary reason has prompted the inclusion of the

Philippine Republic in this study: The young island republic markedly differs in outlook from that of its South East Asian neighbors, for the Philippines have been directly subjected to United States internal administration.

Because of the unique aspects of the United States-Philippines connection, specific issues unlike those which engendered tensions between the United States and other Asian countries troubled relations between the Philippines and the United States. In the political realm, these include the Japanese Peace Treaty, the question of American bases, and American "Domination," in the economic realm, the U. S. tariff, the Bell Act, the Laurel-Langley Agreement, the problem of American Aid, and the MSA land reports.

THE JAPANESE PEACE TREATY

The terms of the Japanese Peace Treaty were a continuous source of irritation in U. S.-Philippine relations both before and after the signing of the Treaty in September, 1951. The Philippines posed two major objections to the Treaty: it did not provide the Philippines with adequate security against a resurgent Japan; and it did not satisfy the Philippines claim to "just and fair" reparations of eight billion dollars.[1]

When the negotiations for the Treaty were in progress, an editorial in the *Manila Chronicle* cited the "unanimous sentiment of the Filipinos against the treaty as conceived by John Foster Dulles," for "to the Filipinos the issue is one of survival, and it is for this (and not any political) reason that they are united in their objection to the Dulles draft." [2]

Philippine leaders felt that the Japanese had been restored too quickly to a position of superiority in Asia. Carlos P. Romulo, a leading advocate of a pro-American

and Western oriented foreign policy and a powerful political leader, thought it "straining human credulity that
Japan, within a brief period of six years, has been completely and permanently transformed . . . into a prac-
tising and thorough-going democracy." [3] Senator Camilio
Osias thought that reports of "wonderful strides made by
Japan along the path of peace and democracy must be
taken with a grain of salt." He cautioned that "Japan, resurgent and rearmed, may become another Germany in
the history of the world." [4]

Embittered by the disregard of Philippine demands for
reparations, Philippine leaders voiced concern that their
country was being discriminated against in favor of the
"Great Powers." Romulo interpreted the treaty as being
"punitive in respect to the claims of the great powers,"
while signifying "forgiveness in respect of the claims of
the smaller countries." [5] Senator Osias asked the American
people to realize "that the shells and bombs intended for
America and the American people did not fall upon the
continental United States but upon the sacred soil of the
Philippines." Thus the people of the United States "must
be convinced that we are right, and righteous in our insistence upon just, fair, and adequate reparations." He reminded the United States pointedly that the Philippines
suffered devastation not because of a war "of our own
making, but because of our involvement in that maelstrom
of war as a result of America's declaration of war." [6]

Much of the Filipino rancor toward the Japanese Peace
Treaty was focused on its architect, John Foster Dulles.
In the summer of 1951, Mr. Dulles was burned in effigy in
Manila.[7] In December, 1952, Senator Rodriguez stated
that the *Nacionalista* Party had not sent delegates to San
Francisco while the Liberal Party—which was then in
power—had joined hands with Dulles in "sabotaging our
true reparations stand." [8]

PHILIPPINE DEFENSE

United States policy regarding Philippine defense was hotly debated by the Philippine Senate when it considered the ratification of the Mutual Defense Pact in 1952. Although the pact was approved unanimously by the Senate, some Senators felt that certain provisions of the agreement discriminated against the Philippines, as compared to similar provisions of defense pacts between the United States and other countries.[9]

First, the provisions that either party could terminate the pact on short notice came under fire. Senator Claro Recto, a *Nacionalista* "Old Guard" leader suspicious of American intentions, expressed fears that the United States could denounce the mutual defense agreement and "leave us defenseless" at any time. Senator Recto pointed out that the United States granted the Philippines less favorable terms than those accorded other allies. The ANZUS Pact and the Japanese defense treaty provided for termination only by mutual agreement.[10]

Second, the United States commitment was deemed unsatisfactory because it did not furnish a categorical guarantee of action, similar to that prescribed in the NATO agreement. The United States-Philippines defense agreement provides that each party "recognizes that an armed attack . . . on either of the parties would be dangerous to its own peace and safety." "In plain language," Senator Recto stated, "the United States promises us nothing." He continued:

> [the United States] may decide to send a mere note of protest against the aggression. It may decide to take up the case in the next meeting of the Security Council and, if we are still alive at the time, . . . we may be the recipients of a powerless resolution of condolence.[11]

The Manila Treaty which established the SEATO alliance in September, 1954 has not been exempt from criticism in the same vein as that expressed toward the earlier United States-Philippines Mutual Defense Treaty. Carlos P. Romulo, personal representative of President Ramon Magsaysay in the United States and one of America's best friends among Asian statesmen, remarked:

> There should be a new orientation in American military strategy in Asia. The Manila Treaty, without commitment of troops, is toothless. Some Asians point to NATO and say, "Why can't a similar plan, on a smaller scale, be prepared for Asia?" They know that the American forces in Asia are not sufficient to cope with the new responsibilities demanded by increasing Communist threats of aggression. The military aid being given to countries that have shown their determination and ability to fight Communism should be stepped up. There is quite a gap between promised aid and deliveries and this should not be allowed to continue.
>
> Asian allies should be taken into the confidence of their Western partners. The exclusion of Asians from military talks between the United States, England, France, Australia, and New Zealand should not be repeated. Since the Manila Treaty considers infiltration and subversion as overt aggression, it is up to the United States, because of its resources and technical skill, to take the lead in conducting researches on how to counter infiltration and subversion by military as well as by other means.[12]

The ghosts of 1941 rise up in Philippine apprehensions about United States defense policies. Senator Laurel concluded that, since the United States did not defend the Philippines adequately in the last war, it would not defend the Philippines adequately in the next war. He declared: "We must not have another Bataan. We cannot face our problems with wishful thinking. We must stop regarding ourselves as the darling of a big colonial power." [13]

New criticism of American defense policy appeared after the Eisenhower administration modified the Truman orders to the Seventh Fleet to enforce pacification of Formosan waters. Senator Recto regarded the new mission of the Seventh Fleet as an "ominous threat to Philippine security." [14] It was feared that the Chinese Communists could now not only attack Formosa, but the Philippines as well. Recto interpreted this as a token of the new administration's policy to "let Asians fight Asians." [15]

Although most Filipinos are grateful to the United States for training Filipino troops—there have indeed been complaints that America is not training and supplying as many Filipino soldiers as she should—there has been some feeling in the Recto camp that America is deliberately training Philippine troops in hopes that they will be used in Asian adventures in place of American soldiers.

AMERICAN BASES

Late in 1954, a major political controversy arose when Philippine critics questioned the United States' right to the land on which military bases were established. The United States claim, namely, that the land was the property of the United States government, met with virtually unanimous rejection.

President Magsaysay, often under attack for his alleged subservience to the United States, was accused of failing to push the Philippine claim aggressively. He sought to calm the opposition by the assurance that, "the U. S. military forces we have here are America's earnest to us of automatic retaliation to aggression." [16] Nonetheless, his conduct of the negotiations with the United States was strongly criticized, as was Magsaysay's willingness to negotiate at all on this issue. The Philippine Government maintained, somewhat lamely, that the United States had a right to present its side of the matter, and that it would be an unfriendly act toward the United States to leave the question unsettled.[17]

Nacionalista Senators took occasion during the discussions of the question in the Philippine Senate to suggest that the negotiations "be used as a lever to gain more trade concessions from the United States." [18] The issue was resolved, presumably permanently, when the United States conceded the Philippine claim to the land, and agreed to lease the land on which the bases were built from the Philippine Government.[19]

AMERICAN "DOMINATION"

The Philippine Government, which is supported in this respect by both major political parties and by the overwhelming majority of the voters, is a "committed" country. Philippine foreign policy is irrevocably tied up with that of the West; the Philippine Republic is a member of SEATO; anti-communism is a keystone of Philippine policy; and the Philippines are not aligned with the Colombo powers or with neutralist Asian groups within or outside of the United Nations.

Since the Philippines do not subscribe to the "neutralist" foreign policy of the so-called "uncommitted" nations of Asia, nor appear even remotely likely to reverse this view, neutralism is a trivial issue in the Philippines, and not a cause of tension in the Philippine relations with the United States.

Exhortations by opponents of the Magsaysay administration that Philippine foreign policy should be more independent of that of the United States sometimes appear to resemble Asian neutralist attitudes. But the unpopularity of neutralism is indicated by the fact that President Magsaysay accused his opponents of "neutralism" to counter their charges that he is a "United States puppet." [20]

The question of relations with the United States became

a major political issue in the electoral campaign of 1953. It is true that as early as 1951, when the Philippine Senate took up consideration of the Mutual Defense Treaty, a "great debate" took place on Philippine-American relations. At that time, as we have seen, *Nacionalista* Senator Claro M. Recto led the attack on the Liberal Party administration of President Quirino, accusing him of truckling to America.[21]

But in the election of 1953 the Liberals used intimations of American influence on the *Nacionalista* Party as the most important plank in their campaign platform, with the possible exception of the "prosperity" issue. Carlos P. Romulo, a leading advocate of cooperation with America, had resigned his candidacy to support Magsaysay. An anti-American faction of the *Nacionalistas,* led by Senator Osias, had defected to the Liberals in protest against the nomination of the ex-Liberal Magsaysay. Magsaysay himself made no secret of his admiration for America and for American institutions, nor of his sympathy for American foreign policy. Senator Jose P. Laurel and others of the *Nacionalista* leadership were also identified with pro-Americanism.

The incumbent President, Elpidio Quirino, had often appealed to the pride which the Filipinos took in their newly gained independence, and claimed to have stood up to American demands and resisted American pressure. Quirino's 1953 campaign platform consisted of the planks of "prosperity" and "sovereignty." His campaign flaunted the bogey of American encroachments upon the "sovereignty" of the Republic. The Liberals made much of an appeal by Senator Laurel to Americans residing in the Philippines to "do something about the preservation of democracy" by using their influence to help ensure clean elections. Such an "invitation to foreign intervention," the Liberals claimed, proved that the *Nacionalistas* were "traitors and Communists," bent on "delivering the country to foreigners." Magsaysay, Quirino charged, was the "candidate of the American people," [22] and his connection with the U. S. Military Mission in the Philippines demonstrated that he was "the United States Army's candidate." [23]

This anti-American Liberal campaign was unsuccessful. Magsaysay's charges of corruption in the Liberal government and the appeal of his forceful and colorful personality resulted in a resounding victory for the *Nacionalistas*. Although it cannot be stated that the election was in any way a victory for pro-Americanism, it does seem clear that the election proved that anti-Americanism is not a significantly effective appeal to the Filipino voter.

U. S. TARIFFS

The contention that the United States has replaced its political dominion over the Philippines with "economic imperialism" is a common charge. "One of the most frequently reiterated criticisms which one hears directed toward the United States by politically conscious Filipinos," stated an American observer in 1952, "is that American economic imperialism is even more vicious than the frank political imperialism of other powers." [24] Even Laurel and his wing of the *Nacionalistas* appeared "to take the position that, although America granted the Philippines political independence, she still holds them in economic shackles." [25]

Much of the charges of Philippine economic subordination to the United States are made in connection with the Philippine Trade Act of 1946 (Bell Act). The Bell Act itself (see below), is far from the exclusive source of Philippine economic grievances against the United States, however, even if it does serve somewhat as a symbol for them.

One writer predicted in 1946 that "the continuation of

free trade after Philippine independence will place the Philippines in the anomalous position wherein her political independence will be nullified by her economic dependence upon the United States. To the average Filipino, free trade has been a noose around his neck." [26]

Charges that the machinations of Wall Street are endangering Philippine independence have been voiced in the Senate. Although the great majority of the American people are friends of the Philippine people, these critics contend, "even the United States Government is sometimes helpless in the hands of Wall Street. This Wall Street, in many ways, and in more ways than we can imagine, has been shaping the economic and import and export ties of the United States. Because of these tariff ties that have been prevailing all along during our tutelage under the United States of America, have we Filipinos been the victims also of Wall Street?" [27] By contrast, "The New Deal economists," unlike the "financiers and monopolists in America . . . backed by Mr. Dulles and Mr. Stassen . . . do not believe in economic invasion of weaker and less fortunate countries, but instead believe in helping them develop their own economy." [28]

Such accusations of American economic imperialism generally were, it seems, deliberately exaggerated for rhetorical effect. Even the severest critics of America or of American business practices will admit that the Philippines "need the aid of the United States. She has money and all that." But the point is that "we don't need her money so badly that we are willing to exchange our dignity for it. We (should be) friendly to the Americans as long as they behave, but . . . ready to drive them out the minute they behave like gringos." [29]

THE BELL ACT

The Philippine Trade Act was enacted by the United States Congress in 1946. It established the legal structure for the special economic relationship between the newly independent country and the former governing power. The Bell Act, as the Philippine Trade Act is usually called, has been a continuous source of economic frictions—perhaps, directly and indirectly, the main source of all tensions—in post-war Philippine-American relations. When the measure was under consideration in Washington in 1946, the onerous provisions of the Bill (the equal rights provision, the tying of the peso to the dollar, imposition of quotas on Philippine goods) became the object of violent attack. Philippine spokesmen assailed the entire measure for being selfish, discriminatory, and imperialistic. The outcry raised from the press and from political platforms was almost hysterical.[30] The issue of the Bell Bill was raised in the first Philippine Presidential campaign, and, by the end of the campaign, the hue and cry raised against America in a portion of the Philippine press threatened to drown out all pro-American voices.[31]

Revision of the act has been constantly demanded. The Bell Mission of 1950, which investigated the operation of the Act in the Philippines, resulted in the Bell Report on The Findings of The Mission.[32] The report was generally welcomed as a step toward revision, but was attacked for its implicit criticism of the Philippines.

Since "many provisions were incorporated into the act that did not exhibit much regard for Philippine national dignity," [33] the prospect of revision was universally hailed. The following excerpt from an editorial in the *Manila Daily Mirror* expresses the more moderate view of the Philippine grievance:

> From the beginning the Bell Act has been opposed as one-sided, unfair, un-American. It was accepted as a

necessary evil, to assure the release of much-needed war damage payments, and on the theory that it would lead to the coming of American capital to offset its disadvantages. Thus if the discriminations are removed a major barrier to real understanding between the two allies will have been removed. At present, despite harmonious relations on the official level, something less than satisfaction is felt regarding our particular position under the Bell trade agreement.[34]

The promise of revision, held out by the Bell Report, was welcomed in most quarters.[35] The Quirino (Liberal) Administration, however, took umbrage at the Report's exposures of official graft and corruption. President Quirino's office issued a virulent statement prior to the release of the Report. This statement (subsequently disavowed by Quirino) attacked the arrogance allegedly displayed by the members of the Bell Mission, and professed to discover implications of an American slur on the moral integrity of the Philippines.[36]

Other criticisms of the United States and of the Bell Report were more reserved. Some persons in the Government took exception to the sections of the Report calling for supervised American aid, since such supervision would infringe on Philippine sovereignty.[37] Several Congressmen, while approving most of the recommendations, objected to the "colonial" aspects of the Bell proposals.[38] Other critics noted "a lack of historical and political perspective," since the conditions of which the Report complained were largely "shaped and conditioned by the demands and responsibilities of a colonial system." [39]

President Quirino said, in January 1953, that the fundamental thing to remember in the question of trade relations with the United States was the Bell Mission's recommendations of future revisions of the trade agreement.[40] The official movement to revise the agreement, which was quite active through 1952 and 1953, had as its purpose "not only to correct the onerous provisions of the trade agreement" but to promote the trade interests of the two countries.[41]

The criticism made of the Bell Act during the move for revision centered upon the adverse effects which the provisions for free trade were thought to have had upon the Philippine economy. The major points in the economic attack upon the Bell Act have been: [42]

1. The free flow of U. S. goods has stunted the growth of consumer industries. Thus, "if the Bell Act is not revised, U. S. goods will continue to pour into the country undiminished in quantity. Cheap U. S. goods will displace any similar items that can be manufactured locally or imported from any other country in the world." [43]

2. The development of a balanced economy is hindered since "only the erection of a sound tariff system can offer substantial hope for the development of the Philippine economy." [44]

3. The system of quota limitations on exports without any corresponding limitation on imports is the source of recurring balance of payment difficulties.

4. A business recession in the United States, the principal Philippine market, would have tremendous adverse effects on the Philippine economy.

5. Trading with other countries is discouraged.

6. The Philippines are prevented from tapping a major source of revenue; namely, duties on imports from the United States.

THE LAUREL-LANGLEY AGREEMENT

Revision of the trade agreement has been one subject on which the *Nacionalista* and Liberal parties have been in accord.[45] The *Nacionalistas* claim to have been the originators and leaders of the movement toward revision,[46] and the Magsaysay Administration has claimed complete credit for the recent successes in revising the agreements.

After preliminary discussions between officials of the United States and the Philippines, negotiations leading to revision of the Bell Act and the United States-Philippines trade agreement were decided upon late in 1954. Magsaysay appointed his political mentor and close friend, Senator Laurel, head of a delegation to the United States.[47] The Philippine mission attempted to secure from America "reciprocal selective free trade" (free trade with certain major commodities still subject to protection); the unpegging of the peso from the American dollar; equalization of immigration quotas—a psychologically significant point; the privileges of equal rights in investment and employment enjoyed by American nationals in the Philippines to be extended to Filipinos in the United States; and the elimination of the United States quotas on sugar, tobacco, and hemp.[48]

After lengthy negotiations in Washington, the Philippine delegation secured an agreement containing extensive concessions to the Philippine viewpoint.[49] This "Laurel-Langley Agreement" (James M. Langley, President Eisenhower's representative, was head of the United States negotiating team) was a victory for Magsaysay and the Philippine position. It was formally signed on May 12, 1955.[50]

However, the Agreement was severely attacked on the floor of the Philippine Senate by both members of the Liberal opposition and by members of Magsaysay's own *Nacionalista* Party. Some *Nacionalista* and Liberal Congressmen proposed a unilateral abrogation of the trade agreement instead of ratification of the Laurel-Langley pact. This, they maintained, would give the Philippines "complete independence for the first time." Though admittedly such a course would cause severe economic hardships, "to be free we must pay the price of freedom."

Abrogation of the trade agreement would "strengthen Philippine character and independence even if it means temporary financial sacrifices." [51] Nothing came of this radical proposal, nor of other parliamentary moves sparked by the Liberals in an attempt to get greater concessions than the United States had offered. [52]

An interesting by-product of the debate was the criticism of the motives of the United States. The Liberals charged that the United States intended to continue to support colonialism through the Laurel-Langley Agreement, that the encouragement of American investment was another device leading to the same end, and that the whole agreement represented the fruits of Magsaysay's subservience to the United States. [53]

The *Nacionalista* majority countered the attacks with the telling argument that it would be "unthinkable to suspect the United States of trying to ruin Philippine industries when it could very well have done that when the Philippines was still a dependency." [54]

THE MSA LAND AND VILLAGE REPORTS

Two extensive surveys were made of land reform and rural conditions in 1952. These, the Hardie Report and the Rivera-McMillan Report, were each the result of co-operation between American and Philippine experts. The published reports of these missions produced a violent controversy, which has become one of the major sources of friction between the United States and the Philippines.

The Hardie Report was prepared under the direction of Robert S. Hardie of the Mutual Security Administration (MSA). (The MSA was succeeded by the Foreign Operations Administration—FOA, the functions of which were transferred in 1955 to the International Cooperation Administration, an adjunct of the State Department.)

The Hardie Report[55] was concerned with land tenure conditions in the Philippines. It recommended extensive land reforms, and intimated that the United States would have to intervene unless extensive improvements were made by Philippine authorities. Land tenure conditions were cited as one of the chief factors in fostering the growth of communism.

The Rivera-McMillan Report[56]—Dr. McMillan of the MSA and Dr. Rivera of the Philippine Council for United States Aid (PHILCUSA)—dealt with Philippine rural life. It charged the Philippine Government with neglecting the needs of the *barrios* (villages). Conditions in the *barrios* were "feudalistic," and nearly half of the village residents were "worse off today than ten years ago."[57]

Philippine criticisms of the Hardie and McMillan-Rivera Reports fell into four major categories: attacks on the substance of the Reports themselves; charges that the Reports advocated U. S. interference in Philippine affairs; allegations that the Reports were communist-inspired and maliciously anti-Filipino; and summary rejections of the Reports as irrelevant and gratuitous since Americans themselves were far from perfect, and so should criticise less and give more unencumbered aid to implement Philippine projects.

The Reports were said to have exaggerated the effects of the land tenure problems with which they dealt.[58] Thus the documents were depicted as "a gross misrepresentation of actual conditions,"[59] since they presented only one side of the situation and left out entirely the work and accomplishments of the government in relieving rural conditions.[60] The critics of the Reports argued that the conditions pointed out in the Reports were of long standing, and although "the utopia that the MSA and PHILCUSA experts have in mind has certainly not been reached," considerable progress has been made toward that goal.[61] Eugenio Perez, then Speaker of the

House of Representatives, asked, "do our well-meaning friends expect us to change these deep rooted systems and customs in seven short years when the Americans themselves failed to cause a dent in the situation during the 47 years in which they ruled the country?" [62] Perez also objected to the fact that "some of the so-called experts sent to the Philippines have sometimes been officious in their enthusiasm and overbearing in their criticism." [63]

The Reports also drew charges that the U. S. was interfering in Philippine internal affairs. Quirino warned that, "the apparent agitation on the part of some Americans for immediate consideration and implementation of the report recommendations can have the effect of American interference with the purely domestic affairs of the Philippines." The Reports represent "subtle threats" of American intervention and "shall not be permitted to exert coercive influence on our thinking and actions." [64]

Some Liberal politicians also declared the Reports to be communist-inspired and maliciously anti-Philippine. Speaker Perez called them communistic, and asked if "their men are bent on putting down instead of setting up our democratic institutions?" [65] A Liberal representative asserted that local MSA officials were "allowing themselves to become tools of certain anti-Filipino elements" instead of "sticking to their jobs" and helping the Filipinos. [66]

Some political leaders also deplored that the United States was giving too much advice in the form of "paper plans and criticisms," and not enough funds. Complaints were also made that too many conditions were attached to American aid. [67] Perez complained that "what we need here are funds to help us to prosecute to success all the proposed remedies that we have already blue-printed. The trouble is America wants to exact its pound of flesh for every half pound it gives to the Filipinos." [68]

Finally, some politicians felt that the United States was mistaken in criticizing the Philippines since Philippine tenancy laws are better than those in most countries in the world, including the United States, and "local social problems cannot be worse than the Negro problem in the U. S." [69]

An interesting criticism of American activities in Philippine rural affairs is that of Jose A. Lansang, an official of the Rural Movement in the Philippines. Accepting the substance of the Reports as true, but claiming that conditions were at least partly attributable to United States neglect during the colonial period, Dr. Lansang stated:

> The truth is that, with the rumble of Communist drums growing audible in the distance, the Filipinos' American mentors have suddenly become frantic and are trying to telescope into the space of two or three years, which they perceive to be critical ones, all that should have been done earlier, in the most favorable decades of the Philippine-American experiment. [70]

Although the criticism of the Reports struck a heavy blow at Philippine-American amity, it did not necessarily reflect the majority opinion of Filipinos. The attack on the United States was largely a partisan affair on the part of the Liberal Party, stung to the quick by the implied censure of the Quirino Administration. The *Nacionalista* Party, then the opposition, considered the Reports factual and helpful. [71] Many Liberals, moreover, attempted to dissociate their attacks on the Reports from attacks on the United States as such. [72]

After the Magsaysay Administration came to power in January, 1954, a new land tenure bill was introduced by *Nacionalista* leadership which was based in part on the recommendations in the MSA Reports.

Criticism was severe in Congress, however, and the Administration bill was soundly defeated by a bi-partisan

Congressional vote.[73] Senator Recto declared the bill to be the "ignoble brainchild" of the United States Embassy and officials of the United States Foreign Operations Administration. He claimed it was designed to create a permanent agricultural economy in the Philippines, dependent on United States industry. "No more conclusive evidence," he declared, "is needed to prove the determined purpose of the foreign advisors of this administration" to advance the aims of the United States.[74]

The land tenure and village conditions reports were released shortly before the 1953 Philippine election campaign. Since Liberal candidate Quirino made a leading campaign issue of Magsaysay's pro-Americanism, the campaign greatly exacerbated Philippine-American tensions. Liberal assertions and *Nacionalista* denials that Magsaysay was a tool of America should be taken into account in judging the significance of the criticisms of the Reports.

AMERICAN AID

Another economic tension arises from the fact that the Filipinos feel that they have not been treated fairly in the distribution of United States aid.[75] "As a leader, America is expected to think in terms of global interest . . . With the same solicitude, therefore, that she regards the situation in Europe she should consider the plight of other nations like the Philippines which is democracy's outpost in the Orient." [76]

While still President, Quirino demanded that the Philippines "must have an equitable share of the world strength to fight a world cause of which the United States is the leader. We are playing a major role in this fight. We need more cooperation, more encouragement, assistance, material and moral, from the United States and from the United Nations." [77] Quirino deemed it only "just, fair, and proper" that the United States should give more aid to the Philippines after having bestowed one billion dollars on Italy, 600 million on ex-enemy South Korea, and two billion on the aggressor Japan. The Philippines are more deserving of aid than the proven enemies of World War II, since she was not only an ally but was involved in the war because of her loyalty to the United States.[78]

American motives in extending aid are often said to be inspired by a desire to continue Philippine subjugation by the United States,[79] and Philippine pride often requires that American aid be extended only in accordance with procedural and substantive limitations designed to protect Philippine freedom of action.[80] The Filipinos, it must be concluded, deeply resent their lack of economic self-sufficiency, and will exert every effort to free themselves from a debilitating dependency on the economy and policies of another nation.[81]

In addition to the dissatisfaction with the scope of American aid, occasional resentment at the very dependence of such aid provokes outbursts as petulant as the following lament of Senator Peralta:

> Oh, my goodness, I sometimes feel convinced that we are a country of beggars asking alms from the United States. As a self-respecting Filipino, I really resent the idea that we shall be called a nation of beggars, beggars forever.[82]

RACIAL ISSUES

Although tensions caused by racial differences are at most only a minor issue in Philippine-United States relations, Filipinos are naturally quick to feel resentment whenever they think American policy is affected by considerations of color.

Such an instance occurred in August, 1952 at a meeting of the nations which had ratified the ANZUS Pact earlier that year. The ANZUS Conference, attended by delegates of the United States, Australia and New Zealand, inspired charges by Filipinos that the participants were practicing racial discrimination.[83] "Because the Philippines were not invited, members of the Opposition thought that the three, or two of the three, were drawing the color line, (and that) Filipinos were being ignored because they were brown."[84]

One Philippine educator asked, "What difference does the color of a skin make? What can two million New Zealanders contribute that twenty million Filipinos cannot?"[85]

The attack on the Conference on the part of the leaders of the *Nacionalista* Party was more violent. Senator Laurel called the meeting "a modern version of prewar colonialism."[86] President Quirino accused the *Nacionalista* critics of "using Communist tactics when they appealed to racial sentiments." He also said they exhibited "colonial inferiority complexes" and a "truculent nationalism."[87] In reply, Senator Claro Recto attacked Quirino for having "brazenly taken the side of 'white Australia' and New Zealand against the *Nacionalistas* who stand for equal rights for the Filipinos and other Asian people in shaping the policies for common defense of the Pacific area." He added:

> We shall be the first to fight if war breaks out, as in 1941. . . . Quirino is ready to send our soldiers into another Bataan to save Australia and New Zealand.

> We *Nacionalistas* are determined that Bataan shall never happen again. . . . No true Filipino will ever forget that in 1942 the Philippine Army was sacrificed in a delaying action to save the skin of the Australians, while vitally needed American convoys were detoured to Singapore and Sydney.[88]

From these statements it is evident that the major antagonism is directed toward Australia,[89] but some antagonism is reflected upon the United States for agreeing to Australia's demands for exclusion of the non-whites.

The Mutual Defense Treaty between the United States and the Philippines, negotiated in 1951 and promulgated in August, 1952, serves in a sense to assuage such hurt feelings as exist among Filipinos because of their exclusion from the ANZUS Pact and its meetings, although, as we have seen above, there has been considerable criticism of the Mutual Defense Treaty as being less favorable to the Philippines than the ANZUS Pact is to its Pacific members.

CONCLUSIONS

In the preceding sections, dealing with Indonesia and the Union of India, the concept, *tensions,* embraces largely those clashes between the outlook, objectives and policies of two countries, which appear to be fundamental and enduring. In short, the term has been used to describe those external strains for which no immediate and effective remedial action could conceivably be applied. In this sense, it can be said that Philippine-American relations are as yet free of that untractable stuff of which tensions are made. With the possible exception of the economic realm, where Philippine reactions to United States policies have displayed the usual inferiority complex of a poor, raw-materials producing country, there exists no essential conflict between the fundamental aspirations of the two nations. Such differences as have emerged center on means, rather than on fundamental objectives. They can be diagnosed as momentary frictions arising from specific issues, but not as deeply rooted tensions.

This is perhaps illustrated best by Philippine conduct in the Cold War. From the onset of the global struggle, the Philippine Republic has been one of the few categorically "committed" nations in Asia. Although they may differ with the United States on such specific political

and strategic issues as the distribution of American military aid and implementative features of the SEATO alliance, Philippine leaders have never lost sight of the
common objective of containing Soviet and Red Chinese
expansion. They differ sharply with the extent to which
American strategy wishes to restore Japan to her prewar strength in Asia—an attitude which is vaguely analogous to the Western European fear of German rearmament. But, whereas many European leaders cloak their
anti-German bias in nebulous, neutralist arguments, the
Philippine attitude has shown a great deal more restraint
and realism.

As we have seen, anticolonialism is probably the
primer movens of Asian hostility toward the West in general and the United States in particular, and forms the
ideological and emotional launching site for neutralist
agitation. It would be presumptuous to assert that the
memories of colonial subjugation have been fully erased
from the consciousness of a nation which has enjoyed
independence for little more than a decade. The Philippines, however, have abstained conspicuously from joining those other Asians who denounce the United States
as a colonial power, bent on perpetuating colonialism
throughout Asia and Africa. Since the Philippines had
direct experience of American "colonialism," this attitude
is encouraging; it is to be hoped that the influence of the
Philippine Republic in Asian councils will, at the very
least, not diminish. As we have seen, Filipino attacks on
America as a "colonial" country are triggered by the belief
that the United States is retarding Philippine economic
development in the interests of American business. Never
absent in such attacks is a distinction between political
and economic groups in America considered sympathetic
and those considered unsympathetic to Philippine interests. Such an approach, treating American "colonialism" as a specific political issue rather than as a national

characteristic of America, or as a basic tenet of American foreign policy, is a far cry from the version of American "colonialism" found in speeches and writings from other areas of Asia.

With its principal prop thus removed, neutralism has been an insignificant factor in Philippine politics. Such quasi-neutralist arguments as can be found represent at best the self-centered viewpoint that a less categorical participation in the power-struggle between East and West would reap greater benefits for Philippine stability. This concept, not entirely dissimilar from the rationale of the Monroe Doctrine or American isolationism, is stated rather hesitantly and vaguely even by its chief spokesmen, such as Senator Claro Recto.

In sum, there appear to be few unbridgeable rifts in Philippine-American relations. Such frictions as have developed are primarily in the nature of family quarrels between nations which have been associated intimately with one another for the greater part of this century. Unequivocal anti-American sentiment is confined to a negligible sector of the Philippine political spectrum, and appears to be activated less by conviction than by political tactics. The fact that anti-American slogans were singularly ineffective in the electoral battle appears to warrant the conclusion that the average Filipino does not respond to the cliché of the American giant who casts a sinister shadow over Philippine independence. He has not a few complaints about the objectives and methods of American policy; he is enough of a realist—and, perhaps, enough of an idealist as well—to take for granted the compatibility of Philippine and American interests in the development of the Philippine economy, in the strengthening of the Free World's defenses in Asia, and in the preservation of democracy.

PART III

*The neutralism of
non-cooperation*

The United States and Egypt

INTRODUCTION

The brief history of United States-Egyptian relations, which date only from the exchange of ambassadors in 1946, has been marked by a number of serious differences of approach to the Middle Eastern situation. These differences have arisen for the most part not out of direct conflicts of interest between the two countries, but rather out of a complex pattern of international relationships involving Washington, London, Tel Aviv, Cairo, Moscow, and the capitals of other Arab states. Egypt and the United States have not, at least up to the early part of 1956, found themselves in a state of ideological tension quite so profound as that which has characterized Indo-American relations since late 1950. True enough, whenever the United States has backed Great Britain in the Middle East, Washington has been tarred with the same anti-imperialist brush as London. Moreover, by creating and sustaining Israel, the United States has been drawn into the whirlpool of the Arabs' ideological struggle against Zionism. Generally, however, Washington and Cairo have been able to understand each other at the practical level, even though they have disagreed on specific issues. Egypt has spoken clearly and frankly about the things she has wanted: military aid and diplomatic support against Israel, the evacuation of all British forces from the Sudan and the Suez Canal, financial assistance to complete the

Aswan Dam project, and so on. It would seem proper, therefore, to distinguish the neutralism of Egypt from that of India. In the former, the tactical component seems more important and the ideological component less important than in the latter.

Egypt's Islamic heritage does not furnish an adequate philosophical foundation for neutralism. It has little in common with Gandhian and socialist pacifism, but much in common with the Judaic and Christian conviction that a universal scheme of ethical values exists and deserves to be defended by force if necessary. The devout Muslim cannot be serenely indifferent to the moral content of the social order, national or international. The ruling classes of Egypt may, in fact, have relied too heavily during the past decade upon the Islamic religion as an impenetrable breastplate against the communist doctrine. Egypt, like all other modern states, has been torn by schism between orthodoxy and secularism. Ideological convictions lose some of their authenticity, finally to be subordinated to political tactics.[1]

At the end of the second World War, relations between the United States and Egypt were cordial. Throughout the Middle East, Americans were thought to be sympathetic to the cause of Arab freedom and welfare. American support was counted upon in the postwar effort to oust the foreigner, especially the Englishman. Egypt also hoped to benefit from the generous policy of giving which the United States had adopted even before the cessation of hostilities. Shortly after Egypt and the United States exchanged diplomatic representatives in October 1946, Washington turned the airfield which had been equipped by the Army during the war over to the Government in Cairo. The Army and the United States Weather Bureau stayed on at the newly named Farouk Field to train Egyptian personnel in communications, navigation aids and meteorology.[2] In the Spring of 1947, the Egyptian Army

Chief of Staff visited the United States to tour military installations. By September of that year, Prime Minister Nukrashi Pasha was asking Undersecretary of State Robert Lovett for United States aid in modernizing his nation's air force and army.[3] This was the first in a long, although vain series of efforts on Egypt's part to procure American military aid.

The Egyptians realized that the wartime discoveries of the world's greatest oil deposits in Iran, 'Iraq and around the Persian Gulf had raised the Middle Eastern stakes of the United States. Egypt voiced her needs as soon as she had established diplomatic relations with the United States. Egypt at that time found herself enmeshed in several complicated problems. She wanted to secure her full national independence, which meant that Great Britain must be persuaded to evacuate the Sudan and the Suez Canal. Egypt could then assert, so her leaders thought, her sovereignty over the Sudan, which had been under the Anglo-Egyptian Condominium since 1936, and thus secure control over the Nile almost to its headwaters. Furthermore, Egypt's strategic and economic importance would be enhanced if she, instead of Britain, were in command of Suez. But she needed arms, if for no other reason than to convince the Labor Government in London that resort to violence was not entirely out of the question as a means of settling accounts.

Throughout the long period of negotiations over the Sudan, the Canal, and the sterling balances which Egypt had accumulated in London during the war, Egyptian attitudes toward the United States were ambiguous, largely because Washington's policy, too, was ambiguous. The United States' position can best be described as a determination to support Britain in a showdown, coupled with a somewhat stronger determination to avoid alienating Egypt at all costs. The U. S. State Department entertained hopes that Egypt, the most populous and potentially the strongest country in the Middle East, might someday be made the cornerstone of a regional defense structure. Egypt welcomed the mediating role of the United States Ambassador, Jefferson Caffery, insofar as he reinforced the natural inclinations of the British Government to postpone a crisis that would make a show of force necessary. Meanwhile, Egypt, throughout 1948, 1949 and 1950, continued to ask Washington for arms. As the Anglo-Egyptian dispute dragged on, Washington became increasingly anxious to secure the defense of the Middle East against possible Soviet aggression. Cairo, however, did not want to be drawn into any military alliance with the Western powers. Such an alliance, it was feared, would operate to prolong the British presence which Egypt was trying to terminate, and hence would be prejudicial to her own national aspirations in the Middle East.

In June 1950, when Egypt refused to participate in the Korean War, her policy was generally attributed to her dissatisfaction with the stand taken on Israel by the United States and the United Nations, and to domestic political and economic problems, rather than to any sort of ideological neutralism. While the United States was helping to arm the nations that were enlisted on the side of the UN in Korea, Egyptian politicians spoke frequently about trying to get arms from the Soviet Union and about entering into a non-aggression pact with the USSR. Their periodic statements dramatized their reluctance to link Egypt with the West in a military alliance. Egyptian attitudes toward the United States after the start of the Korean War continued to undergo rapid fluctuations. American prestige went up whenever Washington was reported putting pressure on London or Tel Aviv to concede a point, but dipped every time attention was called to U. S. support of Zionism or British imperialism. It was not at all uncommon for an Egyptian mob to demonstrate outside the American Consulate in protest against the failure to press harder for British evacuation while, in the same

week, Egyptian newspapers hailed the Point Four talks
which were going on between the representatives of the
two governments. In keeping with the general pattern of
U. S.-Egyptian relations during the first half of the postwar decade, peripheral issues occasionally caused Egyptian
tempers to flare for a while, such as the State Department's warning to American tourists in 1949 about the
perils of traveling in certain parts of war-torn Egypt, and
Life magazine's uncomplimentary treatment of King
Farouk in 1950, for which it was "banned forever." [4] But
these were hardly serious irritants. The focal point of
Egypt's hostility toward the United States from 1948 on-
ward was Israel. The attitudes generated by this issue must
be examined closely before the American efforts of the
last five years to bring about a settlement in that area
conducive to the formation of a Middle East defense system
can be fully understood.

THE ARAB-ISRAELI DISPUTE

It is true enough that the Arab world has neither forgotten nor forgiven Lord Balfour for having promised in 1917
that one day a Jewish "national home" would be created
in Palestine. But immediately after the second World
War, the United States replaced Great Britain as the object of Arab suspicion and ill-will so far as the Palestine
Question was concerned. Problems of empire after 1939
had compelled the London Government to get back into
the good graces of Arab leaders by retreating from its
position as the supporter of the Zionist cause and by re-
stricting Jewish immigration to Palestine. The British in
the course of two wars had undertaken contradictory
commitments to Arabs and Jews and the only way in which
they could extricate themselves from the dilemma was to
turn it over to the United Nations in 1947. From then on,
the United States took the initiative in behalf of Zionist

aspirations which, the Arabs fear, include unlimited Jewish immigration and expansion. Israel proclaimed itself a state in May 1948. President Truman granted it immediate recognition. At first, the Egyptians and all the Arab peoples were indiscriminately angry at the 33 nations in the UN Assembly who had voted for the majority report favoring Israel. In the early part of the year 4,000 students from Fuad I University had demonstrated wildly in Cairo, shouting "Down with Zionist America" and "Down with Communist Russia." [5] As time went on, however, it became clearer to the Egyptians that the new state on their northeastern border, partially blocking them from the Levantine countries, had come into being largely under American auspices. Egyptians were aggrieved by the fact that the United States did not stop with the establishment of Israel, but continued to furnish financial and military aid during her conflict with the Arab states. Such a policy, declared Kamil Abdul Rahim, former Egyptian Ambassador to the United States, "is not helping the relations with the Near East, nor is it strengthening the forces which are fighting communism there." [6]

*The Cairo press, which is the most highly developed press to be found in the Middle East, is the principal mouthpiece of Arab resentment against the Jewish state and its sponsors. All of the original supporters of Israel, with the notable exception of the Soviet Union, come under constant newspaper criticism and are accused of violating their earlier pledges. *Proche-Orient,* a nationalist publication, noted in 1952 that the Powers which had solemnly proclaimed the internationalization of the Holy City had not "so much as raised a finger" to prevent Israel from transferring her capital to Jerusalem.[7] So far as the press is concerned, the possibility that the Arab states might ever concede Israel's right to sovereign existence before settling such problems as the Arab refugees, the definition of the border, water supplies, and so forth is inconceivable.

The magazine *al-Tahrir* was speaking for the great mass
of the Arab peoples, when it urged Arabs to remember
that "as long as this menace exists in their region, they can
never enjoy stability, freedom or independence." [8]

The United States is inevitably singled out as the architect of Israeli power. Egyptians frequently recall that both
the Democratic and Republican platforms in the 1948
presidential campaign contained strongly pro-Israel planks.
Egyptian editors contend that American Middle Eastern
policies are shaped by anti-Arab forces within the United
States, especially the Jews, whose hold on the country
they deem so powerful that "even the American Negro
will be free before American politics are purged from the
domination of . . . [Jewish] newspapers and capital." [9]
Al-Balagh, a Wafdist newspaper, explained President Truman's prompt recognition of Israel in the spring of 1948
by noting that "he was badly in need of votes in the State
of New York." [10] It is significant that the Egyptians tend
to interpret the American position primarily in terms of
practical domestic politics, for it points, regardless of the
accuracy of their analysis, to the Egyptians' preoccupation with the tactical rather than the ideological elements
in their relations with the United States.

The United States has striven to avoid the appearance
of being an unequivocal supporter of Israel and of being
insensitive to the fears and needs of the Arab countries. In
this regard, the State Department has frequently found it
necessary to represent the Arabs' position in Congressional
committees, hoping that legislative process would take a
via media and not displease one side more than the other.
In 1951, for example, when Israel requested from the
United States an economic grant-in-aid in the amount of
$150,000,000, measures to that effect were immediately
introduced in both houses of Congress under bipartisan
sponsorship. The arguments for the most part stressed the
democratic institutions, military strength, and strategic

location of the new state. The State Department pleaded for a regional appropriation of $125,000,000 for purely economic aid to the Middle East (exclusive of Turkey and Greece) and a regional appropriation of $415,000,000 for Middle East military aid, of which the President might assign as much as ten per cent to the Arab states and Israel, according to his estimate of the security situation.[11] Israel was primarily interested in economic aid rather than military, because she was not much more willing than the Arab states to enter into a binding alliance with the Western nations. The final appropriations were just about equal for each side; and $50,000,000 was assigned for Jewish refugees in Israel to balance the sum authorized for the Arab refugees outside Israel.

The Wafdist organ, *al-Misri*, anticipating a Republican victory in the elections of 1952, expressed the hope that the new President would reverse the Middle East policies of his predecessor and thus salvage "the great prestige of America" in the Arab world.[12] The Eisenhower Administration, as a matter of fact, has been somewhat more inclined to back up the State Department's position than its predecessor. During 1953, the pressure on Tel Aviv from Washington increased. The United States induced Israel to release $2,800,000 to Arab refugees from frozen bank accounts, and withheld grant-in-aid funds in an attempt to force Israel to comply with the UN request that she halt work on the Jordan River hydroelectric project, which she had undertaken in violation of the armistice.[13] In November 1953, the United States joined the other members of the Security Council in censuring Israel's raid against Jordan in which the whole border village of Kibya was virtually wiped out.[14] These actions on the part of the United States, however, did not impress the Egyptians, who did not think that a vacillating policy of censures and exhortations addressed to Israel was compensation for the original sin of having created the problem in the first place. The refugee problem especially has defied solution. The United States furnished generous financial assistance to the 870,000 Arabs who were expelled from Palestine. This gesture was not appreciated since it strongly implied United States support of the Israeli contention that these homeless people should be absorbed permanently by the Arab states, whereas the Arabs demanded that they be repatriated. The very existence of the Arab refugees, some of them living in squalid tent communities in the sight of their former homes across the border and others wandering poverty-stricken throughout the adjacent states, is a sore on the body politic and social of the Middle East which poisons Arab-American relations. This problem, according to Henry A. Byroade, then Assistant Secretary of State, "has added to the real and deep-seated bitterness which replaced, to some extent at least, an earlier faith in the United States." [15]

Another aspect of continuing U. S.-Egyptian frictions during the Israeli dispute has been the conflict over Egypt's attempts at economic warfare against Israel. After the Egyptian army had been driven into a narrow beachhead of the Sinai Peninsula in the late spring of 1949, the Egyptian Government decided to resort to blockading and boycotting the enemy. On May 27, Cairo notified American shipping companies that henceforth all vessels carrying Palestine-bound cargoes would be subject to inspection at Port Said, Suez and Alexandria.[16] This announcement naturally evoked a strong protest from the United States. General William E. Riley, the American Chief of Staff of the UN Truce Supervision Organization in Palestine, asserted that the Egyptian action was aggressive and "contrary to the spirit of the general armistice agreement." [17] In the face of mounting international protests, the Egyptians adhered to their blockade-boycott policy. Israel has to trade abroad or perish. The Arab countries were aware of the effectiveness of methods of economic warfare which they had learned from the history of their former British master, and they congratulated themselves on winning the armistice after losing the war. Neither the United States nor Britain could persuade them to release their grip.

When the UN Economic Survey Mission to the Middle East was established under the head of an American, Gordon Clapp, the Egyptian press charged that the State Department in Washington was simply trying another of its tricks to integrate Israel's economy with that of the whole Arab region.[18] The Egyptians remained adamant and unmoved by the argument that the economics of a processing Israel and an agricultural Arab region were naturally complementary and would lead to a rise in the standard of living throughout the entire Middle East. Finally, in August 1951, the United States joined Great Britain and France in sponsoring a Security Council resolution which called upon Egypt to lift the blockade. The United States delegate, Mr. Warren Austin, told the Council:

> The United States is firmly of the opinion that the restrictions which Egypt is exercising over ships passing through the Suez Canal are inconsistent with the spirit of the Armistice Agreement. . . . The result of this hostile act is the engendering of hostility in return, which places in jeopardy the peace and stability of that area.[19]

Egypt nonetheless resisted the Western pressure, convinced that ending the economic isolation of the Jews would once again tip the scales against the Arabs. The armed forces of the Arab countries were not much stronger than they had been when they took a decisive beating from the Israelis. Their only superiority consisted in economic weapons which they had no intention of relinquishing. The Egyptian representative in the Security Council, Mahmoud Fawzi Bey, declared that his government's action was perfectly justified under the Convention of

1888 which had defined Egypt's rights in regard to the
Canal. He then reminded the Americans of the "beam" in
their own eye, suggesting that U. S. control of the Panama
Canal might be similarly challenged.[20] Nonetheless, the
Security Council, with the Soviet Union, China and India
abstaining, adopted the resolution which bade Egypt to
end the blockade. The Egyptian Cabinet, backed up by
the nation's press and by several Arab League spokesmen, assumed a defiant attitude, denying the UN's jurisdiction in the matter, and declaring that they would comply when Israel had acted on other UN peace directives.
During 1952, the blockade was relaxed somewhat, but
Egyptian interceptions of foreign vessels bound for Jewish
ports increased. In 1953 and 1954, when the issue came up
again for debate in the Security Council, the Western
Powers moved another resolution similar to that of 1951.
This time, to the delight of the whole Arab world, the
Soviet Union sustained Egypt's position by vetoing the
resolution.[21] Egypt was gratified that a Great Power had
finally been induced to reverse an earlier stand on the Israeli issue. Cairo and the neighboring Arab capitals detected a shift in the wind. One Arab leader remarked,
"A veto by Vishinsky is worth all the aid of America and
Britain." [22]

Within the last three years, the United States has become acutely conscious of the dilemma which confronts it
in Palestine. Up until 1955, American statesmen have seen
their plans for a Middle Eastern Defense Organization
frustrated by Arab-Israeli tensions, which have invariably
taken precedence in the minds of most of the Arab political leaders over the threat of Soviet communism. By ac-
quiescing originally in the expulsion of the Arab population from Palestine, and by allowing the refugee problem
to drag on until repatriation was practically out of the
question (since it could be effected only at the cost of another terrible dislocation of hundreds of thousands of

people), the West has been burdened with the weight of Arab wrath. The West is being blamed for having created a large class of embittered, discontented émigrés, many of them well-educated and politically articulate, who may constitute that firm social foundation which the anti-Western ideology hitherto lacked in the Middle East. Israel has always tried to persuade the United States that the economic rehabilitation of the Arab refugees would help to smooth the way for a political settlement, while the Arabs have contended that repatriation had to be an integral part of any settlement, and that therefore the refugees could not be absorbed into the economic life of the nations bordering on Israel. Egypt, incidentally, has about 200,000 refugees, most of them concentrated along the Gaza strip.[23] Thus the refugees have been a serious stumbling block to the conclusion of peace.

Israel has argued that the political settlement must precede the construction of a regional security system, while the Arabs for their part find it impossible to talk about a peaceful settlement, because that would involve their accepting Israel as a permanent entity, something which they have shown no readiness to do. Any regional system of which Israel would be a part is, of course, inconceivable to the leaders of the Arab states. In March 1955, Deputy Assistant Secretary of State John D. Jernegan conceded that Israel could not be included in any Middle Eastern defense organization until after the tensions had been resolved.[24] There is a significant difference between the Israeli contention that a settlement must precede the *creation* of the defense organization and the growing U. S. conviction that a settlement must precede the *inclusion* of Israel in the regional defense pattern. Some of the implications of the changing American attitude will be examined in the next section, which deals with the efforts of the West to draw Egypt into a defense arrangement. It is sufficient at this point to note that a significant shift has occurred during the last few years in the United States policy with respect to the Arab-Israeli conflict. In 1951, Washington was distinctly pro-Israel. By 1953, Israel's indignation at the failure of the United States to press the Arabs into peace negotiations was just about as vehement as Arab criticism of the failure of the United States to demand Israeli compliance with the UN Assembly partition resolutions. This "balanced animosity" indicated that the State Department was succeeding in its efforts to bring the United States around to a more neutral posture.

Since 1953, the Israeli policy of retaliation for violations of the truce has served to alienate some of the American support which the Jewish state had formerly enjoyed. U. S. political strategy in the Middle East demands the minimization of the Arab-Israeli tensions, for reasons that will become clear in the next section. Retaliatory attacks, like the ones against Kibya in Jordan, against Gaza in Egypt, and against Galilee in Syria, have served merely to maximize the tensions, without bringing a political settlement appreciably closer. In fact, the raid against the Gaza strip in February 1955, which led to Ambassador Lodge's speech in the Security Council rebuking Israel and commending Egypt for its restraint,[25] may have contributed a great deal to Egypt's eagernesss to conclude the arms deal with the USSR some months later.

The degree to which the United States finds itself caught in the middle of the Palestine dispute was accurately reflected in a speech made by Assistant Secretary of State Henry A. Byroade in the spring of 1954 in which he rebuked both sides for deliberately keeping trouble alive along the frontiers. To the Arabs he said:

> . . . you should accept this State of Israel as an accomplished fact. I say further that you are deliberately attempting to maintain a state of affairs delicately suspended between peace and war, while at present desiring neither. This is a most dangerous policy and one which

world opinion will increasingly condemn if you continue to resist any move to obtain at least a less dangerous *modus vivendi* with your neighbor.

He then gave the Jews this advice:

. . . you should come to truly look upon yourselves as a Middle Eastern state and see your own future in that context rather than as a headquarters, or nucleus so to speak, of world-wide groupings of peoples of a particular religious faith who have special rights within and obligations to the Israeli State. You should drop the attitude of a conqueror and the conviction that force and a policy of retaliatory killing is the only policy that your neighbors will understand. You should make your deeds correspond to your frequent utterances of the desire for peace.[26]

Some of the Arab states might be willing to conclude a settlement now on the basis of the UN Assembly partition resolution of 1947 which originally prompted them to go to war against the new state. But as a result of the fighting in 1947-48, Israel pushed well beyond the boundaries defined by the UN, and refused to consider any withdrawal from her frontiers, won in a war that was not of her own making. The daily violations of the truce continued, and the American head of the UN Truce Supervision Organization, General E. L. M. Burns, tried to reduce the number of border incidents by persuading both sides to tighten their controls. Two plans were proposed by the West during the latter half of 1955. Secretary of State Dulles presented his proposal in a speech before the Council on Foreign Relations in August, calling for an international loan to Israel to compensate the refugees, and international guarantees of agreed, permanent Arab-Israeli frontiers.[27]

The Dulles proposal was well received by Great Britain, France, and the Secretary General of the United Nations. It seemed to offer a genuine opportunity for the Western Powers to reduce the tensions considerably, and to eliminate the possibility of a war in the Middle East. Within a week, however, news of the Soviet-Egyptian arms deal had reached the West, and Egypt lost whatever interest she may have had in Secretary Dulles' solution. The semi-official *Al-Jamhouria* waxed caustic about the West's alarm at the news of the plan to exchange Egyptian cotton for Czech heavy arms, and pointed out that the United States had evaded or refused Arab arms requests for years, while Israel had received all that she needed or wanted from Western sources.[28] This was not a new argument devised for the exigencies of the moment. Several months earlier, another newspaper, *al-Ahram*, had laid down a fairly typical charge when it said that "the United States recognizes for Israel the right of attack but will not recognize for the Arab countries the right of defense." [29] Even though the Jews were complaining throughout 1955 that U. S. policy had turned pro-Arab, the Arab press was less than fulsome in its praise of the United States. Therefore it is not surprising that in November, Prime Minister Sir Anthony Eden felt constrained, in the midst of his efforts to engineer the framework of a Middle Eastern defense system in the form of the Baghdad Pact, to modify the Dulles proposal with his own plan. Sir Anthony's proposal linked a guaranteed settlement on refugees, frontiers, and the waters of the River Jordan, to a projected territorial compromise between the boundaries as first defined in the UN resolution and the present ones.[30] Needless to say, Egypt received this plan much more favorably, and preferred British to American mediation of the Palestine dispute.

UNITED STATES DEFENSE AIMS IN THE MIDDLE EAST

The United States has been deeply concerned with the implications of the changed position which the West has held in the Middle East since the end of the war. The French have left Syria and the Lebanon. The British saw their oil concessions in Iran nationalized, withdrew from 'Iraq and Jordan, and concluded agreements to evacuate the Sudan and the Suez Canal. In the wake of this Western withdrawal and in the ensuing power vacuum the governments of the Middle Eastern states have moved rather unsteadily. As British military and economic influence retreated without being replaced by the influence of any other Great Power, the Arab states failed in their own efforts to achieve regional unity despite the presence of Israel in their midst. Generally speaking, the United States and its Western allies have realized the delicacy of the situation. Aware also that hasty action might precipitate an unfavorable reaction and jeopardize their chances by creating greater, rather than less, instability and hostility, the Western nations have been extremely cautious in their attempts to establish a Middle Eastern defense system.

From the West's point of view, several factors, some of them advantageous and some disadvantageous, must be taken into account. First of all, the British have had considerably more experience than the Russians in dealing diplomatically with the Arabs. Therefore, the United States has tended to defer to British initiative in forging an anti-communist alliance in the Middle East. Secondly, England, France and the United States have maintained schools and universities in the area for several decades, and the Arab nationalists, if they can be said to have borrowed any political ideas from Europe, have taken them for the most part from Locke, Rousseau, Jefferson, Bentham and Mill rather than from Marx and Lenin.[31] The Middle Eastern peoples, however, are not deeply involved in the ideological controversies which have absorbed the older nation states since the end of the first World War. They had no moral stake in the second World War, only a tactical one. The Arabs felt no revulsion at the prospect of a Fascist victory, and they maintained a prosperous neutrality until the tide had clearly turned. The war over, the Arab leaders were preoccupied with consolidating their independence and putting up a united front against the Israeli threat. Neither task has proved to be an easy one. Either one, by itself, might have been sufficiently distracting to obscure the magnitude of the challenge posed by the Kremlin's imperialism. In combination, they defeated —right up to 1955, when the Baghdad Pact began to take shape—all Western attempts to interest the Arab nations in joint defense.

Turkey, the least Islamic of the states which once comprised the Ottoman Empire, but the most keenly conscious of Russian ambitions, was easily induced to enter a military agreement with the West as early as March 1947, while all the members of the Arab League remained aloof for several more years, apparently content to outlaw communism at home and to rest confident in the belief that Islam stood as an impregnable bulwark against Marxist materialism.[32] As one author has observed, in view of the poverty of the *fellah*, the corruption and inefficiency of the political institutions, the social indifference of the *pasha* class, and the growing numbers of educated, professional persons whom the national economies cannot absorb, it is fortunate for the West that in Egypt communism has found so few able leaders.[33]

For the greater part of the postwar decade, Western hopes of buttressing the defenseless Middle East against the Soviet Union foundered on the Anglo-Egyptian impasse. Washington made a determined bid in the fall of 1951 to bring about a settlement between London and Cairo by linking it to the formation of an Allied Middle East Command which was to include the United States, Great Britain, France, Turkey and Egypt.[34] But the Egyptian leftists and nationalists protested vehemently against

these Four Power proposals which they branded as a sub-
terfuge to perpetuate Western economic and military
domination. *Proche-Orient* characterized the plan as one
more example of the "desperate assaults of the imperialist
powers who are striving to maintain their ancient positions in this coveted portion of the world." [35] Egypt was
not at all averse to entering an alliance with the United
States which would have gained for her military aid and
guarantees against Israel without involving any broader
commitments on Egypt's part. Azzam Pasha, former Secretary General of the Arab League, pointed out early in
1952 that he had frequently proposed such a bilateral
U. S.-Egyptian Pact. "If they want it," he said, hinting that
the offer still stood, "we are ready. We have no fear of
America at all." [36] Egypt, however, was definitely not interested in any regional agreement which would align
Egypt or other Arab League states with Washington, London and Paris in the Cold War. By the summer of 1952,
legislation was being urged in Cairo making it "treason
against the people of Egypt and the cause of world peace
to negotiate with the imperialist powers for concluding
aggressive alliances." [37]

It is important to note that the Egyptians have always
distinguished sharply between an agreement for supplying Egypt with arms against Israel and one for the organization of the region against communism. While advocat-
ing the first, they persistently shunned the second, and
remained unconvinced that the Middle East faced the
threat of external aggression from Soviet communism.[38]
Cairo moreover was very much afraid that an alliance for
broad political and military purposes with the West would
vitiate the progress which the nation had been making
along the road to independence and territorial consolidation. There was more to this attitude than a mere emotional bias against the West. The Sudanese and Suez
questions were vitally related to Egypt's policy concerning

a regional defense agreement. When the five-nation command was suggested, the negotiations over the future of the Sudan were in full swing. Britain, which has ever since the disintegration of the Ottoman Empire favored the separate existence of several entities in the Middle East rather than the development of fewer and stronger states through mergers, insisted on self-governing rights for the Sudan, whereas Egypt wanted the fusion of the Sudan and herself under the "common crown." If Egypt were to let herself be persuaded to soften her stand on the Sudan issue in return for an alliance, she risked being outmaneuvered by London and its allies. The hopes for a "greater Egypt" might then have to be postponed indefinitely. As one writer remarked, discussing Egypt's unwillingness to permit the use of the Nile Valley as a base for foreign troops, Egypt "did not seek to rid herself of one 'allied occupation' only to become saddled with an occupation by 'four allies.'" [39] Egypt demonstrated her opposition to the Western overtures by abrogating the Anglo-Egyptian Treaty of 1936.

The United States and Britain hoped that Egypt might prove more amenable to proposals for regional defense after a satisfactory agreement was finally reached on the Sudan in February 1953. But another reason for Egypt's reluctance to commit herself still obtained: her desire to win the most favorable terms possible in the negotiations over Suez, which were next on the Anglo-Egyptian diplomatic calendar. Colonel Gamal Abdel Nasser demanded the immediate and unconditional withdrawal of British troops from the Canal Zone. Foreign Minister Sir Anthony Eden wanted a gradual evacuation of British forces, and that only after guarantees were given permitting Great Britain to re-occupy the base in the event of war, and retaining either British or NATO technicians at the Suez installations. The United States, quite naturally, was interested in the strategic aspects of the problem, even though the value of the Canal had diminished since the advent of nuclear weapons. Washington was sympathetic to the English demand for guarantees. At the same time, the United States came very close to entering the Suez talks as a third party. Ambassador Jefferson Caffery, who had been congratulated by General Mohammed Naguib for having smoothed the way for the accord on the Sudan, was reported ready to promise U. S. economic aid to Cairo after the Suez question was resolved in a way that would not prejudice Western strategic interests. But Colonel Nasser, fearing that the formal presence of the American Ambassador in the Canal conferences would tip the scales against Egypt, was opposed to such participation. Ambassador Caffery immediately clarified the atmosphere by announcing that the United States had no wish to enter the talks unless invited by both sides.[40] Two months later, when Secretary of State Dulles visited Cairo, *al-Misri* complained that he was trying to put pressure on Egypt to accept Eden's demands.[41] Secretary Dulles then proceeded to dramatize his country's "tactical neutrality" in the dispute by presenting General Naguib a pistol as a gift from President Eisenhower—a gesture which offended the British almost as much as the Secretary's appearance upon the scene had originally aroused the Egyptians. The Cairo Government responded to the friendly tone of Mr. Dulles' visit by arresting a number of communists who had distributed pamphlets attacking the American Secretary of State.[42] The whole episode served to improve U.S.-Egyptian relations temporarily at Great Britain's expense, but the situation in the Middle East remained substantially unaltered.

Shortly thereafter, Prime Minister Jawaharlal Nehru of India traveled to Cairo in an attempt to induce Egypt to draw closer to the Asian neutralist bloc (India, Indonesia and Burma) and thereby enhance her bargaining power in the Suez discussions. Prime Minister Mohammed Ali of Pakistan also stopped at Cairo in June 1953 to review the

Suez situation with Naguib and Nehru. Pakistan, which had not as yet signed the military agreement with the United States, joined India in morally supporting Egypt against Great Britain. Later that same summer, the Egyptian Cabinet approved a proposal for the conclusion of a trade pact with the Soviet Union in the hope that arms and oil might be had in exchange for cotton.[43] A trade agreement with the USSR and Czechoslovakia was actually signed in August 1953, but it brought no arms to Egypt. Moscow obviously was not yet impressed by the neutralist overtures of the new military oligarchy in Cairo. Western observers, however, noting the increasingly frequent references to arms-for-cotton and the possible recognition of communist China, combined with the establishment of closer ties with Marshal Tito, detected the beginnings of a new activist phase of Egyptian neutrality.

After his tour of the Middle East, Secretary Dulles reassessed the prospects for the development of a firm alliance there in these words:

> A Middle East Defense Organization is a future rather than an immediate possibility. Many of the Arab countries are so engrossed with their quarrels that they pay little heed to the menace of Communism. However, there is more concern where the Soviet Union is near. In general, the northern tier of nations shows awareness of this danger.[44]

This represented a new departure in American policy, for it meant that the effort to build a defense structure with Egypt as its foundation was being abandoned. Egypt, it is true, had an army which was equivalent to the combined armies of 'Iraq, Syria, Jordan and the Lebanon, but the Egyptian force, even though trained by British and German officers, was inadequately equipped and still smarted under the sting of the defeat which the Israeli army had inflicted. Moreover, with each passing year the

Suez Canal was becoming less vital in international politics, even as it was becoming more important to Egypt's prestige. Considerations like these made it possible for the United States to accept Cairo's opposition to regional defense with equanimity. Doubtless the United States would have preferred a Middle East Defense Organization with Egypt in it. American military assistance could have converted its army into a formidable enough force for present purposes. But the United States was not willing to hold its plans for Middle East defense indefinitely in abeyance until Egypt should decide to participate.

Egypt, as a matter of fact, appeared to be getting farther away from the kind of regional unity which the West looked for rather than closer to it. She pressed the Arab states to ratify the Arab League Collective Security Pact which had been drafted in 1950 to integrate military forces in case the Palestine fighting flared up again. This pact, which by 1953 had been ratified by all the League members except Libya, was quite different from the regional organization that many Western statesmen hoped to see grow out of Arab initiative insofar as its *raison d'être* was the threat from Israel, not the threat from the Soviet Union. This distinction is central to an understanding of Middle East developments during the last three years, for it points to the most persistent reason behind Egypt's position: the fear that any Western-oriented defense system would involve the decline of the Arab League as an independent power bloc in international politics and, more serious for the Egyptians to contemplate, would probably jeopardize their erstwhile leadership of the Arab League because it would shift priority away from the challenge of Israel (the League's chief *casus unitatis*) toward the challenge of Soviet communism, against which Egypt, because of her geographical location, could not assume the leadership of the Middle East. These implications were plain to Cairo. As early as October 1951, *al-Misri* noted that the Four Power Proposals posed the question of whether or not the League would continue to function as an instrument of Arab solidarity, and editorially warned the other members that if they permitted their unity to be disrupted by the proposed arrangements they, not Egypt, would be the losers.[45] When Egyptians talk about the disruption of Arab unity, they generally mean the seizure of Arab leadership by one of their potential rivals.

Egypt's leadership of the Arab states has never been unchallenged. The original move for the creation of the Arab League was made during the second World War by Nuri Sa'id, Foreign Minister of 'Iraq, who envisioned the integration of all the countries in the Fertile Crescent, which would have excluded Egypt.[46] Cairo, however, managed to seize the initiative by calling a wider conference in 1944, and has since held the field against all competitors, of which 'Iraq and Pakistan have been the chief ones. Therefore the signing of the U. S.-Pakistan pact in Karachi on May 19, 1954, had implications for Arab solidarity which were not to Egypt's liking. 'Iraq, which had become disillusioned about the prospects of an Arab military victory against Israel, and which had never completely abandoned its own aspirations for a lesser Arab unity centered on the Levant, made her last serious bid for regional leadership at the meeting of the Arab League Council in Cairo in January 1954, when she proposed political unification and the formation of an all-Arab army to be financed largely from her oil revenues. Egypt, as was to be expected, would have no part of a plan which looked like a play for the hegemony of the Hashemite countries.[47] A few months later Egypt pushed through the League Council a resolution under which the members agreed not to "accept any responsibility undermining their sovereignty and independence, or incompatible with their responsibilities as members of the Arab League."[48] That was adopted on the same day on which Pakistan signed a pact with Turkey, a member of NATO and a secularized Islamic state whose indifference to the Israeli problem was an object of Egypt's suspicion and resentment.

The cleavage in the Middle East became more apparent in January 1955 with the announcement by Turkey and 'Iraq of their decision to conclude a regional defense agreement that would be open to all other neighboring states except Israel. This announcement, the first sign that an active member of the Arab League was ready to abandon tactical neutrality in favor of a pro-Western alignment, came as a distinct reverse to Egypt's aspirations. Salah Salem, then Minister of Public Guidance (Propaganda), declared that the pact threatened the Arab League. The Government invited the Premiers of five Collective Security Pact members to Cairo for an emergency conference. Premier Nuri Sa'id was unable to attend because of "illness." At the hastily summoned caucus, Egypt attempted to muster support for a condemnation of all alliances outside the Collective Security Pact, but at the same time she wanted it clearly understood that Western military aid would still be welcome, so long as it left the recipient nations free to dispose of it as they wished. If 'Iraq and Turkey went through with the projected pact, Nasser declared, Egypt might well withdraw from the Arab League and sponsor a new grouping of states pledged to avoid external alliances. Notwithstanding the threat of the League's collapse, the pact was signed, and the ensuing month saw Egypt and 'Iraq engaged in a furious scramble for the allegiance of the smaller states. Meanwhile, the United States watched from the sidelines, preferring to allow two of its allies, Turkey and Britain, to explore the highly fluid situation.[49] Turkey bore the brunt of the Egyptian press attacks for the unfavorable turn which events were taking from Cairo's point of view. *Al-Ahram*, for example, charged that Turkey was trying to persuade the NATO powers to give her a free hand in the

Middle East, and warned the Arab states that they were being converted into a "Turkish sphere of influence." [50] Britain and the United States took advantage of the domestic instability of the French Government and its preoccupation with North African problems throughout most of 1955 to minimize its role in the move to build up Middle East defenses, a judicious arrangement in view of the Arabs' bitter Francophobia. It is interesting to note that all of the countries which finally came together in the Baghdad Pact in August 1955 had formerly been in the British, not the French mandated sphere of influence in the Middle East.

The United States did not regard it as particularly disastrous that two regional groupings should appear in the Middle East, one consisting of Great Britain, Pakistan, Iran, 'Iraq and Turkey, the other of Egypt, Saudi Arabia and Syria, with Jordan, Yemen and the Lebanon holding off the longest before committing themselves. For one thing, an important step had been taken at last toward organizing the defense of a spacious and vital area of the world which might at some future time provide the West with a new chain of major air bases, now strategically more valuable than canals, armies and oil wells. For another thing, the political mitosis of the Arab League took the United States "off the hook" with respect to the Arab-Israeli dispute, at least temporarily. Israel expressed considerable alarm at the appearance of the new coalition, predicting that any arms aid earmarked for the Northern Tier countries would ultimately be turned against her. The Egyptian newspapers leaped to the opposite pole, charging that Washington had plans for drawing the Arab states into an alliance that would sooner or later include Israel. It would be quite inaccurate to interpret the accession of 'Iraq to the Baghdad Pact as 'Iraq's defection from the Arab cause. In June and again in August 1955 'Iraq reiterated her pledge to come to Egypt's aid if Israel should attack. She denied that her other commitments precluded her participation in the defense of the Arab states were Israel to break the truce in Palestine.[51] This is one of the reasons, and by no means the least important one, why the United States was so concerned at the announcement at the end of the summer of 1955 that Egypt was expecting to receive arms from Czechoslovakia in exchange for cotton. The arms deal could serve only to heighten the tension between Egypt and Israel and complicate 'Iraq's position in the Baghdad Pact. Nasser insisted that unless Egypt availed herself of the communist offer, Israel's military superiority over the states touching her borders would be increased decisively in 1956, since American and British firms were supplying weapons to Israel while Egypt was receiving nothing but demands from the West.[52]

The United States now faces in the Middle East a precarious situation which might be compared to a delicately poised see-saw. On the one side, Egypt has reason to fear that the Baghdad Pact, against which the "Voice of the Arabs" transmits its daily invectives from Cairo, may wreck Arab unity on the Israeli issue. On the other side Washington has reason to fear that any flare-up in the Palestine sector, sparked perhaps by the desire of some Israeli leaders to wage a preventive war against Egypt before the flow of communist arms can alter the power distribution, may wreck the Baghdad Pact before it really jells into a military, not just a psychological, *cordon sanitaire.* The United States, at the time of this writing, is still reluctant to enter the Northern Tier Alliance as a formal member since such a move might further estrange Egypt and lead to increased Jewish demands for a mutual defense treaty with Washington.

The prospects for a U. S.-Egyptian rapprochement on the question of Middle East defense are far from bright at the present time. There is no urgency about bringing

Egypt into the Baghdad Pact—even were Nasser willing to take so unlikely a step—in order to reap strategic fruits from MEDO, since Egypt is screened on the map by Turkey and flanked by 'Iraq and Libya, in all of which countries additional air bases can probably be constructed if they are needed. Egypt's importance is political rather than strategic. MEDO's fortunes hinge upon the West's ability to dissuade Egypt from exploiting the Israeli dispute as a means for regaining the unquestioned leadership of the Arab world.

ECONOMIC PROBLEMS

Since the end of the second World War, Egypt has had to grapple with some extremely serious economic problems. In the years ahead, these are bound to absorb the increasing attention of her leaders, if not because of their concern with the welfare of their people then at least for reasons of military power. Within a relatively short time, the Egyptians have learned several lessons about the integration of economic and political policies.

Quite simply, Egypt's primary economic problem consists in the lag of production behind population growth. The population stands today at approximately 22.5 million and is expanding at the rate of some 300,000 per year.[53] This makes Egypt one of the most densely populated countries in the world, if the ratio of population to cultivatable land be taken into account.[54] The surplus rural population is estimated to be from five to six millions, depressing the entire nation's standard of living to an appalling level of undernourishment, bad sanitation, poor housing and disease. At present, about six million acres of land are under cultivation. Another two and a half or three millions could be rendered arable with expanded irrigation. This means that no more than five per cent of the national land area is suitable for agriculture. The problem is further aggravated by the latifundian ownership structure, under which 37 per cent of the good land is held by only one half of one per cent of the owners, while 70 per cent of all landholders have only one acre or less each. These data lead one economist to conclude that Egypt's problems cannot be permanently solved by building dams, expanding irrigation, introducing improved techniques, and attracting foreign investment unless the land tenure system undergoes basic reform.[55] Much of the land is given over to cotton which Egypt has to sell abroad in exchange for manufactured goods. When the cotton market is strong, as it was at the beginning of the Korean War, Egypt enjoys an export boom and artificial prosperity. When the world price of cotton slumps, as it did in 1953, Egypt suffers.[56]

The Government's financial policy calls for opening up new land for growing purposes through the more efficient use of the Nile waters, thereby easing the food shortage and permitting greater crop diversification. Simultaneously, it hopes to encourage industrialization and productivity through increased foreign investment.[57] All of these objectives depend to a great extent upon aid from the West. But that aid has been slow to arrive. In October 1951, the United States Congress appropriated $125,000,-000 for technical assistance in the Middle East (exclusive of Greece and Turkey, for whom larger amounts were earmarked). However, despite the fact that Egypt and the United States had concluded a Point Four Agreement, Cairo found that its implementation encountered political obstacles, largely because of Egypt's truculence. In March 1953, the prospects brightened when Cairo and Washington announced arrangements for a $25,000,000 land reclamation project in the Nile Delta, to which the United States was to contribute 40 per cent of the cost.[58] Windfalls like this, however, were few and far between, and Cairo noticed that even the plans for this project were

delayed. Egypt and her Arab neighbors particularly resented the fact that the United States appeared to be-
grudge whatever it gave the Arabs while it lavished gifts
upon Israel. Between 1946 and 1954, all the Arab states
together had received from the United States a total of
$87,000,000 chiefly in the form of technical assistance and
credits, while Israel had received $350,000,000, 60 per cent
of which was in the form of aid grants.[59]

General Mohammed Naguib, then President and Prime
Minister, wrote to President Eisenhower in July 1953,
strongly hinting that Egypt would be more willing to conclude a settlement over the Suez Canal if she could receive some assurance that economic aid would thereafter
flow from the United States. President Eisenhower delayed answering until a year later. In July 1954, he informed the Egyptian Government that simultaneously
with the conclusion of the Suez agreement the United
States was ready to enter into "firm commitments" regarding economic assistance. Meanwhile, the United States
was reported to be holding up $20,000,000 worth of aid
already earmarked for Egypt, pending final accord on the
Canal pact.[60] Twelve days after President Eisenhower's
letter arrived, the agreement was signed. The way now
seemed to be open for the promised grants. A few months
later, in November 1954, Foreign Minister Mahmoud
Fawzi Bey and Ambassador Caffery signed the economic
assistance instruments under which the United States was
to furnish $40,000,000 during the coming fiscal year. Even
this amount, while undoubtedly welcome, fell considerably below the figure of $100,000,000 per year which the
Egyptians had asked be guaranteed for a ten-year period.[61]
Washington was disappointed that Egypt still seemed cool
to the suggestion of a defense alliance now that the evacuation of British forces was definitely in sight, and Egypt
had to be content with less than she had hoped to receive.
During 1955, the most significant development in

Egypt's economic life was the consummation of the barter agreements with the Soviet Union and its satellites. She signed a trade pact with the USSR and Rumania whereby she would exchange E£3,000,000 worth of cotton for petroleum products; a pact with Hungary under which 93 Diesel switch locomotives would go to Egypt in return for E£2,000,000 worth of cotton; a three year pact with Peiping calling for the export of E£10,000,000 worth of cotton and superphosphate to China for the import of industrial and agricultural products valued at only E£2,-000,000; and finally a three year extended agreement with Czechoslovakia whereby cotton and rice would be shipped to pay for an undisclosed amount of heavy arms. At the end of 1955, the five biggest suppliers of goods to Egypt were still Western Powers (Great Britain, United States, West Germany, France and Italy), while the five leading purchasers of Egypt's products were, in order of importance, France, India, communist China, West Germany and the United States.[62]

The announcement of the arms deal with Czechoslovakia in August 1955 had the effect of hastening the decision of the United States and Great Britain to help finance the Aswan Dam on the Nile, a ten year project expected to cost $1,300,000,000. This dam, which has already been raised twice since it was constructed in 1902, holds a central place in Egypt's future plans. The High Dam will create the largest artificial lake in the world, add two million more acres to the total of irrigated land, generate 750,000 more kilowatts of electrical energy per year, and facilitate general development by permitting the construction of a much needed fertilizer plant and a steel mill to process the iron ore deposits near Aswan.[63] To finance the work, the Egyptian Government had vainly sought a loan from the International Bank for several years. In the Fall of 1955 the Soviet Union, following up its strategic success in offering arms, indicated that it would give

Egypt the necessary financial and technical assistance. In December, Washington and London transmitted their combined offer of assistance to the Egyptian Finance Minister, promising an initial grant of $70,000,000 of which sum the United States would contribute 80 per cent. Egypt was also assured that aid would be forthcoming for later phases of the work, but the United States was careful to explain that one Administration in Washington could not bind future Administrations or Congresses to long-range appropriations commitments. The proposed Anglo-American aid was intended to supplement a $200,000,000 loan which the International Bank for Reconstruction and Development was now ready to make.[64] The day after the Western offer was revealed, Soviet Ambassador Daniel S. Solod said in Cairo that his country still intended to participate in the Aswan project "unless there is something in Egypt's agreement with the West which specifically excludes us." [65] It was taken for granted in London and Washington that the exclusion of the USSR was implicit in the offer, in view of the growing suspicion on the part of the Western allies that Moscow, in its new policy of "competitive co-existence," had launched a serious effort toward the economic penetration of the Middle East. In some respects, the United States and Britain are bound to regard the Soviet Union's economic overtures more formidable than the arms offer. The ultimate effect of the Soviet Union's economic penetration of Egypt would be much more difficult to control than the shipment of arms. Egypt's reliance on Soviet economic aid and trade would secure for Moscow its first solid, friendly outpost in the Eastern Mediterranean.

NEUTRALISM

One of the most difficult tasks confronting American policy-makers in the Middle East is that of placing a correct evaluation on Egypt's neutralism. Is it to be distinguished from India's neutralism, and if so, how? In the introduction to this part of the study, it was argued that Egypt's neutralism is more tactical and less ideological than India's. This does not mean that the ideological factor can be ignored in the case of Egypt, or the tactical factor in the case of India; the problem is one of emphasis. The explanation for Cairo's policy is to be sought primarily in concrete circumstances, needs and aspirations rather than in any overarching philosophy of anti-Westernism or of a sublime refusal to conceive the international situation in terms of the bipolar struggle. Egypt has adhered to a fairly sensible schedule of objectives during the last ten years: to oust the British from the Sudan and Suez in order to promote her own national unification, independence and prestige; to reduce the threat of Zionism to manageable proportions by gaining first the support of Britain against the United States, then the support of the State Department against the Congress at Washington, and finally the support of the United Nations against Israel; to maintain the solidarity of an Arab League led by Egypt and catalyzed by Israel; and to obtain as much military, technical and economic aid at the lowest cost of concessions and commitments. Sometimes, these objectives proved simultaneously incompatible, and delicate priority choices had to be made. By protracting the talks over the Sudan and Suez, by turning her back on Middle East defense, and by refusing to discuss the possibility of a settlement with Israel, Egypt herself raised obstacles to her quest for the economic aid of the United States. But at other times her objectives reinforced each other and thereby improved her bargaining position. Holding out against regional defense, for instance, served several important purposes. It induced the United States to put gentle pressure on Great Britain to grant concessions in the Sudan and Suez talks. It postponed the day of reckoning for the unity of the Arab League. It aroused the benevolent interest of Moscow in the potentialities inherent in the situation which could be exploited by offers of arms and financial support of the Aswan Dam project. Especially since 1953, the strategic, political and economic tendencies of the region have been subtly interwoven with those of the globe. As a result, Egypt has found ready at hand a variety of bargaining alternatives at each new diplomatic juncture.

Egypt rarely criticizes the United States in the abstract. It cannot be denied that anti-American utterances have frequently emanated from Cairo, but almost invariably they can be linked to *ad hoc* objectives, usually relating to Israel, British policy, regional defense, and economic assistance. Perhaps the best way to savour the flavor of Egypt's anti-American sentiments is to juxtapose a number of typical official and journalistic statements:

> What excuse has a great nation which hoisted the flag of freedom and self-determination during the two world wars for persisting in a policy toward Arabs and Jews which has made us lose any appreciation or confidence we had in America? . . . America will learn that it will lose much by satisfying five million Jews in the United States at the expense of antagonizing seventy million Arabs. Twenty-nine nations at Bandung voiced support of the Arab case in Palestine. America should have heard this by now.[66]

> (There) has been talk of "Communist infiltration" in the various Arab and African nationalist movements. It would be unwise for the United States to take that view of nationalist activities, led by sincere patriots whose only desire is to see their nations free from foreign domination. Americans recognize this to be the inalienable right of every man, yet balk at supporting these nationalists for fear of annoying some colonial Power that has refused to move with the times. . . .

> There would not be any Communist infiltration in any part of the Middle East and Africa if the United States

could develop a courageous policy—and the only morally correct one—of supporting those who are anxious to get rid of foreign domination and exploitation.[67]

The free world which Dulles asks us to join is the world which sabotaged the national cause from within and without.[68]

The American mentality is preoccupied with two principal things—fighting communism and exploiting raw materials.[69]

On the whole, it appears as if American interest in the Middle East will not be aroused until Russia arouses it, and then it will be too late.[70]

Deep as may be the current of hostility against the United States, minor rivulets seem to flow in the opposite direction. Tactical considerations have impelled the Egyptians to say many things designed to please the United States. As the Suez talks were getting under way, an official publication scored the British for undermining "the traditional friendship between the United States and the people of the Middle East for imperial and commercial motives." [71] In July 1953, General Mohammed Naguib wrote to President Eisenhower that Egypt was seeking a peaceful settlement of the Suez question so that she might cooperate on a new basis with the West in the spheres of Arab defense and economic development.[72] It is interesting that only a few months earlier, Major Salah Salem, Minister of National Guidance (Propaganda), had declared that in her fight against British imperialism Egypt "will take any devil in the world as an ally." [73] No immediately fruitful results flowed from Naguib's letter. At the beginning of 1954, Egypt indicated that she was ready to strike out on the bold course hinted at by Salim. The Egyptian Ambassador to Moscow, Lieut. General Aziz el Mazri, said: "We have to find ways and means of enlisting Soviet help for our struggle and we have to give the Russians some *quid pro quo.*" [74] Not many weeks later, the Cairo Government notified the United States that it had had enough of American "good offices" in the Suez dispute. Speaking for the President and Premier, Minister Salem told the press:

> I hereby announce that Egypt has taken practical steps to bolster cooperation in all its forms in the other nations of the world, in the East and West equally. We will not discriminate between one state and another except according to its response to our demands and its support of us in various fields, whether economic or political.
>
> Egypt has submitted all its principal projects to many countries in the world, including Russia. There are now continuous contacts in this respect . . . [A] trade delegation has been sent to Russia and to the Eastern European countries. There is a great possibility that Russia may execute some of these projects in Egypt if there should be a final agreement on details. [75]

Here was the classic enunciation of what might aptly be called the doctrine of tactical neutralism. He who wants to be taken for a neutralist, even if he has publicly announced that it is just for tactical reasons, has to talk like one, and may have to retreat a few steps from his philosophical position later on. Hence on April 13, 1954, Deputy Premier Gamal Abdel Nasser called U. S. Point Four Technical Assistance a form of "American colonial penetration" in the Middle East, but on May 2 he withdrew that criticism and replaced it with another and far milder one, declaring that American technical assistance had not produced noteworthy results as yet. [76] Egypt did not want to alienate the United States. On May 31, Egypt agreed to hire British and American technicians to staff the installations at the Suez Canal Base. The only obstacle then to reaching a final accord on Suez was Britain's insistence upon the right to reoccupy the base in the event of war. Daniel S. Solod, Soviet Ambassador to Egypt, visited Nasser on July 14 to register a protest against Cairo's reported readiness to concede the British demand. One day later the letter from President Eisenhower arrived, informing President Naguib that Egypt would get "firm commitments" relating to American aid upon the conclusion of a Suez settlement. After that assurance was received, the Anglo-Egyptian accord, containing a guarantee of Great Britain's re-occupation rights in the event of an attack on any Arab League state or Turkey within a period of seven years, was promptly signed.[77]

The question still remained whether Egypt would allow herself to be drawn into an alliance with the West. Premier Nasser declared in August 1954 that:

> after the Suez settlement there is nothing standing in the way of our good relations with the West. But this hammering . . . for pacts will only keep alive the old suspicions in the minds of the people. . . . It is a matter of group psychology with deep roots and until the Arabs realize that there is no longer any hidden domination or control in pacts, any pressure to obtain them will be dangerously premature.[78]

The following month, the Egyptian Government furnished to the foreign newsmen in Cairo a "background paper" in which it stated that "Egypt today stands in every respect with the West," that she was still opposed to communism, and regarded the USSR as the major threat to the region. This latter statement represented a concession to the West which official sources had hitherto been reluctant to make. Nonetheless, a defense pact was held to be out of the question at that particular time on the grounds that Egyptian public opinion was bound to regard such a treaty as a new form of colonial domination.[79]

During 1955, Egypt acted out the rôle of a full-fledged "neutralist" state, particularly with respect to official visits, receptions and international conferences, all of which have come to play such an important part in the symbolism of "neutralist" diplomacy. The year began with Premier Nasser calling on Marshal Tito in Yugoslavia, and ended with Marshal Tito repaying the visit in Cairo. In between times, at the Bandung Conference, Nasser engaged in friendly talks with Foreign Minister Chou En-lai, mostly about the Arabs' case against Israel, and about the possibility of diplomatic and trade relations between Cairo and Peiping. Upon his return from the Asian-African Conference, Premier Nasser addressed a crowd from the balcony of his office in such words as made it appear that he had been won over completely to the anti-colonialist neutralism of Prime Minister Nehru:

> The states of Asia and Africa met for the first time without the participation of those powers which dominated them, to proclaim to the world at large that it is high time for Asia and Africa to be liberated, and that henceforth these areas cannot remain under the domination of imperialism or its lackeys. . . . I went to Bandung to announce that Egypt has been liberated, and that it speaks for the cause of self-determination and freedom of the nations, the suppression of imperialism, and the independence of all states. Egypt desires that the world go hand in hand, and that its states not be playthings of the big powers in the arena of political competition.[80]

When it became known toward the latter part of the summer that Egypt was to exchange cotton for Czech arms, Nasser's neutral policies, although tactical rather than ideological, were beginning to pay tangible dividends. For a short time, the United States was ready to try to forestall the Soviet-Egyptian arms agreement by an offer of arms aid. This strategy was quickly abandoned, for to make such a counter-proposal was tantamount to submitting to "blackmail," a term used by Prime Minister Eden. Washington and London held back on the arms, but hastened the completion of their plans for financing the Aswan Dam project—after the Soviet Union had expressed interest in advancing the necessary credits. Thus within a three-month period, the USSR offered Egypt the two things which she had been trying hardest to obtain for several years. In both cases, the initial American reaction was to give Egypt what she wanted, and quickly. The United States refrained from matching the Soviet contribution to Premier Nasser's arsenal. However, the American offer of economic aid is being translated into action. For the economic penetration of the Nile Valley by the Soviet Union, with all its future implications for the orientation of the Middle East and interior Africa, would pose a more formidable threat, one that would be much more difficult to counter than the menace of Egypt's not-so-formidable army.

At the time of the completion of this study, early in 1956, it still seems safe to conclude that Egypt's brand of neutralism, because of its manifestly tactical aspects, is indeed unique. Neutrality has served Egypt well, bringing her more diplomatic support than she had been getting in her struggle with Israel, the assurance of arms aid from the communist bloc, American support in the negotiations over the Sudan and Suez, and the prospect of help at Aswan. The possibility cannot be discounted, however, that Egypt, having achieved several of her tactical objectives, and having watched the withdrawal of the "imperialist occupier," may gradually move, elated by her sensational successes, from tactical to ideological neutralism. What started as an improvisation might still grow into a dogma as far-fetched and casuistic as that which inspires the apostles of neutralism East and West.

CONCLUSIONS

Since 1948, the Arab-Israeli conflict has loomed larger than the Anglo-Egyptian conflict as a focal point of tension between Egypt and the United States. The Anglo-Egyptian conflict proved negotiable, and the United

States was able to play a mediating role in it. The Palestine question, the primary ideological issue on Egypt's
political horizon, has not proven negotiable, and all American efforts to bring about a settlement have thus far
failed. This comparison suggests that the fear of Zionism
overrides that of Western imperialism, so far as Egypt
is concerned. Egypt recognized the legitimate interest
of the United States in the Suez agreement, at the conclusion of which Washington and Cairo sounded a cordial note. But Egyptians remain firmly convinced that by
sponsoring and sustaining Israel the United States has
done the Arabs a grave and continuing injustice which
cannot be blotted out by mediation. Despite the discerni-
ble shift since 1953 in the American attitude, which has
become more critical of Israel and more sympathetic toward the Arabs, Egypt is still inclined to be suspicious
of Zionism's power to obtain support in the United States.

At the time of this writing, each side demands that the
United States take a clear and unequivocal stand in its
favor. Washington does not appear the least bit willing
to do anything at present which might upset the precarious balance between Israel and her neighbors, since the
prevention of renewed large-scale hostilities is essential
for the gradual establishment of a Middle East defense
system. As Secretary Dulles stated in his letter of February 6, 1956 to a group of Congressmen concerning the
Arab-Israeli question, "the problems of this area must be
studied in the larger context of the free world's unceasing
struggle against international communism." [81]

If a serious outbreak of large-scale hostilities should
threaten as a result of the Soviet's arms shipments to
Egypt or Israel's attempt to spoil Arab preparations for an
attack, the United States, Britain and France may find
that they have no alternative but to enforce by arms the
border guarantees originally given in the Tripartite Declaration of May 25, 1950. President Eisenhower and Prime

Minister Eden, in their joint statement issued after the Washington Conference of January 1956, called attention to the three-power obligation to take action "both inside and outside the United Nations" in the event of the use, or the threat or preparations to use force, to violate the armistice lines. They added: "We are bound to recognize that there is now increased danger of these contingencies arising. Accordingly, we have made arrangements for joint discussions as to the nature of the action which we should take in such an event." [82] Should such action become necessary, Egypt's attitude toward the United States could be expected to take a turn for the worse because American intervention would be deemed more to Israel's advantage than to her own. Nonetheless, the forcible imposition of the border guarantee is probably preferable to the renewed outbreak of war. Pressure might then have to be brought to bear on Israel to grant some territorial concessions to Egypt, perhaps in the form of a corridor across the Negev to Jordan. Meanwhile, the United States would continue to assist in the solution of the Arab refugee problem. A policy comprising these elements, while it would not be too popular in the Arab world, at least would not jeopardize the progressive "firming up" of the Northern Tier countries as much as a new Palestine war would. If war comes, it will be difficult indeed to prevent 'Iraq from trying to match Egypt's bid for military leadership of the Arabs by diverting to Palestine arms which have gone to her under the Baghdad Pact. The United States would then have no choice but to give massive aid to Israel, alienating again, as in 1948, the Arab world.

There is at least a good possibility that the Baghdad Pact is strong enough to survive a Tripartite guarantee. Much of the Arab resentment, of course, would be directed against Britain, a prospect which cannot give comfort to the United States since Britain holds the key position in the

Middle East alliance. But with the easing of Arab-Israeli tensions, or at least the realization by both parties that they must be held in abeyance temporarily, the Northern Tier countries will have an opportunity to take the measure of the Soviet Union's ambitions in the Middle East and to formulate concrete defense plans. Meanwhile, the breathing spell would enable Egypt and her neighbors to concentrate on internal economic development without having to worry about the domestic economic disturbances and the flight of foreign capital which war would surely cause. If Great Britain and the United States can convince Egypt that she must choose between war and the Aswan Dam, the danger that Cairo will trigger the conflict would be considerably reduced. With the threat of war removed, by Tripartite action if necessary, the period of domestic development in Egypt, supported by Anglo-American aid, may witness the end of Egypt's "non-cooperation" with the West, or the transformation of neutralism into neutrality—the conventional rather than the "dynamic" type.

PART IV
General conclusions

General conclusions

The purpose of this study has been to determine the nature and extent of tensions existing between the United States and certain selected countries of Asia, from Egypt to Japan. Not every friction, of course, which arises between two countries deserves to be called a tension. A genuine international tension exists when two or more nations are striving for incompatible foreign policy objectives over a period of years. Tension relates, in other words, not to a specific misunderstanding which lends itself to diplomatic settlement, but rather to the major orientation of the foreign policies of the states involved. The term should be applied to those areas of important, continuing disagreement which prevent nations from cooperating with one another along a broad front for any considerable length of time. Allies who are united for broad purposes (as in NATO, for example) may experience intermittent frictions over questions of national prestige, economic welfare, or methods of dealing with specific situations as they arise within the framework of their agreement on the over-all problem. Such minor irritations have frequently marked the relations of Washington with London and Paris during the last decade. Though these frictions placed a strain upon the diplomats from time to time, they never broke up the alliance because the NATO countries had a common objective: their own security. On the other hand, a state of tension can be said to exist when nations cannot cooperate with one another on a broad front, precisely because their major foreign policy objectives are mutually exclusive. They might occasionally find themselves working together on an *ad hoc* basis, but when this happens it should not be construed to mean that there is no underlying tension.

Disagreement over the priority of political challenges and tasks confronting the world has become the gravest *single* source of tension between the United States and certain Asian nations, especially India and Indonesia. Prime Minister Jawaharlal Nehru has put the problem this way: "We talk about the crisis of our time and many people view it in different ways. Probably in the U. S. A., the crisis of the time is supposed to be Communism vs. anti-Communism. It may be so to some extent. But the crisis of the time in Asia is colonialism vs. anticolonialism. Let us be quite clear about it." * India, having won its own national independence only eight years ago, now wishes to assign top priority on the international political agenda to the elimination of every trace of "white imperialism" in Asia—and Africa, too. Anticolonialism has become the cornerstone of its foreign policy. This anticolonialism is always couched in the highest moral tones, as if it were an absolute principle that should be applied universally, without any exceptions. But India apparently reserves its political epithets for the policies of the Western nations toward Asia and Africa. She ignores all other forms of imperialism, whether it be that of the Soviet Union in Eastern Europe and Outer Mongolia, or that of the Chinese People's Republic in Tibet, North Korea and Indo-China. Indian policy-makers have succeeded brilliantly in narrowing the meaning of colonialism to the category of white people versus colored. They close their eyes to the categories of white versus white and colored versus colored, and to this extent they have contributed to an in-

* *The Times of India*, August 27, 1954.

tensification of the race problem at the international level. The Indian leaders have also succeeded to no mean extent in simplifying the term "Asian," thereby enhancing their claim to speak with the voice of Asia. Their viewpoints have often been identified as Asian, even though they have often been at variance with the viewpoints of other Asian statesmen.

India is obviously convinced, and she is trying to convince her neighbors, that Western white colonialism or neo-colonialism poses a more serious threat to the colored continents than communism does. She regards every military, economic or political link which the Western nations attempt to forge with the governments of the Afro-Asian countries as an instrument of neo-colonialism. By way of contrast, she does not consistently look upon communism as a foreign policy instrument of the Soviet Union or of Red China. Rather, when communism invades the countries of South and Southeast Asia, it is looked upon primarily as a domestic political opposition which feeds upon social and economic discontents, as well as anticolonial feeling. Indians frequently charge that whenever Asian nations are drawn into alliances like the Southeast Asia Treaty Organization (SEATO), their independence is jeopardized and the propaganda of the communist parties needlessly scores another point. Nehru believes that communism cannot bring about a successful revolution in that part of the world except under the guise of a struggle to liberate a nation from its colonial overlords, and therefore regards SEATO as an unnecessary irritant in the Asian environment. India, however, has not been able to persuade all the countries of the Middle East and the Far East that her analysis of the situation is the correct one. The three Asian nations which have had the most intimate contacts with the United States in this century do not concur in this analysis. The Philippines have had direct experience of American colonial rule. Japan has undergone six years of American occupation. South Korea is the only Asian country which has been an area of extended U. S. military operations. All of these countries, every bit as Asian as India, are allies of the United States. A number of other countries have allied themselves with the United States and Great Britain. Thailand, the Republic of China on Formosa, Pakistan, Turkey, Iran and Iraq have all shown that in their foreign policies they place the defense of the free world against the threat of Sino-Soviet aggression above the passions of anti-Westernism.

India, in contrast to the SEATO and Baghdad Pact countries, refuses to conceive of the needs and aspirations of the United States—its quest for security and its image of a free society—in terms of the bipolar struggle. Her leaders attempt to employ ideology, without backing of armed force, to thrust India into the position of the third power center in a tripolar world. They are well aware of their country's military, economic and political weakness during the period of painful transition from a colonial territory to a national state. Consequently, they rely mainly upon the anticolonialist theme, which they have welded to the related theme of antimilitarism. Both of these themes loom large in the propaganda campaign of the Soviet Union. Since India usually applies these twin shibboleths only against the "white imperialists" of the West, her foreign policy objectives coincide increasingly with the strategic goals of the Sino-Soviet bloc. The Indians are willing to overlook the fact that the Russians, who are also white, maintain vast colonial holdings of their own, conclude military alliances with China and the Warsaw Pact satellites, continue their own H-bomb experiments in central Asia, and refuse to accept President Eisenhower's "open sky" proposal for mutual aerial inspection, designed to show that neither side is preparing to start a war.

India, in striving to assume the leadership of the emer-

gent states, is exploiting the predisposition of the Asian and
African intellectuals, journalists, and politicians to accept
the Leninist explanation of imperialism as the final stage
of capitalism. According to the Leninist theory, the colonial
markets and sources of raw materials are essential to capitalist survival. (Switzerland, of course, one of the world's
leading capitalist states, has never engaged in imperialism;
and the Mongols, Arabs and Spaniards, to mention only a
few of history's outstanding empire-builders, never developed a capitalist system.) India is partial to the Marxist
analysis, and whenever the opportunity presents itself, her
leaders such as Nehru, Menon and Panikkar question the
motives of the West. No matter what the West does, its
motives are never given the benefit of the doubt. The purpose of the economic aid programs to the underdeveloped
countries is taken to be the economic or political subjugation of the countries receiving it, and, simultaneously, the
alleviation of Western capitalism's own problems of production, consumption and investment. In view of her
suspicions of dollar-imperialism, India would prefer to see
technical aid coming from the Soviet Union, provided that
Moscow could give what India wants.

Doubtless India chooses to emphasize the anticolonial
argument because it is the one ideological appeal most
likely to strike a responsive chord throughout the colored
continents. In order to come forth with clean hands as
the champion of the anticolonial cause, India must react
with consummate indignation to the lingering presence of
European colonial rule on her own doorstep—Goa. Quite
consistently with her anticolonial philosophy, India measures the moral rectitude of the foreign policies of other
countries by examining their stand on Goa. Indians frown
and take offense when Secretary Dulles refers to Goa as a
Portuguese province. They smile and take comfort when
Bulganin and Krushchev declare that Goa belongs to
India. Speaking at Agra about the Soviet declarations

of support for India on the controversies over Goa and Kashmir, Nehru said: "Our friends living in other countries did not like these speeches. They have said and written in newspapers that the statements made by Bulganin and Krushchev did not please even Nehru. The Soviet leaders have expressed their opinions after due consideration and great deliberation. It is foolish to think that I or any of us did not like these statements." *

A complex relationship exists between India's anticolonialism and her antimilitarism, insofar as the achievement of her objectives is concerned. Ideological pacifism is a powerful component in Indian thought, rooted in Hindu spirituality and reinforced by the imported Socialist strain. But no nation can subscribe completely to pacifism as a working policy. India maintains troops along the Kashmir and Tibetan frontiers. Moreover, so evil does she deem Western colonialism, that she condoned the use of force by the Viet Minh to drive the French out of Indo-China. Today the leaders of India realize that in their dialogue with the peoples of Africa and Asia, they must emphasize the struggle to throw off the colonial yoke and mentality, rather than merely declaim against the use of physical force. Pacifism, after all, is not very deeply ingrained in the cultures of Islam and tribal Africa, where the anticolonial slogans can be expected to produce their most telling effect. India has just begun to perceive the potentialities latent in this ideological theme. Hence the absence of Afro-Asian unity exhibited at the Bandung Conference was perhaps hastily interpreted by Western correspondents as signifying a severe setback to Nehru's aspirations to speak with the voice of Asia and Africa. Bandung certainly did not mean that India's efforts to rally the colored peoples of the world under the banner of anticolonialism are doomed to failure.

What does all of this mean for the future of Indo-Amer-

* New York *Times,* January 4, 1956.

ican relations? It means, unfortunately, that the fissure which has opened between the two countries is likely to widen into a chasm. As time goes on, India will press with increasing urgency for the withdrawal of European and American influence from the colonial areas. She will protest the storage of arms in the Afro-Asian lands, as well as the testing of nuclear weapons in the Pacific—the "yellow man's ocean." She will sound the alarm against the maintenance of Western air bases in those areas, and criticize the SEATO and Baghdad Pacts as intolerable symbols of Western encroachment upon the independence of the new nations of the East. She can never be content with compromises, reforms, or renegotiations designed to place the colonial territories or emergent nations on a more favorable footing *vis-á-vis* the West. India is already playing a decisive catalytic role in the United Nations by hammering away at the colonial question until it has become the most emotion-charged issue in the General Assembly. Under Nehru, India is making her influence felt far beyond the confines of Asia. By demanding the liquidation of Western "white colonialism" without offering any alternative guarantee for the security of the free world, India is moving perilously close to the disruption of the NATO defense structure, especially in North Africa, where troubles in Morocco and Algeria have caused 200,000 French troops to be siphoned from the North Atlantic Treaty Organization.

The question confronting American policy-makers is this: What, if anything, can be done on the initiative of the United States to reverse the deteriorating trend in Indo-American relations? It seems that the area in which an understanding can be reached is quite narrow indeed. There are very few concrete, non-ideological issues into which the diplomats can sink their teeth. Anomalous as it may sound, it is not inaccurate to say that there is almost nothing to be negotiated between the two countries.

Practically everything that India would like to see the United States do involves, not Indian interests directly, but the interests of other countries. She would like the United States to abandon the French in North Africa, the Portuguese in Goa, Rhee in Korea and Chiang on Formosa. She would like to see the United States withdraw from its treaty commitments with Asian states, especially Pakistan. She would further like it to consent to the admission of the Chinese People's Republic into the United Nations. All of these desiderata would, of course, represent strategic or psychological setbacks for the West. In the nature of things, they can carry with them no guarantee that they would make the United States a bit more attractive to the Indians for any considerable period of time. The United States simply cannot negotiate away either its own security or the security of its allies to placate the Indian Government and public. Washington obviously cannot discuss the problem of thermonuclear weapons with New Delhi, any more than Moscow could. There is only one potential channel through which India and the United States might engage in face-to-face contacts, and that is the channel of economic assistance. India, however, while anxious to reap the benefits of such assistance, will not want it put on a face-to-face basis. She will shy away from long-term loans supplied by American private capital, and will prefer to have government-to-government loans routed through the United Nations and the international banking institutions, lest they come with political strings attached. To sum up, it appears that the initiative for an improvement in Indo-U. S. relations will have to come from New Delhi.

Japan's relations with the United States have been comparatively cordial since the Peace Treaty went into effect in 1952. No serious tensions, springing from incompatible foreign policy goals, have appeared. Most of the things which have thus far irritated the Japanese are rooted in the transition from occupation to full independence. There have been minor cultural frictions arising out of the continued presence of Americans in Japan. Some hostility has been generated against the lingering symbols of dependence upon the United States which frustrate the achievement of complete national sovereignty. An apparent reluctance on the part of the United States to come to grips with Japan's international trade situation is another source of ill-feeling. But the United States has found that it is possible to negotiate workable settlements with the Japanese Government. This was amply demonstrated in the case of the joint-defense agreement by the revision of the clause governing jurisdiction over U. S. troops, which the Japanese regarded as "extra-territorial" in its implications. Settlements have been concluded precisely because the Government of Japan, as distinguished from the press and the public, has refrained from taking ideological positions in its dealings with Washington. When it does complain, it couches its complaints in realistic terms of the national welfare. A perfect example of this attitude was the Government's reaction to American hydrogen experiments in the Pacific. A certain segment of the press (but not all of it) raised an impassioned protest, but the Government confined itself to a request that the United States schedule the tests with a consideration for the seasonal interests of the fishing industry. While editors, labor unions and leaders of the opposition parties demand that the United States abandon its bases in Japan and pull out its troops, the Government follows the more moderate line of arguing about its share of the joint defense costs. Instead of railing against SEATO on pacifist or antimilitarist grounds, Tokyo contents itself with repeatedly pointing out that it does not want to be drawn into an alliance which would deprive it of the freedom of decision to employ Japan's forces outside of the home islands. At least up until this time, the Government has invariably taken its stand within the traditional framework of national economic and political interests. Japan seeks to regain her prosperity and independence as a Great Power. To achieve these objectives, she seeks foreign markets and the return of her former island possessions, and thus to be able to chart her own course.

There is no doubt that Japanese-American relations are entering a crucial phase. The situation is fraught with imponderables. No one can see how many foreign policy issues may be turned into domestic political issues by the partisan struggle for control of the Japanese parliament. The Soviet Union can be expected to spare no efforts to neutralize Japan, for Japan has nearly reached the saturation point so far as gaining concessions from the United States is concerned, while the Soviet Union has not yet begun to exploit its bargaining position. Without any doubt, Japan will try to get as much as she can from the USSR in negotiating for a peace settlement. The Russians can hint at territorial concessions, the return of the war prisoners, the use of their influence toward the re-establishment of Japan's trading position in China, and admission of Japan to the United Nations. These are significant pawns at the disposal of Moscow in its bargaining for Japanese neutrality. Needless to say, the Soviets will not wrap all of their negotiable assets into one large package deal, but rather will parcel them out one by one, waiting after each concession for further evidence of Japanese "good will." It is significant that the Soviet Union just prior to the resumption of the London talks in January 1956 unveiled another weapon in their arsenal of bargaining devices: The Soviets made it clear that their veto is the last hurdle to be overcome by Japan in her quest for membership in the United Nations. The Soviets are certain to make the seating of Red China to the United Nations a pre-condition of Japan's admittance. This will bring the United

States into conflict with another ally, the Republic of China on Formosa, which, too, holds the veto power in the U. N. Security Council.

American diplomacy in the Far East must strive to reconcile the major goal of Japanese policy, which is restoration to Great Power status, with its own major objective in that area, namely, the security of the free world against the Sino-Soviet threats of aggression or subversive penetration. The pace of Soviet diplomatic initiatives in Asia has quickened. Hence difficulties, which, if not resolved, might develop into real Japanese-American tensions, now call for prompt attention. Closer diplomatic and economic contacts between Japan and the communist countries are almost certainly in the offing. Furthermore, Japan can be expected to make overtures to the neutralist countries. In fact, some of the United States' present economic policies are calculated to steer the Japanese into closer contacts with the countries of Southeast Asia. These policies involve the risk of reinforcing, at least temporarily, the various pressures that now militate in favor of Japanese neutrality. They are not, however, totally devoid of future possibilities that would be advantageous to the West, provided that the West can place confidence in Japan's ability to serve as a bridge between the West and Asia, interpreting each to the other. The problem confronting American statesmanship in this regard is to make sure that Japan, in her understandable efforts to win as many concessions as she can from the communist bloc, does not drift out of sight. At the present time, it seems highly unlikely that Japan will acquiesce to any Soviet demand if it would prove seriously detrimental to vital American interests in the Pacific. But it would be fatal for the United States to take continued Japanese friendship too much for granted, as though it were a much-deserved reward for its generous occupation and peace policies. It would be equally fatal to underestimate the Soviet Union's genius for bargaining and propaganda. Keeping Japan committed to the camp of the free nations will call for consummate skill on the part of U. S. policymakers.

To bolster the Japanese Government against the domestic critics of its pro-Western policy, the United States will have to proceed along several fronts. American authorities should continue to strive toward minimizing the cultural frictions which flow from the presence of U. S. personnel in Japan. They should continually reassess strategic needs with a view toward making the American military establishment as unobtrusive and inoffensive as possible. Perhaps the relocation of the Headquarters of the Far Eastern Command on Okinawa could be taken into consideration. Greater care must be taken in the future not to provoke emotional outbursts against the United States by committing unnecessary blunders such as using the slopes of the venerated Mount Fujiyama as an artillery range.

With regard to Japan's economic problems, the United States will do well to weigh the combined effect upon Japanese attitudes of the American protective tariff wall and the lure of trade with Communist China. It may be advisable for the Administration in Washington to publicize widely the need for revising the tariff schedule in favor of some Japanese products. There is no reason to assume that the United States will have to absorb the major part of Japanese exports. The Japanese are realistic enough to look to other markets. But there certainly is a reason for the United States to demonstrate its willingness to make moderate adjustments in its economic policy for the sake of maintaining the friendship and good will of the Japanese people. At the same time, a moderate increase in Japan's trade with the Chinese mainland appears inevitable. It goes without saying that Washington must continue to hold the line firmly on the shipment of strategic items. This will pose no serious difficulties so long as American strictures on commerce in prohibited goods are transmitted mainly through diplomatic channels rather than over the international press wires.

The United States, in short, must avoid giving the impression that it still looks upon Japan as a country which requires external direction. Legally, the Japanese are independent, and they expect to be treated as a sovereign nation. Their leaders should no longer have to beg and cajole invitations to visit Washington, not knowing whether their overtures will be rebuffed, as has happened on occasion in the past. Japan will chafe in her subordinate position until she is welcomed into the councils of the free nations as an equal partner. Ultimately, she should be taken into Washington's confidence on Pacific affairs as much as Britain is on Atlantic affairs. To help to achieve such a harmonious working relationship, the United States should make it a point to send able and top-ranking spokesmen to Japan, who can effectively interpret American motives in the Far East and who can encourage Japan to grow strong within a climate of freedom, until she takes her place as a leader of Asia and a bastion of peace in the Pacific.

Nothing short of brilliant diplomacy will be called for if the United States is to counter growing Soviet efforts to manufacture Japanese-American tensions. The USSR hopes to inject an ideological element into the frictions between the United States and Japan. It cannot exploit the ideology of anticolonialism in the case of Japan because of the Nipponese Empire's own imperial ventures in the thirties and forties. Therefore, the Kremlin has chosen to stress the ideology of nationalism, which is linked to Japan's efforts to restore her Great Power status. It will attempt to shift to the United States the onus of frustrating Japan's efforts to restore Japan's sovereignty over all of her former national territories. The Soviets realize that the nationalist and irredentist ideologies may be fraught with considerable tension possibilities and are beginning to focus attention upon the islands as the most fetching symbol of Japanese resentment against American domination. The question of the islands might create a serious impasse between the United States and Japan, since Japanese demands for an immediate and comprehensive solution would impinge upon strategic concepts which the United States cannot compromise. The United States can forestall the Soviet tactical offensive to some extent, and deflate the communist propaganda balloon, by returning the strategically unimportant Bonin Islands to Japanese control at the appropriate time. They should be given back before the Soviet Union can return—as it probably will—the Habomai and Shikotan Islands. The transfer of control should be turned into a dramatic event, accompanied by official, ceremonial exchanges of pledges of friendship in the two national capitals. There should be a reminder that the United States returned the Amami Oshima Islands in December 1953, while the Soviet Union has thus far kept all of its World War II acquisitions. Finally, the return of the Bonins should be represented as a gesture of good faith on the part of the United States, demonstrating that it has no intention to hold on to Japanese possessions permanently. The Japanese could be assured that Okinawa will be returned when the strategic situation in the Pacific no longer warrants its retention as a major base of deterrent power. The return of the Bonins would force the Soviet Union to offer Japan much more handsome prizes than tiny Habomai and Shikotan. To impress the Japanese, the Russians might then have to withdraw from the Kuriles and South Sakhalin. The Soviet Union would be confronted with a dilemma: It would either have to delay the full exploitation of the islands until the beneficial effects of the American gesture wear off, or else be compelled to play its trump cards earlier than it had anticipated. Whichever the course of action

the Soviet Union would choose, the possibility of manufacturing tensions between Japan and the United States
would be diminished as a result of the American diplomatic initiative.

India, Japan, Indonesia, the Philippines and Egypt, important as they are in the councils of Asia, cannot be
taken *singly* as being "representative" of Asian attitudes
toward the United States. The countries of the Middle
East, South and Southeast Asia, and the Far East do not
fit into neat categories such as "pro-Western" or "uncommitted," but rather are ranged along a wide political spectrum. It does not help American policy-makers to know
that a certain country is "neutralist," since neutralism is of
many different shades of meaning and motivation. Both
Egypt and India have frequently been assigned by Western commentators to the neutral, anticolonial bloc, yet it
would be a mistake to assume that Premier Nasser and
Prime Minister Nehru are of the same mind on the great
issues in international politics. The reasons for Egypt's
refusal to commit herself to the West are much more
plausible in terms of economic needs and aspirations for
regional hegemony than they are in terms of pacifist
and anti-Western ideologies. There are sufficient historical
and cultural grounds for distinguishing sharply between
Egypt's attitudes and those of India. For one thing, Egypt
is an Islamic state and hence lacks a spiritual tradition
of pacifism. For another, Egypt has known several varieties
of imperialistic domination during the last twenty-five
centuries, most of which have been non-Western. Moreover, Egypt's modern period of Western tutelage was
considerably shorter than India's and that tutelage itself
took the form of a protectorate which operated through
the existing political structure rather than direct colonial
rule. Whatever xenophobia Egypt harbors can hardly be

the same as India's. In any case, it has not yet been elevated to the dignity of a moral absolute.

The Government in Cairo sees economic development as the primary task confronting it at home. It resorts to a *tactical* neutralism for the purpose of raising the stakes by inducing the West and the communist countries to engage in competitive bidding for Egypt's support. Only within the last two years has Egypt become fully aware of the advantages to be derived from a policy of putting a price tag on neutrality or alignment in the Cold War. In this respect, too, Egypt parts company with India and Indonesia, since the latter countries refuse to conceptualize their foreign policy within the framework of the Cold War, while Egypt exploits the Cold War for her own purposes. The visit of Marshal Tito to Cairo in December 1955 lends weight to the view that Egypt has learned a lesson from Yugoslavia on how to obtain economic results from a neutral stance. To meet her financial needs, Egypt has shown herself willing to deal with any power that is ready to invest in her economy, regardless of ideology.

The Israeli dispute, which complicates Egyptian-U. S. relations more than any other issue, is closely related to Egypt's tactical neutralism. This dispute must be understood in its proper perspective: It is meaningful politically only within the Arab world. It is bound up integrally with Egypt's struggle for the leadership of the Arab community, for it serves as a cohesive factor in the absence of which Arab unity would be seriously diminished. The Israeli dispute constitutes the genuine ideological tension in the Middle East, or at least an important part of it, and this explains why it is practically non-negotiable. But the presence of Israel as an irritant in the Middle Eastern environment has, in a way, proved to be a boon to Egypt in her nationalist aspirations. Just as Trieste served to unify Yugoslavia behind Tito, so Israel can be used to unify Egypt and her Arab neighbors behind Nasser. Sometimes it is more advantageous to aggravate a dispute than to remove its causes.

By shouldering a major share of the burden in the Palestine fighting during 1948 and 1949, Egypt forcefully asserted her claim to the leadership of the Arab League. That, after all, is her primary foreign policy objective. No Middle Eastern state is in a position to engage in full-scale world politics; the scope of its autonomous action is regional. But Egypt made the most of being the strongest among the Arab states and her leverage upon one of the world's most important strategic areas. Her optimum expectancy was to provoke a diplomatic encounter between Washington and Moscow that could not but redound to her benefit. Israel furnished the occasion. Washington's support of Israel drew upon the United States the full weight of Egypt's popular indignation, and the Government in Cairo was finally able to arouse Soviet interest. Incidentally, it is not inconceivable that the Kremlin grasped the future Cold War possibilities latent in the Palestinian question before instructing its Security Council delegate to vote "yes" on that rare day in October 1947 when the Big Five achieved unanimity on the resolution establishing Israel.

Cairo, taking stock of Egypt's international position in 1955, made no bones about its disappointment at not having received as much as it had expected from the United States. The development of electric power at the Aswan Dam site had been in the talking stage ever since the end of the war, but no financial aid was forthcoming. Premier Nasser deftly joined in his calculations the two things he needed most: arms and economic assistance. First, he stepped up his appeals to the United States for weapons to be used in defense against the would-be "aggressor" on Egypt's northeastern border. But U. S. policy since 1949 has been to give arms aid only in connection with a security alliance. Nasser, who could not have been ignorant of American practices, was not ready to commit himself to an alliance with the West. He refused to move closer to the Baghdad Pact countries, not because he considered a Western military alliance "neo-colonialist," but because he feared that Egypt would be relegated to a position inferior to that of her arch-rival, 'Iraq. If a higher priority were assigned to the defense of the Northern Tier against Soviet communism than to the defense of the Arab lands against Israel, regional leadership would gravitate eastward, closer to the Soviet border and farther away from Egypt.

Egypt's main foreign policy asset is proximity to Israel. Moscow, grasping the importance to Egypt of keeping alive the Palestine issue, offered Premier Nasser Czech arms in return for cotton. The Soviets could not fail to note that a new military crisis in Palestine would place a severe strain upon the Baghdad grouping, which had not yet been developed into a firm military alliance, complete with air bases. The opening gambit completed, the Soviet Union began to talk about investing in the construction of the High Dam at Aswan. It appears that the United States' first and somewhat hasty reaction to the Soviet bid for Egypt's friendship was to ponder a quick way for giving arms to Egypt before the USSR could do so. Such a course of action would have been tantamount to submitting to blackmail, as Prime Minister Eden put it. After a diplomatic pause, Secretary Dulles advanced a much more suitable proposal, namely, a guarantee of the Arab-Israeli border against any violations. This proposal, which circumvented the non-negotiable character of the Arab-Israeli dispute, offered the best practical hope for minimizing the explosive tensions in the Middle East. If Washington remains firm in its intention not to enter a security agreement with Israel alone, Israel would find the border guarantee vastly preferable to an arms build-up in Egypt's favor. But Egypt stands to lose much if she accepts the border guarantee, for Israelophobia would diminish in importance as a rallying point for the Arab lands.

The United States and Britain followed up the guarantee proposal by announcing their joint offer to assist in the financing of the Aswan Dam project—provided that Soviet participation be excluded. This is the current status of the dialogue between Egypt and the United States. Its tenor, on Egypt's side, is not ideologically neutralist, pacifist, or anti-white-imperialist. It is, at least up to the time of this writing, rather strategic and economic.

In summation of the foregoing study, the following generalizations can safely be made:

1. Serious tensions exist between the United States and some of the countries of Asia. Some of these tensions lend themselves to settlement by diplomatic negotiation, while others do not. Where tensions do not seem to be negotiable, it is because an ideological difference bars agreement.

2. The ideological differences which have arisen between the United States and certain Asian nations during the last decade do not spring so much from a basic disagreement about the relative values of the democratic and the communist social systems as they do from a conflict over the priority of tasks confronting the world at this particular juncture of history.

3. Two fundamental interpretations of the world situation and historical imperatives are, while not totally contradictory, simultaneously incompatible: The Western allies are primarily concerned with the organization of the security of all the areas of the world which are threatened by Sino-Soviet imperialism. The neutralist countries of Asia, led by India, place the liquidation of colonialism at the top of the international political agenda. The older nations of the Atlantic Community are united by considera-

tions of the strategic defense of freedom against totalitarianism. The new nations of the Middle East, South and Southeast Asia, and the Far East are mainly so preoccupied with the challenges of national unification and independence and the elimination of the last vestiges of European colonialism, that they deprecate the need for defense against communist expansion.

4. The United States does not find itself equally at odds with all the countries of Asia over the problem of priorities. Turkey and Japan, the two Asian nations to be first admitted to the modern state system, are allies of the United States. The Philippine Republic, a former colonial possession, is also an ally of the United States, along with Thailand and Pakistan, under the Manila Pact which set up the Southeast Asia Treaty Organization. Iran and Iraq, inasmuch as they are joined with the West through Great Britain under the Baghdad Pact, receive military aid from the United States. These countries are by no means disinterested in the political and economic problems of the colonial areas and the newly emergent nations, but they are willing to see them approached within the framework of strategic security.

5. The principal reason why the tension between India and the United States is so serious is because India's anticolonial ideology, which identifies all military alliances with the West as a form of intolerable neo-colonialism, jeopardizes the retention by the West of vital bases in the colonial areas and elsewhere throughout Africa and Asia. To this extent, India's foreign policy lends powerful moral support to the Soviet Union's primary strategic objective, viz., to roll back the base system upon which the West's policy of deterrence rests. By equating the terms "imperialism" and "Western colonialism," while keeping silent about the iniquities of Soviet and Chinese colonialism, India appears to countenance the Leninist thesis that only capitalist countries can be imperialistic.

Such "sloganization" of a complicated political problem serves to obscure its real nature and reduces the possibility of its orderly, decent solution. The United States cannot share Prime Minister Nehru's faith that the emergent nations of the world would really stand to gain, at this crucial juncture of the Cold War, from the West's strategic withdrawal, or that the Soviet Union is bound to mellow into a genuine democracy once it is no longer subjected to encirclement by the West.

6. The problem of the economic development of the nations of Asia is integrally linked to the issue of strategic defense versus anticolonialism, and frequently serves to complicate it vastly. It seems highly doubtful that the United States will be able in the future to carry on with the countries of Asia any *purely economic* relations totally divorced from strategic and political considerations. The United States may not be able, even if it wished to do so, to keep its international trade and investment policies toward the uncommitted world free of political considerations. Even though Washington does not always insist upon welding economic policies to strategic desiderata, the neutralist Asian nations tend to view—or profess to view—the foreign economic policies of all the Western capitalist states in the light of the Leninist interpretation of capitalism in its last, imperialist stage of development.

7. In some instances, the tensions which exist between the United States and certain Asian nations can be traced to direct Soviet initiative. This is patently true, for example, in the case of the Japanese Islands. More often, existing tensions are exploited and aggravated by Soviet propaganda and diplomacy, the most obvious instance being the offer of arms to Egypt.

Notes

THE UNITED STATES AND INDIA

[1] Speech before the House of the People, June 12, 1952, *Parliamentary Debates*, Vol. II, No. 1, p. 1662. For discussions of Indian neutrality, the reader is referred to the article by T. M. P. Mahadevan, "India's Policy of Non-Alignment," in the *Indian Yearbook of International Affairs*, Madras, 1953; Robert A. Scalapino, "Neutralism in Asia," *American Political Science Review*, Vol. XLVIII, March 1954, 11. 49-62; Taya Zinkin, "Indian Foreign Policy," *World Politics*, Vol. VII, January 1955, pp. 179-208.

[2] *Manchester Guardian Weekly*, September 3, 1953.

[3] Editorial, "Moscow Declaration," in *The Hindu*, December 30, 1945. It was suggested that the proper solution for Korea would be "complete withdrawal of forces by both Russia and America, which would be consistent not only with the promise made during the war, but also just under the circumstances. But because of mutual suspicions it is now provided that there should be a Russo-American 'trusteeship' for five years." *See also* Editorial, "Korean Hopes Fading," in *National Standard*, December 31, 1952.

[4] *Indiagram*, December 31, 1952. Mavrik, a political columnist of the *Free Press Journal*, had written on August 11, 1951: "The tragic part of it all is that those who are so anxious to make the world safe for democracy always see to it that they do the fighting part of the job as far away from themselves as possible. . . . Korea is already impoverished and all but wiped out because some powerful neighbors had a dispute to settle. The dispute still being unsettled, now Korea must go off the map." *See also* Nehru's speech of August 9, 1951.

[5] *The Hindu*, October 12, 1953.

[6] *Free Press Journal*, October 6, 1953. On the same day, *The Times of India*, in an editorial entitled "Treachery," commented: "Treachery is a strong word to be used among friends and allies, but the U. S. would do well to realize that there is a point beyond which forbearance ends."

[7] *The Hindu*, October 12, 1953.

[8] *Free Press Journal* and *The Times of India*, October 6, 1953.

[9] *Hindustan Times*, October 11, 1953.

[10] Krishna Menon said this in an address to a group of lawyers at Madras. *The Times of India*, January 14, 1955. For further treatment of India's position with respect to Korea since the end of hostilities, see the Indian Resolution in the United Nations Assembly, December 3, 1954;

Nehru's Press Conference in Peking, October 26, 1954; and the Congress Party Resolution at Madras, January 1955.

11 *The Overseas Hindustan Times,* April 7, 1955.

12 *The Hindu,* August 29, 1951. Cf. also the editorial, "Waiting May Pay," in *The Statesman,* February 9, 1955.

13 Editorial, "War of the Islands," *The Statesman,* November 30, 1954.

14 Editorial, "Far East Powder Keg," *The Statesman,* January 29, 1955.

15 Editorial, "Keeping the Peace," *The Hindu,* February 22, 1955.

16 Editorial, "U. S. Lead," *The Times of India,* February 9, 1955.

17 *The Statesman,* November 30, 1954.

18 Chester Bowles, *Ambassador's Report,* New York, Harpers, 1954, pp. 180, 371.

19 Review of *Ambassador's Report* in the *Illustrated Weekly of India,* March 20, 1955, p. 51.

20 *The Statesman,* November 30, 1954. Cf. also Norman Cliff's article, "Formosa," *Times of India,* February 8, 1953, p. 8.

21 *Amrita Bazar Patrika,* April 24, 1955. On the same day *The Hindustan Standard* declared that "if proof of good intentions and good behavior is needed, it must also come from Washington," and it added that "Chou En-lai had put the cold-war strategists on trial."

22 Editorial, "U Nu in Peking," *The Hindu,* December 13, 1954.

23 *The Statesman,* February 19, 1947.

24 All India Congress Committee Statement, *Hindu Weekly Review,* September 13, 1954.

25 Editorial, "Peace in Indochina," *The Hindu,* July 26, 1954 (*Weekly Review*). At the same time, the pro-American *Thought* pointed out that the Geneva agreement would never have been possible had not America agreed to it. April 9, 1955.

26 *The Times of India,* April 19, 1955.

27 *Ibid.*

28 *Ibid.,* March 17, 1955. *The Hindu* charged that "an explosive situation exists in Indo-China, where the Americans are engaged in drilling the army of South Viet Nam as anti-Communist crusaders." February 28, 1955 (*Weekly Review*).

29 Editorial, "Divided Viet Nam," *The Statesman,* March 30, 1955.

30 Editorial, "Cambodian Crisis," *The Times of India,* March 5, 1955.

31 *Ibid.*

32 *New York Times,* November 8, 1949.

33 *The Statesman,* November 6, 1954.

34 *The Hindu,* August 10, 1953 (*Weekly Review*).

35 Nehru's speech at Mirzapur, U. P., July 12, 1954. More than a year previously, the Prime Minister had said in an address to the Indian Parliament, "The United Nations, which presumes to be a universal organization in this world has ceased to be that, because of the major fact that a great country which is obviously a running country, obviously a stable and strong country, is not represented there." (February 18, 1953.)

36 *The Times of India,* August 20, 1952.

37 *National Herald,* August 23, 1952; *The Tribune,* October 30, 1951.

38 *The Hindu,* August 10, 1953 (*Weekly Review*).

39 *The Statesman,* October 4, 1953.

40 Editorial in *United Asia,* December 1954, p. 263.

[41] *The Hindu*, December 13, 1954.

[42] *Ibid.*, January 17, 1955.

[43] *Hindustan Standard*, December 24, 1950.

[44] "Vedette" made this observation after a trip to China where he found "a grim strain in the Chinese character . . . no exhibitionism but an essential part of the collective national mind . . . a determination to resist armed attack." *The Statesman*, February 5, 1955.

[45] Sardar Panikkar, after a four-year stay in China as the Indian Ambassador, was convinced that "a community of approach, a commonness of understanding," linked the leaders of India and China. "Political issues apart, there were no differences at all . . . on matters like the freedom of Asian peoples and the need for social and economic justice." *The Times of India*, August 26, 1952. Many Indians agreed with V. K. Krishna Menon in preferring to call Chinese Communism "Maoism."

[46] Editorial, "Bandung Balance Sheet," *The Statesman*, April 30, 1955.

[47] Prime Minister Nehru, in a speech to the Lok Sabha (Lower House of Parliament) on February 25, 1955.

[48] *The Hindu*, November 16, 1953 (*Weekly Review*).

[49] *The Statesman*, April 30, 1955.

[50] *The Times of India*, January 18, 1952.

[51] *Ibid.*, January 25, 1952.

[52] *National Standard*, January 3, 1953. On January 3, 1953, Dr. A. Appadorai, Secretary General of the Indian Council of World Affairs, stated in an address of welcome to Ambassador Chester Bowles his belief that the two main reasons for the recent deterioration in Indo-American relations were Kashmir and Asia, and exhorted Americans to cultivate a "better appreciation of the Kashmir issue." In reply, Mr. Bowles admitted that it was "too bad and unfortunate . . . (that) the factual outlines behind the basic issues in the Kashmir story" were not fully understood by the American people. *Hindustan Times*, January 4, 1953.

[53] *The Statesman*, March 18, 1954.

[54] Dispatch from Correspondent Homer Bigart in the New York *Herald Tribune*, April 7, 1955.

[55] *The Statesman*, March 4, 1954. This comment was provoked by Prime Minister Ali's interview with *U. S. News and World Report*. The newspaper also took note of the fact that Pakistan's U. N. Representative, Ahmed S. Bokhari, had "undiplomatically related the Kashmir question to U. S. arms aid."

[56] *The Hindu*, February 15, 1954 (*Weekly Review*).

[57] *Ibid.*, March 8, 1954.

[58] *Indiagram*, March 3, 1954.

[59] *The Hindu*, March 8, 1954.

[60] The full text of Nehru's speech is to be found in *Indiagram*, March 3, 1954.

[61] *The Statesman*, March 8, 1954. When in reply to India's request for the withdrawal of American nationals serving on the U. N. Mission in Kashmir, U. S. and U. N. circles insisted that U. N. employees became denationalized by virtue of their position, *The Hindu* retorted: "After all, it was the U. S. which claimed in a different context that her nationals, serving the U. N. Secretariat, did not become 'denationalized'

on that account." March 22, 1954. In suggesting that the American officers be withdrawn, Mr. Nehru was supported by the overwhelming majority of Indians, including those who are usually his severest critics. Thus the Politburo of the Indian Communist Party declared that the pronouncement "will receive wholehearted support from every patriotic Indian." *The Statesman*, March 4, 1954.

62 *The Statesman*, March 8, 1954.

63 *The Hindu*, March 8, 1954.

64 *Indiagram*, March 3, 1954.

65 *Hindustan Times*, October 22, 1953 (Overseas Edition).

66 *Ibid.*, December 12, 1953.

67 *Thought*, December 26, 1953.

68 *The Statesman*, January 26, 1954.

69 Editorial, "The Japanese War Criminals," *The Hindu*, May 24, 1954 (*Weekly Review*).

70 Nehru's speech in the Indian Parliament on February 18, 1953, was reported the following day in the Indian press. The Prime Minister said: "A soldier is a very excellent person in his own domain, but as somebody, I think a French statesman once said, war—even war—is too serious a thing to be handed over to a soldier to control, much less peace."

71 *Ibid.*

72 *Eastern Economist*, February 6, 1953.

73 Editorial, "Wrong Tactics," The *National Standard*, February 13, 1953.

74 *The Hindu*, April 12, 1954 (*Weekly Review*).

75 Surveyor, "Thermonuclear War or Co-Existence?" *Times of India*, April 19, 1955.

76 Nehru's speech to the House of the People, September 13, 1954.

77 V. K. Krishna Menon's speech in the Council of State, August 27, 1954.

78 Editorial, "A Threat to Security," *Hindustan Times*, September 16, 1954 (Overseas Edition).

79 Editorial, "An Area of Peace," *The Hindu*, September 6, 1954 (*Weekly Review*).

80 *Hindustan Times*, August 26, 1954.

81 Editorial, "An Imposed SEATO," *Hindustan Times*, August 26, 1954 (Overseas Edition).

82 *The Hindu*, September 13, 1954.

83 Nehru's speech in the House of the People, February 25, 1955.

84 *Hindustan Times*, March 3, 1955.

85 Nehru's press conference in Rangoon, reported in *The Statesman*, April 1, 1953.

86 *Indiagram*, March 3, 1954.

87 *The Hindu*, September 7, 1953.

88 *United Nations Daily Report*, October 1, 1953, p. 12.

89 Editorial, "What Next?" The *National Standard*, January 3, 1953.

90 Chester Bowles, *Ambassador's Report*, New York, Harpers, 1954.

91 Editorial, "Indians in the U. N.," *The Hindu*, May 9, 1955. The case of Pakistan was cited in view of its holding fifteen posts, whereas its quota was between six and ten. "Mr. Hammarskjold has replaced an Indian Assistant Secretary General with a Pakistani. By all means let a Pakistani hold an important job of this kind. But why should an Indian be removed to make place for him?"

[92] *National Standard,* February 13, 1953.

[93] *The Statesman,* October 4, 1953.

[94] Address of John Foster Dulles before the National Publishers' Association, January 17, 1947, *New York Times,* January 18, 1947. *See also* the letter by Dr. L. Sundaram in the *New York Times,* February 2, 1947.

[95] Editorial, "Dulles the Double," *Indian Express,* December 29, 1952.

[96] The *Times of India,* December 29, 1952.

[97] Recently, the same newspaper carried this critical judgment: "Certainly Mr. Dulles' unctuous sermons on the 'craven purchase of peace' come strangely from a master of absolutes on the one hand and a vendor of compromises on the other. . . . The net result is not merely a loss of face, but a loss of both faces." Column by Onlooker, April 15, 1955.

[98] The Premier of Egypt, Gamal Abdel Nasser, makes this point in his recent article, "The Egyptian Revolution," in *Foreign Affairs,* Vol. 33, January 1955. Speaking of the importation of Western political ideas to the Middle East, he says: "Overwhelmed and unsettled, Eastern minds lost almost all national values, yet could not absorb Western values. Misapplication of Western patterns of government brought a confused mixture of political systems and philosophies. Democracy was only a veil for dictatorship. Constitutions framed in the interest of the people of the Middle East became instruments for their exploitation and domination." (p. 199)

[99] Article by Onlooker, "Through Indian Eyes," *Times of India,* April 15, 1955.

[100] *The Hindu,* September 12, 1953.

[101] Article by Onlooker, cited in Note 99.

[102] Editorial, "U. S. Policy," *Indian Express,* February 3, 1953. "Even supposing the 'liberation' promised by the Eisenhower Administration can be achieved only through greater stress, there should be something more to enthuse the millions of Asians to welcome the new policy. . . . The obvious course to dispel suspicion is to induce Britain, France and the other Colonial Powers to immediately recognize the rights of these peoples to self-government."

[103] Letter from Nehru to the Arab-Asian delegations to the United Nations, New York *Times,* April 30, 1952. Cf. also speech by V. K. Krishna Menon before the General Assembly, in *United Nations Daily Report,* October 1, 1953, p. 12.

[104] *Free Press Journal,* August 31, 1951 and the Indian Express, February 3, 1953. *The Tribune,* September 12, 1951, said, "India has no faith in military pacts to contain communism if the alternative to communism is colonialism and the denial of economic and political freedom to the people."

[105] *The Times* (London), August 20, 1951.

[106] Article by Edouard Sablier, *Le Monde,* March 8, 1951.

[107] *The Times of India,* April 15, 1955.

[108] *The Statesman,* April 11, 1955.

[109] Editorial, "Apartheid," *Hindustan Times,* April 14, 1955. (Overseas Edition).

[110] *The Times of India,* August 29, 1952.

[111] L. Natarajan, *American Shadow Over Asia,* Bombay, 1952, p. 6.

112 *The Hindu,* November 2, 1953.
113 *Ibid.,* April 6, 1955.
114 Nehru's broadcast address, January 24, 1955 on the occasion of U. N. Day.
115 Nehru's speech before the Madras meeting of Congress Workers, *The Hindu,* October 3, 1953. A few days earlier, Nehru said: "It is going to be less and less feasible in the future for any world organization to leave Asia out of account or to consider it only as a playground for their [Europe's and America's] politics or conflicts. Inevitable, Asia is bound to resent this kind of treatment." *The Hindu,* September 24, 1953.
116 *The Times of India,* April 26, 1954.
117 *Hindustan Standard,* April 26, 1954.
118 *United Asia,* December 1954, p. 263. "Two contrary and contradictory forces are at work today moulding the future course of Asian history. One of these, represented by Manila, is a continuation of the unwanted and embarrassing Western solicitude for Asia. The other, represented by Bogor, exemplifies the new Asian assertiveness at least in so far as purely Asian matters are concerned." Manila was the site of the SEATO Pact, and Bogor the meeting place of the Colombo Premiers.
119 Cf., e.g., the interview of Indian Finance Minister C. Deshmukh with C. L. Sulzberger, "Seeing Ourselves as Others See Us," New York *Times,* February 19, 1955. Indians tend to connect the creation of SEATO with their belief that Americans hold Asian lives more expendable than Western lives. *Hindustan Times,* August 12, 1954 (Overseas Edition), declared that SEATO ". . . can only heighten tension in Asia and in the ultimate reckoning leave Asians to fight Asians."
120 Report of Sardar J. J. Singh's trip through India, *New York Times,* May 6, 1947.
121 Address by Secretary of State George C. Marshall at Harvard University, June 5, 1947, *New York Times,* June 6, 1947.
122 Editorial, "Asia and U. S. Aid," *The Hindu,* February 3, 1955.
123 This comment was made by Dr. Krishnalal Sridharani, who added that India's financial policy makers were disappointed principally because they had fashioned the Five Year Plan with substantial American aid in mind. *Amrita Bazar Patrika,* September 24, 1952.
124 *Economic Weekly,* January 12, 1952, p. 2. Meanwhile, *The Statesman* contrasted U. S. investments in India of $38 million with $726 million in the Persian Gulf, $285 million in France, $198 million in Australia, and $140 million in South Africa. December 25, 1952.
125 Editorial, "Outside Aid for the Plan," *National Standard,* January 5, 1953.
126 Editorial, "Asia and U. S. Aid," *The Hindu,* February 3, 1955 and editorial, "India and SEATO," *The Hindu,* August 23, 1954. The *Hindustan Times* admitted that "American aid is very useful for the Indian economy, yet the question arises how great is the danger that Indian independence and foreign policy would be jeopardized by such aid." Editorial, "Aid Without Strings," September 18, 1952.
127 *The Hindu,* September 6, 1954. The Indians have also discussed the possibility of receiving aid from private sources in the United States.

The *Hindustan Times* recently carried an editorial entitled "Constructive Philanthropy," in which it expressed appreciation for the help given by the Ford Foundation. "The Ford Foundation's assistance remains entirely outside the political arena, and seeks only to promote the general good of the people. Aid without political strings attached has been the cry of underdeveloped countries . . ." February 13, 1955.

128 *Thought*, April 23, 1955, p. 5.
129 *United Asia*, December 1954, p. 260.
130 *The Modern Review*, September 1954, p. 178 and *Times of India*, August 27, 1954.
131 *New York Times*, October 5, 1955.

THE UNITED STATES AND INDONESIA

1 Walter H. Mallory, "Making a Friend of Indonesia," *Foreign Affairs*, January 1954, p. 283.
2 Claude A. Buss, *The Far East*. New York: Macmillan, 1955, pp. 598-604.
3 *Ibid.*, p. 715.
4 *Times of Indonesia*, December 30, 1952.
5 *Harian Rakjat*, as quoted in the *Times of Indonesia*, November 4 and 13, 1952.
6 *Times of Indonesia*, February 3, 1953.
7 *Times of Indonesia*, February 4, 1953.
8 *New York Times*, November 25, 1953.
9 *New York Times*, November 20, 1954.
10 *New York Times*, December 11, 1954.
11 Mallory, *op. cit.*, p. 283.
12 *Duta Masjarakat*, quoted in the *Times of Indonesia*, December 22, 1954.
13 *Indonesia Raya*, as quoted by Radio Jakarta, April 26, 1955, in Indonesian.
14 *Berita Indonesia*, as quoted by Radio Jakarta, April 5, 1955, in Indonesian.
15 The vote on November 30 was considered a victory for Indonesia, since the resolution did not recognize the validity of the Dutch claim to western New Guinea and recommended continued negotiations between Indonesia and the Netherlands. There is a good account in the *New York Times*, December 1, 1954.
16 *New York Times*, December 1, 1954.
17 *New York Times*, December 3, 1954.
18 The Dutch also criticized the United States for not supporting the Netherlands claim. *New York Times*, December 12, 1954.
19 The Sastroamidjojo Government, led by the *Partai Nasionalis Indonesia* (PNI), accepted only the parliamentary votes of the Communist Party. Although the Communists considered it advantageous for their purposes to support the Cabinet, it must be remembered that there was no evidence that the Communists were consulted by the Government or that they exerted any influence on the determination of Government policy.

[20] This is well illustrated in an article by Mohammed Hatta, Vice President of Indonesia and former Premier. "Indonesia's Foreign Policy," *Foreign Affairs*, April 1953, pp. 441 ff.

[21] *Report on Indonesia* (Indonesian Embassy, Washington), August-September 1954, p. 8.

[22] *Report on Indonesia, loc. cit.* Natsir, who was Prime Minister at the time, defined Indonesia's foreign policy on May 18, 1950 in terms not at variance with those used before and since by Indonesian leaders: "Indonesia has resolved on an independent foreign policy. In pursuing this independent policy, the interest of the people will be the main directive of the Government. Besides, it will endeavor to support world peace, or support any undertaking to that purpose." Quoted in Lawrence Finklestein, "Indonesia's Record in the United Nations," *International Conciliation*, November 1951, p. 516.

[23] *Indonesian Review* (Ministry of Defense, Jakarta), February-March 1951, p. 83. Cf. *The Times* (London), April 26, 1951, p. 5.

[24] *Pedoman,* quoted in *Report on Indonesia* (Embassy of Indonesia, Washington), February 27, 1953, p. 3.

[25] *Times of Indonesia,* May 20, 1952. The same paper stated, on January 23, 1953, that "too many Americans tend to simplify things by thinking that not being anti-Russian, being pro-Asian, and wanting to be independent of the two conflicting groups is similar to being anti-American. Such thinking betrays a complete lack of understanding and insight into the forces now working in a new Asia."

[26] *Merdeka,* quoted by Radio Jakarta, June 9, 1951, in English.

[27] Sastroamidjojo, on the occasion of his appointment as Premier, declared that "We expect to continue the already existing friendly relationship with the United States and improve and strengthen it." *New York Times,* August 2, 1953.

[28] The possibility exists that a greater identification of the PNI with China and a more critical attitude toward China on the part of the Masjumi and Socialists might develop as a result of the polarization of the major parties around political issues during the 1955 election campaigns. Masjumi and Socialist expressions of good will toward China appear to be significantly less frequent since the PNI has been more actively cultivating Chinese friendship.

[29] Justus M. Van der Kroef, "Indonesia, Independent in the Cold War," *International Journal* (Canadian Institute of International Affairs), Autumn, 1952, p. 285.

[30] *Times of Indonesia,* February 14, 1953.

[31] *Merdeka* regarded this as an important advance toward peace: Since Britain would be unacceptable to China and India to the U. S., Indonesia would be the likeliest candidate for mediator. Quoted by Radio Jakarta, May 14, 1955, in Indonesian.

[32] *Suluh Indonesia,* quoted by Radio Jakarta, May 11, 1955, in English.

[33] *Merdeka,* as quoted by Radio Jakarta, May 11, 1955, in English.

[34] *Abadi,* as quoted by Radio Jakarta, April 30, 1955, in Indonesian.

[35] *Times of Indonesia,* April 27, 1955.

[36] *Times of Indonesia,* April 25, 1955. The text of the treaty is reproduced in *Far Eastern Survey,* May 1955, pp. 75-76.

[37] *New York Times,* April 29, 1955.

[38] *Times of Indonesia,* April 28, April 29, 1955.

[39] "The two Prime Ministers declare that it is the inalienable right of the people of any country to safeguard their own sovereignty and territorial integrity. They express sympathy and support to the efforts of either of the two countries in safeguarding its own sovereignty and integrity." Text from the *New York Times,* April 29, 1955.

[40] *New York Times,* October 3, 1955.

[41] Mallory, *op. cit.,* pp. 285-286.

[42] Roeslan Abdulgani, "Ideological Background of the Asian-African Conference," *United Asia* (Bombay), April 1955, pp. 43-44.

[43] *The Provisional Constitution of the Republic of Indonesia* (Act No. 7, 1950) Gazette 1950, No. 56.

[44] Radio Jakarta, May 19, 1955, in Indonesian. The speech continued: "I have made this remark to every correspondent . . . who has considered that the so-called Asian-African diseases could be cured by technical, economic, and military aid. Billions of dollars may be thrown to Asia and Africa; however, if there is no realization of the fact that Asian & African nations are living with a feeling of nationalism and desire freedom from imperialism, it will be useless."

[45] George M. Kahin, "Indonesian Politics and Nationalism," in W. L. Holland, ed., *Asian Nationalism and the West,* New York: Macmillan, 1953, pp. 111-198.

[46] The form in which the agreement was signed was probably stronger than the Department of State required. The Indonesian Government clearly misjudged the Indonesian public reaction. Virtually all countries receiving aid previous to the passage of the Mutual Security Act of 1951 signed the agreement and continued to receive aid. (Ireland was an exception, but Ireland refused to sign the agreement on other grounds than neutralism.) Thus Indonesian neutralism does not necessarily provide a full explanation of the political crisis over this affair.

Nationalism and not communism was the basis for the opposition to the agreement. The cancellation of grant aid, in the words of a *New York Times* correspondent, "was more a result of fierce independence than of leftist influence." (October 2, 1953, p. 3)

[47] Quoted in the *New York Times,* December 14, 1952, p. 4. A *Times of Indonesia* editorial accused America of attempting to prevent Indonesian economic self-sufficiency through the device of the MSA agreement. (January 23, 1953, p. 6)

[48] Dr. F. L. Tobino, Minister of Information, pointed out on May 7, 1955 that only $7,000,000 in U. S. aid was allocated to Indonesia in 1955, while the Philippines, with their much smaller population, received $20,000,000 and Japan $100,000,000. This was in response to criticism of the Government for accepting American aid. Radio Jakarta, May 7, 1955, in English.

[49] *Time,* September 5, 1955, p. 27.

[50] Justus M. Van der Kroef, "Indonesia's Economic Difficulties," *Far Eastern Survey,* February 1955, pp. 17-24.

[51] *Ibid.,* p. 18.

[52] *Report on Indonesia* (Embassy of Indonesia, Washington), August 15, 1952.

[53] Mallory, *op. cit.,* p. 287.

[54] *Ibid., loc. cit.*

[55] 70% of Indonesia's total exports are in tin, rubber, and copra. 50% of

Government revenue is from import-export duties, and 25-27% of the national income is gained through foreign trade. *Ekonomi dan Keuangan Indonesia,* December, 1953, p. 733. (Quoted by J. M. Van der Kroef in *Far Eastern Survey, op. cit.,* p. 18.)

[56] *Abadi,* quoted by Radio Jakarta, June 23, 1951, in English.

[57] Cheh-Yung Chen, *Future Trade of Indonesia,* Philadelphia: University of Pennsylvania, M.B.A. Thesis, 1952, pp. 103-104.

[58] *Sin Po,* as quoted by Radio Jakarta, April 12, 1955, in Indonesian.

[59] *Pedoman,* quoted by Radio Jakarta, March 8, 1952, in English.

[60] Leslie H. Palmer, "Modern Islam After Independence," *Pacific Affairs,* September 1954.

[61] Even the Masjumi disavow Darul Islam. *Times of Indonesia,* April 15, 1955. Cf. Amry Vandenbosch, "The Indonesian Political Scene," *Far Eastern Survey,* October, 1953, pp. 146-147 and *Indonesia* (Embassy of Indonesia, Bangkok), January 17, 1955.

[62] Robert C. Bone, Jr., "The Future of Indonesian Political Parties," *Far Eastern Survey,* February 1954, pp. 21-22. Moslems who desire a theocratic state have largely left the Masjumi for less liberal Moslem groups. See Robert Van Niel, "Indonesian Political Developments," *Far Eastern Survey,* June, 1953, p. 86.

[63] Mallory, *op. cit.,* pp. 285-286.

[64] *Times of Indonesia,* editorial, May 15, 1952.

[65] Bone, *op. cit.*

[66] "Conference Bureau and the Indonesian Government," *Socialist Asia* (Rangoon), Vol. 3, No. 1, May, 1954, pp. 2 ff.

[67] Justus M. Van der Kroef, "The Dutch Position in Indonesia Today," *Far Eastern Survey,* June, 1954.

[68] But the Indonesians "think of the United States as a 'white' country." Mallory, *op. cit.,* p. 285.

[69] Cf. *Harian Rakjat* (Indonesian-language Communist journal), as quoted in the *Times of Indonesia,* April 21, 1955.

THE UNITED STATES AND JAPAN

[1] Kazuo Kawei, "Sovereignty and Democracy in the Japanese Constitution," *American Political Science Review,* Vol. XLIX, September 1955, pp. 663-672.

[2] Paul M. A. Linebarger and others, *Far Eastern Governments and Politics,* New York, Van Nostrand, 1954, pp. 464-468.

[3] Lily Abegg, "Japan Reconsiders," *Foreign Affairs,* Vol. 33, April 1955, p. 410.

[4] *Nippon Times,* August 17, 1951.

[5] *Ibid.,* Peace Treaty Supplement, September 25, 1951.

[6] *Mainichi,* October 27, 1953.

[7] *Ibid.,* September 9, 1951.

[8] *Nippon Times,* March 10, 1952.

[9] *Ibid.,* February 9, February 29, and March 1, 1952.

[10] *Ibid.,* February 20, 1952.

[11] *Yomiuri Shimbun,* February 22, 1952.

[12] "Yokata Airs Views on Garrison Issue," *Nippon Times,* February 23, 1952.

[13] This was sent in February 1952. Another letter of protest in the same vein was dispatched a month later. *Nippon Times,* March 19, 1952.

[14] *Ibid.,* November 15, 1952.

[15] *Japan, Her Security and Mission,* Ministry of Foreign Affairs, Japanese Government, April 28, 1952, pp. 9-11. See also Article XVII, "Administrative Agreement with Japan," for provisions on jurisdiction over offenses committed by U. S. armed forces. Reprint from the *Department of State Bulletin,* March 10, 1952, pp. 386-387.

[16] *Mainichi,* September 29, 1953.

[17] *Nippon Times,* April 22, 1952.

[18] *Mainichi,* December 31, 1952.

[19] Survey conducted by the Japanese Ministry of Agriculture and Forestry, February 1953; reported in *Nippon Times,* February 4, 1953.

[20] *Ibid.*

[21] *Tokyo Evening News,* February 18, 1953, and *Mainichi,* March 11, 1953.

[22] *Mainichi,* April 28, 1955.

[23] *Asahi Picture News,* August 6, 1952.

[24] *Mainichi,* November 20, 1952; *Nippon Times,* January 6 and 24, 1953.

[25] *Mainichi,* May 1, 1954.

[26] Report of Doctors Myoshi and Kumatori to the International Medical Convention at Kyoto, in *Mainichi,* April 3, 1954. Cf. also *Oriental Economist,* April 1954, p. 164.

[27] *Oriental Economist,* May 1954, pp. 215-216.

[28] *Mainichi,* March 31, and April 11, 1954.

[29] *New York Times,* July 29, 30, and 31, and August 6, 7, 8, and 9, 1955.

[30] Japanese Constitution, Chapter II, Art. 9. Text in Paul M. A. Linebarger *et al., op. cit.,* p. 605.

[31] Tashikazu Kase, "Japan's New Role in East Asia," *Foreign Affairs,* Vol. 34, October 1955, p. 46. Kase is author of *Journey to the Missouri* and Permanent Observer of Japan at the United Nations. Recently, he headed the Delegation of Japan to the Bandung Conference.

[32] Preamble to the Security Treaty, *Conference for the Conclusion and Signature of the Treaty of Peace with Japan: Record of Proceedings,* Washington 1951 (Pub. No. 4392, International Organization and Conference Series II, Far Eastern 3).

[33] *Nippon Times,* September 25, 1951.

[34] *Yomiuri Shimbun,* February 8, 1952.

[35] *Nippon Times,* September 16, 1952 and November 8, 1952.

[36] *Mainichi,* September 3, 1954.

[37] *Nippon Times,* November 5, 1952.

[38] Editorial, "National Strength and National Defense," *Mainichi,* November 8, 1952.

[39] "Japanese Politics Behind the Scenes," *Nippon Times,* November 10, 1952. Cf. also Robert P. Martin, "New Eisenhower Policy Requires Clarification," *Mainichi,* November 27, 1952.

[40] *Mainichi,* October 16 and December 4, 1953. The fact that MSA aid has actually been shipped to the NSF does not resolve the question conclusively, since the defense of Japan itself, in view of the 12 major bases which the United States maintains there, would make the NSF eligible to receive such military aid.

[41] Tashikazu Kase, *op. cit.,* p. 44.

[42] Treaty of Friendship, Alliance and Assistance. See pamphlet, *The Sino-Soviet Treaty and Agreements*, Peking, Foreign Languages Press, 1951.

[43] Kase, *op. cit.*, p. 44.

[44] Commission on Foreign Economic Policy, *Report to the President and Congress*, January 23, 1954, p. 44.

[45] *New York Times*, February 6, 1955.

[46] *Ibid.*, October 2, 1954.

[47] *Mainichi*, January 4, 1955.

[48] *Ibid.*, March 17, 1955.

[49] *Ibid.*, February 9, 1955.

[50] *Nippon Times*, February, 1953.

[51] *Mainichi*, April 29, 1955.

[52] *New York Times*, February 6, 1955.

[53] *Ibid.*, September 12, 1955.

[54] *Nippon Times*, September 13, 1951.

[55] *Ibid.*, April 4 and May 21, 1952; *Tokyo Evening News*, March 25, 1953.

[56] *Yomiuri Shimbun*, May 23, 1952.

[57] *Transcript of Proceedings at the Asian Socialist Conference*, Leftist Socialist Party, Tokyo, January 31, 1953.

[58] *Mainichi*, April 4, 1953.

[59] *Ibid.*, September 5, 1953.

[60] *Mainichi*, January 19, 1954.

[61] *Ibid.*, October 6, 1953.

[62] Address by Harold Stassen, then Foreign Operations Administrator, to the Asahi Chamber of Commerce, *Asahi Evening News*, March 11, 1955.

[63] "Japan and GATT," *Mainichi* Overseas Edition, February 15, 1953; "U. K. Is Urged to Oppose Japan's Entry into GATT," *Nippon Times*, March 12, 1953.

[64] *New York Times*, September 26, 1954.

[65] *Oriental Economist*, September 1954, p. 430.

[66] Statement by Aiichiro Fujiyama, President of the Japanese Chamber of Commerce and Industry, *Nippon Times*, November 6, 1952.

[67] Tanzan Ishibashi, member of the House of Representatives, and former Minister of Finance, "Current Thoughts on Economic Reform," *Contemporary Japan*, Vol. XXI, Nos. 4-6, 1952, p. 224.

[68] "The Coming Dilemma," *Nippon Times*, November 13, 1952. Cf. also, "Rearming Scope to Be Surveyed," concerning the Economic Survey of the nation's rearmament potential, and "Japan Unable to Arm Now," in the *Nippon Times*, January 25, 1953.

[69] *Mainichi*, April 28, 1954.

[70] *Ibid.*, September 5 and October 21, 1953; February 9, March 9 and April 13, 1955.

[71] *Asahi Evening News*, March 8, 1955.

[72] *Mainichi*, March 12, 1955.

[73] *Mainichi*, February 20 and March 8, 1955.

[74] *Oriental Economist*, May 1955, p. 209.

[75] *Mainichi*, April 28, 1955. See also issue of April 13, 1955 and *Asahi Evening News*, April 12 and 15, 1955.

[76] *Korean Survey*, Vol. I, No. 4, December 1952, p. 11.

77 "Sea Defense Zone," *Nippon Times,* October 26, 1952; "Stern Protest on Incident Given Koreans," *Mainichi,* February 20, 1953.
78 "Big Fishery Rally Set," *Nippon Times,* February 8, 1953.
79 *New York Times,* December 25, 1953.
80 Ralph Braibanti, "The Ryukyu Islands: Pawn of the Pacific," *American Political Science Review,* XLVIII, December 1954, p. 973.
81 "Ryukyus Return to Nippon Urged," *Nippon Times,* August 11, 1951. Cf. also "Leftist Socialists Want Islands Back," *Nippon Times,* February 5, 1953; "Japan Seeks Civil Rule at Okinawa," *Nippon Times,* February 8, 1953; "Return of Okinawa, Bonins Being Pressed," *Tokyo Evening News,* February 8, 1953; and "On the Territory Problem," *Mainichi,* September 28, 1952.
82 *Contemporary Japan,* Vol. XX, Nos. 7-9, July-September 1951, p. 410.
83 *Asahi Evening News,* January 13 and January 17, 1955.
84 Ralph Braibanti, *op. cit.,* p. 984.
85 Hatoyama's Statement to the Diet, *Mainichi,* March 26, 1955.
86 Japanese concern for the return of the Soviet-held possessions began to be displayed in 1953. Cf. "Nippon Government Airs Views on Sakhalin," *Nippon Times,* February 4, 1953; "Britain O. K.'s Russian Hold on Kuriles," *Nippon Times,* February 13, 1953; "Kuriles Return Seen U. S., British Obligation," *Nippon Times,* February 25, 1953; "Japan Is Sceptical of Regaining Isles," *New York Times,* February 6, 1953.
87 *New York Times,* June 7, 1955.
88 Tashikazu Kase, "Japan's New Role in East Asia," *Foreign Affairs,* Vol. 34, October 1955, p. 43.

THE UNITED STATES
AND THE PHILIPPINES

1 Senator Osias made this speech on the Senate floor: "There has not been a single problem in contemporary Philippine politics, not even the question of Philippine independence, upon which the people were so clearly, so unanimously united as on the question of demanding just, fair, and adequate reparations from Japan in virtue of her war activities, in virtue of her lust for conquest, and in virtue of the incalculable losses of property and lives inflicted upon this country and the people of the Philippines." *Congressional Record,* Senate, Vol. III, No. 41, March 24, 1952, p. 630.
2 *Manila Chronicle,* quoted in "Philippine Newsletter," September 1, 1951. It continued, "the issue of the Japanese treaty is not a political issue, nor is it being used as a political weapon, as some ill-informed persons in Washington have averred."
3 See statement by Carlos P. Romulo at the Japanese Peace Treaty Conference, September 7, 1951, mimeographed by the Philippine Delegation to the Conference at San Francisco, pp. 2-3.
4 See Senator Osias' speech before the Senate, *op. cit.,* pp. 633-635. *The Manila Daily Mirror* warned in an editorial: "From the record of the Japanese, it is impossible to expect a permanent adherence to democratic ways without a watch-dog around. It is, therefore, up to the United States, while placing so much hope in its protege, not to tempt

probability too much by yielding complete power to them prematurely." Quoted in *Philippine Newsletter,* October 1, 1951.

5 Carlos P. Romulo's speech at the Japanese Peace Treaty Conference, *op. cit.*

6 Senator Osias' speech before the Senate, *op. cit.,* p. 631.

7 *New York Times,* July 17, and July 19, 1951. An unofficial report that Dulles had made a deal with Premier Yoshida of Japan not to press the reparations claims of ten countries in exchange for an assurance that Japan would cooperate in U. S. Far Eastern policies was officially denied. *New York Times,* January 11, 13, 1952.

8 Quoted in *Manila Times,* December 27, 1952. One of the campaign issues in 1951 was the *Nacionalista* Party's contention that the acceptance by the Liberal Party's administration of the Japanese peace treaty was "a virtual surrender of the people's rights." See campaign statement by Felixberto M. Serrano, *Nacionalista* campaign coordinator, in *Philippine Free Press,* November 10, 1951.

9 For a discussion of the Senate reaction to the treaty, see T. M. Locsin, "How Safe Are We?" *Philippines Free Press,* May 17, 1952.

10 Senator Recto said: "Under this article the U. S. has the right to denounce our mutual defense agreement for any reason at all, and at any time, with a mere year's notice. . . . It may abandon us to our fate if it disapproves our internal policies, or the results of our election, or, which is even more likely, if a new administration of Republican isolationists gains power in the American Presidential elections." *Ibid.*

11 *Ibid.*

12 *New York Times,* June 19, 1955, Sec. 6, p. 61.

13 Much political capital has been made of the fact that the U. S. was unable to defend the Philippines in the first few months of 1942. This statement of Senator Laurel is cited as one of the points of the indictment of anti-Americanism by Teodoro M. Locsin in "Pro-Americanism —the Issue of 1953," *Philippines Free Press,* October 4, 1952.

14 Statement by Claro Recto reported in *Manila Daily Mirror,* February 3, 1953.

15 *Philippines Herald,* February 4, 1953. The *Manila Chronicle,* in an editorial entitled "Fears Dispelled," in its issue of the same day, expressed a sense of relief at General Bradley's announcement that the U. S. would continue to protect Formosa.

16 *New York Times,* January 25, 1955, p. 5. The *Manila Chronicle* editorialized, "We know only too well that a great many people must needs be humored in their sublime belief that the concentration of American bases in the Philippines would be the strongest guarantee of our security. From this point of view, American bases would seem to be necessary." Editorial by I. P. Soliongco, May 22, 1955.

17 *Manila Chronicle,* May 8, 1955.

18 *Philippines Herald,* May 11, 1955.

19 *Manila Chronicle,* May 11, 1955.

20 *New York Times,* June 8, 1954, p. 7; July 28, 1954, p. 3.

21 See Claude A. Buss, *The Far East.* (New York: Macmillan, 1955) pp. 623-624.

22 Willard E. Elsbree, "The 1953 Philippine Presidential Elections." *Pacific Affairs,* March 1954, pp. 8 ff.

23 Donn V. Hart, "Magsaysay: Philippine Candidate." *Far Eastern Survey,* May, 1953, p. 68.

24 L. Edward Shuck, Jr., "Democracy: Success or Failure in the Philippines?" *Pacific Spectator,* Vol. 6, No. 1, Winter, 1952, p. 9.

25 Marc T. Greene, "Power Politics in the Philippines." *Eastern World,* January, 1952, p. 11.

26 Hernando J. Abaya, *Betrayal in the Philippines,* New York: A. A. Wyn, 1946, p. 187.

27 From a speech by Senator Verano, Republic of the Philippines, *Congressional Record,* Senate, Vol. III, No. 6, February 4, 1952.

28 The *Manila Chronicle,* April 30, 1955, p. 13.

29 I. P. Soliongco's strongly anti-American column, "Seriously Speaking." *Manila Chronicle,* May 8, 1955.

30 *Seventh and Final Report of the High Commissioner to the Philippines,* Covering the period September 14, 1945 to July 4, 1945-July 4, 1946. Washington: Government Printing Office, 1947, p. 39.

31 *Ibid,* p. 2.

32 *Report to the President of the United States by the Economic Survey Mission to the Philippines,* Washington: Government Printing Office, October 9, 1950.

33 Benito Legardo, Jr., "America and the Philippine Economy," *Philippine Quarterly,* March 1952, p. 26.

34 Editorial in the *Manila Daily Mirror,* reproduced in the *Philippine Newsletter,* June 1952.

35 Benito Legardo, *op. cit.,* even stated, "what was most significant about the Bell Mission Report was that it was probably the first official U. S. public document that admitted the necessity of modifying the Bell Act." p. 29.

36 *New York Times,* October 26, 1950, pp. 1 and 4. The statement reads in part: "Philippine bankruptcy and corruption have an intimate relation to the American example in racketeering and to the . . . inspiration provided by conspicuous consumption, otherwise known as the so-called American standard of living. . . . With more time and greater chances, [the Filipinos] will yet show they can equal or even surpass the stink familiar and now taken for granted in Washington. . . . The Filipinos are now getting it in the neck because they are not rich enough to cover up their own stink and be lofty and moral about it before a hungry and devastated world."

37 Shirley Jenkins, "Philippine White Paper," *Far Eastern Survey,* January 10, 1951, p. 5.

38 *New York Times,* November 3, 1950.

39 Shirley Jenkins, "The Philippine Economy," *Foreign Policy Bulletin,* February 1, 1952, p. 6.

40 Statement by former President Quirino at a press conference, the *Manila Times,* January 16, 1953, p. 14.

41 Quirino, *loc. cit.* The 15-man committee appointed by the President proposed revision of the Trade Agreement on the following lines:

1. A limited selective free trade plan, envisioning duty-free trading on certain essential items and an exchange of goods on non-essentials under customary impost.

2. Unpegging the peso from the dollar.

3. Reconsidering the parity arrangement which gives Americans the same rights as Filipinos in developing Philippine natural resources. *Philippines Herald,* January 22, 1953, p. 4.
Note the similarity with the demands of the Philippine delegation to Washington in late 1954, discussed below.

42 These points were emphasized in the 12-point report of the 15-man committee appointed by President Quirino, reproduced in the *Philippine Newsletter,* June, 1952.

43 Teodoro Vanencia, "Business Over a Cup of Coffee," *Philippines Herald,* January 1, 1953.

44 Miguel Guaderno. "The Bell Trade Act and the Philippine Economy," *Pacific Affairs,* December, 1952, p. 331.

45 *Philippines Herald,* January 22, 1953, reports unanimous agreement on revision reached in the bi-partisan council of state.

46 Senator Rodriguez of the *Nacionalista* Party said: "We fought the Bell Act in the 1947 plebiscite, waging a country-wide campaign to warn the people against its disastrous effects on our economic welfare and independence . . . The *Nacionalista* Party has been upheld by the logic of facts and events." *Manila Times,* January 17, 1952, p. 8.

47 *New York Times,* August 26, 1954.

48 *Ibid.*

49 However, Senator Recto maintained that "The United States certainly had the initial advantage because, to begin with the Bell Act itself was all benefits for the United States and therefore gave her negotiators much leeway for making concessions." *Manila Chronicle,* April 28, 1955, p. 2.

50 *Manila Chronicle,* May 12, 1955.

51 *Manila Times,* April 29, 1955.

52 *Philippines Herald,* May 11, 1955.

53 The definitive attack on the Laurel-Langley Agreement is an extremely long speech by Senator Recto, reprinted in three installments by the *Manila Chronicle,* April 28, 29, and 30, 1955.

54 *Manila Bulletin,* April 16, 1955.

55 *Philippine Land Tenure Reform: Analysis and Recommendations,* by Robert S. Hardie, Special Technical and Economic Mission, Mutual Security Administration, Manila, 1952, 287 p.

56 *The Rural Philippines,* by Generosa F. Rivera and Robert T. McMillan. Cooperative Project of Philippine Council for United States Aid and the United States Mutual Security Administration, August, 1952, 217 p.

57 See the consideration of the Hardie and Rivera-McMillan Reports in the *Philippines Free Press,* January 3, 1953. Arguments on both sides are presented.

58 President Quirino saw an exaggeration by the MSA of the possible effects of the land tenure system. *Manila Times,* December 26, 1953, p. 3. Speaker Perez also saw exaggeration, caused by a "warped vision" of investigators who "did not bother to look into all the circumstances behind the conditions." *Manila Times,* January 5, 1953, p. 12.

59 Diosdade Macapagal (Chairman of the House Foreign Affairs Committee—Liberal) *Manila Times,* December 27, 1953, p. 1.

60 President Quirino, upon saying the McMillan-Rivera Report was one-sided, listed 15 measures the government had taken to improve barrio

conditions. *Manila Times,* January 5, 1953. Perez claimed the MSA "deliberately" ignored Philippine efforts to improve the situation. *Manila Times,* December 25, 1952.

[61] Quirino's statement, January 5, 1953, *Manila Times.*

[62] Quoted in *Philippines Herald,* December 22, 1952.

[63] *Ibid., loc. cit.*

[64] Quoted in *Philippines Herald,* January 1, 1953.

[65] Speaker Perez' charges are reported in the *Manila Times,* December 24 and 25, 1952. Representative Tirzon also implied there was Communist participation in the drafting of the Reports. He said the reports could be used as a text in Stalin University. *Manila Times,* January 15, 1953.

[66] Representative Floro Crisologo, quoted in *Philippines Herald,* January 7, 1953, p. 10.

[67] Speaker Perez complained about "American bureaucracy, Washington red tape, as well as uncertain and indefinite policies" which "delayed many of our projects." *Philippines Herald,* December 22, 1953. There were also too many conditions—"strings"—attached to U. S. aid. *Ibid.,* January 7, 1953.

[68] Quoted in *Manila Times,* January 5, 1953, p. 12.

[69] Representative Cipriano S. Allas (Liberal), reported in *Manila Chronicle,* December 26, 1952.

[70] Lansang, Jose A., "The Philippine-American Experiment: A Filipino View" *Pacific Affairs,* September, 1952, p. 229.

[71] See the *Manila Times,* January 2, 1953 and "The Big Choice," *Philippines Free Press,* January 3, 1953.

[72] Liberal Representative Allas, defending Perez, said it was foolish to dub Speaker Perez' proposal to screen MSA officials for Communism as anti-American. The Republican Party, Allas said, won the 1952 American election on the issue of screening Communists. Allas added that Adlai Stevenson had been accused of being pro-Communist, and that 36 million Americans demonstrated in the election that they approved of Perez' suggestion. *Manila Times,* December 26, 1952.

[73] *Manila Chronicle,* May 19, 1955.

[74] *Manila Chronicle,* May 24, 1955.

[75] U. S. aid allocated to the Philippines from 1945 to January 1, 1953 amounted to $2,239,400,000 ($149,200,000 in the year 1952). Much of this total was in Veterans' Administration payments to Filipino veterans.

[76] Dr. Albino Z. SyCip, *American Economic Help to the Philippines.* (pamphlet) Reproduced through the courtesy of the Philippine Association, Manila, August, 1950, pp. 11-12.

[77] Quoted in the *New York Times,* October 27, 1952, p. 3.

[78] Statements to this effect by President Quirino were reported in the *New York Times,* March 24, 1951, and by Senator Osias in the *Congressional Record* (Republic of the Philippines), Senate, February 28, 1952, p. 349, and March 24, 1953, p. 631.

[79] *Manila Chronicle,* May 22, 1955 complained that "the test of loyalty among our people has been made their pro-Americanism," and that dependence on aid has weakened the Philippine character. (Editorial, p. 4.)

[80] A $9,500,000 U. S. military aid grant was delayed at the last minute

because of sudden minor Philippine objections. See *New York Times,* April 27, April 28, 1955.

[81] See Senator Recto on American investment and its effect on the Philippine economy in the *Manila Chronicle,* April 30, 1955, p. 13.

[82] *Congressional Record* (Republic of the Philippines), Senate, February 1, 1952.

[83] See Richard L. Walker, "Allied Unity in the Pacific," *New Leader,* February 16, 1953, pp. 9-10, and E. D. Killen, "The Anzus Pact and Pacific Security," *Far Eastern Survey,* October 8, 1953, pp. 137-141.

[84] Teodoro M. Locsin, "The Fuss-Much Ado About Anzus," *Philippines Free Press,* August 23, 1952, p. 2.

[85] Quoted in Walker, *op. cit.,* p. 9 (note 1).

[86] *New York Times,* August 5, 1952, p. 3.

[87] Quoted in Locsin, *op. cit.,* p. 2 (note 2).

[88] Quoted in *ibid.,* p. 2. Recto went on to tell Quirino he should emigrate to Australia (p. 54).

[89] Note the editorial in *Bataan,* May, 1952 on "The White Australia Policy." "It was reported in Manila that the Australian Government reiterated its policy of discriminating non-Caucasian Filipinos from membership in the proposed Pacific Defense Council. Obviously, the Filipinos resented vehemently such an unfriendly act and made clear their stand that under no conditions will the Filipinos seek membership in the Council."

THE UNITED STATES AND EGYPT

[1] For general background on Egypt and the postwar Middle East, a number of helpful works are available, such as Anthony Galatoli, *Egypt in Mid-Passage,* Cairo, Urwand and Sons, 1950; Clare Hollingworth, *The Arabs and the West,* London, Methuen and Co., Ltd., 1952; the *Middle East Journal,* published quarterly since 1947, is a valuable source of data on developments in the region; cf. also *Nationalism in the Middle East,* Addresses at the Sixth Annual Conference on Middle East Affairs, pub. by Middle East Institute, Washington, D. C., 1952.

[2] George A. Brownell, "American Aviation in the Middle East," *Middle East Journal,* Vol. 1, pp. 404-405.

[3] *Middle East Journal,* Chronology, Vol. 1, p. 309 and Vol. 2, p. 62.

[4] *New York Times,* June 22, 1949 and April 11, 1950.

[5] This happened on January 24, 1948. *Middle East Journal,* Chronology, Vol. 2, p. 206. For an understanding of the efforts made in the United Nations to solve the Israeli question, see L. Larry Leonard, "The United Nations and Palestine," *International Conciliation,* pub. by Carnegie Endowment for International Peace, October 1949, No. 454; also Hal Lehrman, *Israel: The Beginning and Tomorrow,* New York, William Sloane Associates, 1951, especially pp. 234-297.

[6] Kamil Abdul Rahim, "Conflict Between Communism and Democracy in the Near East," Address at Princeton University, June 2, 1952, pub. by Egyptian Embassy, Washington, D. C., mimeo., u. d.

[7] *Proche-Orient,* July 1952.

[8] Quoted by *Radio Cairo,* Egyptian Home Service, May 10, 1955.

9 *Akhbar al-Yaum,* October 18, 1952.

10 *Al-Balagh,* November 12, 1952.

11 Lehrman, *op. cit.,* pp. 311-312. Between 1946 and 1954 all the Arab states together received a total of $87,000,000 from the United States in the form of technical assistance, exchange of persons, loans and credits, while Israel had received $350,000,000, 60 per cent of which was in the form of economic aid. Testimony of Arthur Z. Gardiner, Political and Economic Adviser in the Bureau of Near Eastern Affairs, Department of State, before the House Committee on Foreign Affairs, May 10, 1954.

12 *Al-Misri,* as quoted in *Egypt News,* November 12, 1952.

13 Cf. Moshe Brilliant, "Israeli Case Against Arabs," *New York Times,* IV, October 25, 1953.

14 *New York Times,* November 25, 1953.

15 *Department of State Bulletin,* April 26, 1954.

16 *Middle East Journal,* Chronology, Vol. 2, p. 322.

17 *New York Times,* July 27, 1951.

18 Lehrman, *op. cit.,* pp. 254-257.

19 United Nations Security Council, *Official Records,* 552nd Meeting, August 16, 1951, pp. 9-10.

20 *Ibid.,* 549th Meeting, July 26, 1951, pp. 14-15.

21 *New York Times,* March 30, 1954.

22 Dr. Hussain Fakhry al-Khalidy, Foreign Minister of Jordan. *New York Times,* April 21, 1954.

23 See James Baster, "Economic Aspects of the Settlement of the Palestine Refugees," *Middle East Journal,* Vol. 8, Winter 1954, pp. 54-68; and Don Peretz, "Problems of Arab Refugee Compensation," *ibid.,* Autumn 1954, pp. 403-416.

24 *New York Times,* March 7, 1955.

25 *Ibid.,* March 5, 1955.

26 *Ibid.,* April 10, 1954. Four days later, the Syrian Foreign Minister, Fayadi al-Atosi commented on the Byroade speech as follows: "As for the Arabs, what does Byroade want from them? Would he induce the Arabs to do things in the interest of Israel, and yet, would he not induce Israel to cease its conceit and aggression? . . . Is Byroade ignorant of the fact that Israel is a religious and racial fanatic with means of explosives within its recesses, to be used to establish an empire?" *Damascus Radio,* April 14, 1954.

27 See text in the *New York Times,* August 27, 1955.

28 *Al-Jumhuria,* August 31, 1955.

29 *Al-Ahram,* May 9, 1955. On the same date, *Al-Jumhuria* pointed out that ever since the Jewish state was established in Palestine it had been receiving "care and help" from private and public sources in the United States. It added that Israel was on the verge of collapse under the weight of the Arabs' boycott, and complained that "despite all this, the United States insists on helping Israel, while the ruling authorities in Israel still insist on beating the drums of war and launching aggressive attacks on the Arabs."

30 See the text of the Eden proposal in the *New York Times,* November 10, 1955. Simultaneously, President Eisenhower, in a move perhaps calculated to take the edge off the Eden proposal in the eyes of Israel, announced that the United States will weigh requests for

arms needed for legitimate self-defense. *New York Times*, November 10, 1955.

[31] Cf. N. Marbury Efimenco, "American Impact Upon Middle East Leadership," *Political Science Quarterly*, Vol. LXIX, June 1954, pp. 202–218. C. Howard Worth, Dean of the American University of Cairo, reported in 1952 that 70,000 Egyptian children were still attending European and American schools within the country, most of them conducted by Christian missionary orders. "Education in Egypt of Today," *Nationalism in the Middle East, op. cit.*, pp. 39-40.

[32] Kenneth Cragg, "The Intellectual Impact of Communism Upon Contemporary Islam," *Middle East Journal*, Vol. 8, Spring 1954, pp. 127-138.

[33] Clare Hollingworth, *op. cit.*, Chap. XV. In the Spring of 1954, the United States Information Agency estimated Communist strength in Egypt to be less than 3,000, concentrated principally among students, industrial workers, feminists and minority groups. *New York Times*, May 10, 1954.

[34] *Ibid.*, October 14, 1951. Cf. also James W. Spain, "Middle East Defense: A New Approach," in *Middle East Journal*, Vol. 8, Summer 1954, pp. 251-266, and Dankwart A. Rustow, "Defense of the Near East," in *Foreign Affairs*, Vol. 34, January 1956, pp. 271-286.

[35] *Proche-Orient*, October 1951.

[36] *Times* of London, January 9, 1952.

[37] *Al-Ahram*, August 2, 1952.

[38] *Al-Misri*, February 26, 1952.

[39] Abu Muhammad, "Persia and Egypt Against Imperialism," *Islamic Review*, January, 1952.

[40] *New York Times*, March 16, 17, and 19, 1953.

[41] *Al-Misri*, May 11 and May 12, 1953. *Al-Akhbar* echoed the charge on the following day.

[42] *New York Times*, May 16, 1953.

[43] *Ibid.*, August 12, 1953.

[44] Text in the *Department of State Bulletin*, June 15, 1953.

[45] *Al-Misri*, October 31, 1951.

[46] Cf. Stephen H. Longrigg, *Iraq 1900 to 1950*, London, Oxford University Press, 1953, p. 331, and Cecil A. Hourain, "The Arab League in Perspective," *Middle East Journal*, Vol. 1, April 1947, pp. 125-136.

[47] James W. Spain, *op. cit.*, pp. 255-256.

[48] *New York Times*, April 2, 1954.

[49] Cf. *ibid.*, for the following dates: January 9, 13, 17, 18, 30 and 31; February 3, 16, 17, and 21; and March 4 and 7, 1955.

[50] *Al Ahram*, May 10, 1955.

[51] *New York Times*, June 9 and August 15, 1955.

[52] *Ibid.*, October 3 and 6, 1955.

[53] *Review of Economic Conditions in the Middle East, 1951-1952*, U. N. Doc. E/2353/Add. 1, p. 16; and Alfred Bonne, "Land and Population in the Middle East," *Middle East Journal*, Vol. 5, pp. 39-56.

[54] Charles Issawi, *Egypt: An Economic and Social Analysis*, London, Oxford University Press, 1947, p. 48.

[55] Cf. Afif I. Tannous, "Land Reform: Key to the Development and Stability of the Arab World," *Middle East Journal*, Vol. 5, pp. 1-20.

[56] *New York Times*, January 5, 1954.

[57] Robert C. Doty, "Egypt Lays Troubles to England and Economics," *New York Times*, IV, July 19, 1953.

[58] *New York Times*, March 20, 1953.

[59] See Footnote No. 11.

[60] *Middle East Journal*, Chronology, Vol. 8, p. 449. The text of the *Anglo-Egyptian Agreement Regarding the Suez Canal Base* will be found in the same volume, p. 460.

[61] *New York Times*, November 7, 1954.

[62] Osgood Caruthers, "Egyptian Trade with Soviet Bloc Is Arousing Concern in the West," *New York Times*, January 4, 1956.

[63] Leon Feiner, "The Aswan Dam Development Project," *Middle East Journal*, Vol. 6, 464-467.

[64] *New York Times*, December 17, 1955.

[65] *Ibid.*, December 19, 1955.

[66] *Al-Ahram*, May 9, 1955.

[67] Gamal Abdel Nasser, "The Egyptian Revolution," *Foreign Affairs*, Vol. 33, January 1955, p. 211.

[68] *Al-Misri*, May 12, 1953.

[69] *Al-Ahram*, June 3, 1953.

[70] *Egypt*, Winter 1951-52. Quarterly publication of the Egyptian Information Bureau, Washington, D. C.

[71] "The Present Egyptian Crisis," Egyptian Embassy, Washington, D. C., mimeo., u.d.

[72] The sending of this letter was revealed on February 14, 1954. See *New York Times* for that date.

[73] *Akhbar al-Yaum*, February 3, 1953.

[74] *Times* of London, January 5, 1954.

[75] *New York Times*, February 14, 1954.

[76] *Ibid.*, April 14 and May 3, 1954.

[77] See Footnote No. 60.

[78] *New York Times*, August 20, 1954.

[79] *Radio Beirut*, September 2, 1954. In May 1955, Nuri Sa'id of Iraq declared that opinion in the Arab world did sanction a political alliance with the West. *New York Times*, May 18, 1955.

[80] *Radio Cairo*, Egyptian Home Service, May 2, 1955.

[81] *New York Times*, February 7, 1956.

[82] *Ibid.*, February 1, 1956.

Index